Mastering Kotlin

Learn advanced Kotlin programming techniques to build apps
for Android, iOS, and the web

Nate Ebel

BIRMINGHAM - MUMBAI

Mastering Kotlin

Commissioning Editor: Richa Tripathi
Acquisition Editor: Karan Gupta
Content Development Editor: Tiksha Sarang
Senior Editor: Rohit Singh
Technical Editor: Romy Dias
Copy Editor: Safis Editing
Project Coordinator: Prajakta Naik
Proofreader: Safis Editing
Indexer: Priyanka Dhadke
Production Designer: Nilesh Mohite

First published: October 2019

Production reference: 1111019

Published by Packt Publishing Ltd.
Livery Place
35 Livery Street
Birmingham
B3 2PB, UK.

ISBN 978-1-83855-572-6

www.packtpub.com

To my wife, for being a constant source of support and encouragement, and for being understanding during all the late nights and early mornings; I couldn't have finished this book without you. To my parents, for always believing in me and teaching me to do the same, and for raising me to dream big; I wouldn't be here without you. To the educators, mentors, and friends over the years: Steve, Steve, Shawn, and Scott—the kindness, encouragement, knowledge, and support you've given me will never be forgotten.

Packt.com

Subscribe to our online digital library for full access to over 7,000 books and videos, as well as industry leading tools to help you plan your personal development and advance your career. For more information, please visit our website.

Why subscribe?

- Spend less time learning and more time coding with practical eBooks and videos from over 4,000 industry professionals

- Improve your learning with Skill Plans built especially for you

- Get a free eBook or video every month

- Fully searchable for easy access to vital information

- Copy and paste, print, and bookmark content

Did you know that Packt offers eBook versions of every book published, with PDF and ePub files available? You can upgrade to the eBook version at www.packt.com and, as a print book customer, you are entitled to a discount on the eBook copy. Get in touch with us at customercare@packtpub.com for more details.

At www.packt.com, you can also read a collection of free technical articles, sign up for a range of free newsletters, and receive exclusive discounts and offers on Packt books and eBooks.

Contributors

About the author

Nate Ebel is a software developer who enjoys building great software and helping others do the same. He has worked with Android since its early days, across a variety of projects, from creative and educational apps, mapping and navigation applications, to the evolution of robotic controllers.

Nate has a passion for technology, education, and software development, and enjoys opportunities to combine the three. He enjoys being involved in the Android developer community and is an active contributor through conference speaking, blogging, and event organizing.

He is working to help himself and others dream, learn, and create in an effort to positively impact others.

About the reviewer

Ashok Kumar Srinivas is a Google-certified Android developer from Bengaluru, India. He is an expert in the web and mobile engineering domains. He has authored books on Android Wear and Firebase, and has reviewed books on subjects including web and mobile applications. He is one of the top open source contributors. He is a passionate YouTuber and runs a channel called AndroidABCD. He is also a speaker at international conferences. He has a keen interest in the quality, architecture, and unit testing of the code. When he can find the time, he writes and reviews books. He also likes to travel inside India and further afield.

I would like to thank T. Subhash Chandra, my teacher in college and life. He has been an incredible support for a diverse range of students, and I am proud to say that I am one such student. I would also like to thank my wife, Geetha Shree Ashok, for supporting me in every way during my work on this book. I would also like to thank my sister, Shylaja Shripathi, my father, Srinivas, my mother, Lalitha, and my entire family.

Packt is searching for authors like you

If you're interested in becoming an author for Packt, please visit `authors.packtpub.com` and apply today. We have worked with thousands of developers and tech professionals, just like you, to help them share their insight with the global tech community. You can make a general application, apply for a specific hot topic that we are recruiting an author for, or submit your own idea.

Table of Contents

Section 2: Putting the Pieces Together – Modeling Data, Managing State, and Application Architecture

Section 3: Play Nice – Integrating Kotlin With Existing Code

Section 4: Go Beyond – Exploring Advanced and Experimental Language Features

Preface

This book is written for software developers looking to expand their experience and understanding of the Kotlin programming language. It aims to bridge the gap between simple, practical examples and advanced language topics.

This book is designed to not only demonstrate how to write code in Kotlin, but to help you to understand the history of Kotlin and some of the motivations behind the language itself. Additionally, the book will demonstrate how features of the Kotlin language work behind the scenes. The goal is to help you to more fully understand Kotlin as a whole, rather than just as a language syntax.

Once a strong introduction to Kotlin and its features has been covered, the book will spend several chapters exploring a variety of more advanced topics, including how to build with Kotlin on a variety of platforms. These chapters aim to act as a quick-start guide for understanding what is possible with Kotlin and where and how you can apply the Kotlin language skills that you have learned for the development of real-world applications.

Who this book is for

This book is aimed at beginner and intermediate Kotlin developers who are looking to improve their understanding of the language, as well as experienced Java developers looking for simple, practical examples of how to solve familiar problems using Kotlin. You should be familiar with object-oriented programming and have some familiarity with Java.

What this book covers

Chapter 1, *A New Challenger Approaches*, provides context for what Kotlin is, how it came about, and why it is gaining popularity. It provides a high-level overview of where the book is headed and lays the foundation for the following chapters' focus on language features, patterns, best practices, and the ability to target multiple domains and platforms.

Chapter 2, *Programmers' Multi-Tool – Flexible, Expressive, and Concise*, dives into the basic details of the Kotlin language. It highlights some of the most popular language features, such as first-class functions, non-null types, and multiple programming paradigms. For each of these features, you will begin to understand how to take advantage of the feature, and what impact it can have on the overall application architecture.

Chapter 3, *Understanding Programming Paradigms in Kotlin*, provides an overview of different programming paradigms that Kotlin supports, including imperative, functional, and reactive programming. The chapter describes these paradigms, and details how Kotlin supports, but does not enforce, all three.

Chapter 4, *First-Class Functions*, introduces you to Kotlin's support for first-class functions. It describes, in detail, how Kotlin functions are flexible, concise, and powerful. You will learn how to leverage Kotlin features such as default parameter values, infix functions, extension functions, and higher-order functions.

Chapter 5, *Modeling Real-World Data*, exposes you to the fundamentals of inheritance and composition in Kotlin. This chapter details the differences between enums, data classes, sealed classes, and type classes, and aims to illustrate when and why you should choose one over another.

Chapter 6, *Interoperability as a Design Goal*, provides background into the design goals behind interoperability in Kotlin, why interoperability is so important to Kotlin, and teaches you how to quickly add Kotlin to an existing project.

Chapter 7, *Crossing Over – Working across Java and Kotlin*, explores the practical ramifications of adding Kotlin to an existing Java code base. It details how to work with both the language within the same project, and about some of the challenges associated with adding a second language to a project.

Chapter 8, *Controlling the Story*, details how Kotlin code can be modified to provide a better interoperability experience with Java. It highlights how to apply annotations, and how to design Kotlin APIs to make working with Kotlin from Java more idiomatic and enjoyable.

Chapter 9, *Baby Steps – Integration through Testing*, explores how to integrate Kotlin into an existing project through testing, and demonstrates how the testing experience can be improved using Kotlin and Kotlin-specific features such as DSLs.

Chapter 10, *Practical Concurrency*, introduces you to advanced threading concepts. It does so by starting from basic threads and working up to Kotlin coroutines as an idiomatic solution for writing asynchronous, non-blocking code.

Chapter 11, *Building Your Own Tools – Domain-Specific Languages (DSLs)*, introduces the concept of custom **Domain-Specific Languages** (**DSLs**) written in Kotlin and how they can be used as a powerful tool to solve a variety of challenges.

Chapter 12, *Fully Functional – Embracing Functional Programming*, provides a deep dive into achieving functional programming with Kotlin. It focuses on how to effectively use the Kotlin Standard Library to write more functional code, and it also takes a look at the Arrow library for writing truly functional code with Kotlin.

Chapter 13, *Kotlin on Android*, explores the use of Kotlin for Android development. It details why Kotlin is so popular for Android development, how it makes a developer's life easier, and what Kotlin tooling is available for building Android applications.

Chapter 14, *Kotlin and Web Development*, introduces the use of Kotlin for frontend web development. This chapter will help you to understand where Kotlin can be used for web development, how to get started by building a simple project, and what the limitations of Kotlin for frontend web development are.

Chapter 15, *Introducing Multiplatform Kotlin*, explores the use of Kotlin for multiplatform projects. It describes how the Kotlin multiplatform approach is different from other cross-platform solutions, how to package and write code that targets multiple platforms, and where the current limitations exist. In this chapter, you will learn how to set up a multiplatform project that targets iOS, Android, and the web using common Kotlin code.

Chapter 16, *Taming the Monolith with Microservices*, introduces the use of Kotlin for backend services that can be used within a microservices architecture. It will describe how and where Kotlin can be used to write backend services and how those can interoperate with other services.

Chapter 17, *Practical Design Patterns*, revisits familiar Java design patterns and demonstrates how to reimagine those patterns using Kotlin features that have been explored throughout this book.

To get the most out of this book

You should be comfortable creating and running Kotlin projects from an IntelliJ-based IDE, installing IDEs such as IntelliJ, Android Studio, and Xcode, and also be familiar with how to run command-line tools on your machines. With the exception of Chapter 15, *Introducing Multi-Platform Kotlin*, all examples in this book should run regardless of your OS of choice. For Chapter 15, *Introducing Multiplatform Kotlin*, the portions of the example dedicated to setting up an iOS project require a computer running macOS and Xcode. You should be comfortable using GitHub and downloading or cloning a GitHub repository in order to make use of the examples presented in this book.

Download the example code files

You can download the example code files for this book from your account at www.packt.com. If you purchased this book elsewhere, you can visit www.packt.com/support and register to have the files emailed directly to you.

You can download the code files by following these steps:

1. Log in or register at www.packt.com.
2. Select the **SUPPORT** tab.
3. Click on **Code Downloads & Errata**.
4. Enter the name of the book in the **Search** box and follow the onscreen instructions.

Once the file is downloaded, please make sure that you unzip or extract the folder using the latest version of:

- WinRAR/7-Zip for Windows
- Zipeg/iZip/UnRarX for Mac
- 7-Zip/PeaZip for Linux

The code bundle for the book is also hosted on GitHub at https://github.com/PacktPublishing/Mastering-Kotlin. In case there's an update to the code, it will be updated on the existing GitHub repository.

We also have other code bundles from our rich catalog of books and videos available at https://github.com/PacktPublishing/. Check them out!

Code in Action

Visit the following link to check out videos of the code being run: http://bit.ly/325fQhz

Conventions used

There are a number of text conventions used throughout this book.

CodeInText: Indicates code words in text, database table names, folder names, filenames, file extensions, pathnames, dummy URLs, user input, and Twitter handles. Here is an example: "Demonstrations of null and non-null types."

A block of code is set as follows:

```
data class Language(val name: String)

fun main(args: Array<String>) {
  val language = Language("Kotlin")
  println(language.name)
}
```

When we wish to draw your attention to a particular part of a code block, the relevant lines or items are set in bold:

```
fun main(args: Array<String>) {
    var language: String = "Kotlin"
    language = null // Error: Null can not be a value of a non-null type
String
}
```

Any command-line input or output is written as follows:

```
$ mkdir css
$ cd css
```

Bold: Indicates a new term, an important word, or words that you see on screen. For example, words in menus or dialog boxes appear in the text like this. Here is an example: "Next, under the **Client** section, select **Jetty HttpClient Engine** and then click on **Next**."

Warnings or important notes appear like this.

Tips and tricks appear like this.

Get in touch

Feedback from our readers is always welcome.

General feedback: If you have questions about any aspect of this book, mention the book title in the subject of your message and email us at customercare@packtpub.com.

Errata: Although we have taken every care to ensure the accuracy of our content, mistakes do happen. If you have found a mistake in this book, we would be grateful if you would report this to us. Please visit www.packt.com/submit-errata, selecting your book, clicking on the Errata Submission Form link, and entering the details.

Piracy: If you come across any illegal copies of our works in any form on the internet, we would be grateful if you would provide us with the location address or website name. Please contact us at copyright@packt.com with a link to the material.

If you are interested in becoming an author: If there is a topic that you have expertise in and you are interested in either writing or contributing to a book, please visit authors.packtpub.com.

Reviews

Please leave a review. Once you have read and used this book, why not leave a review on the site that you purchased it from? Potential readers can then see and use your unbiased opinion to make purchase decisions, we at Packt can understand what you think about our products, and our authors can see your feedback on their book. Thank you!

For more information about Packt, please visit packt.com.

Section 1: Kotlin – A Modern Solution to Application Development

1

Kotlin is a modern language for modern-day application development. It builds upon decades of experience with Java and modern influences to provide a programming experience that is powerful, flexible, and delightful. In this part, you'll learn about the Kotlin programming language, its goals, its features, and why it's one of the fastest-growing programming languages in the world.

This section comprises the following chapters:

- Chapter 1, *A New Challenger Approaches*
- Chapter 2, *Programmers' Multi-Tool – Flexible, Expressive, and Concise*

A New Challenger Approaches 1

In this chapter, you'll gain an understanding of what Kotlin is, how it came about, and why it's quickly gaining popularity. You'll find a high-level overview of key language features, as well as the design principles behind the language itself. Finally, this chapter will lay the foundations for the following chapters' focus on features, patterns, platforms, and best practices for improving your understanding of the Kotlin programming language.

This chapter covers the following topics:

- Creating a modern language for the **Java Virtual Machine** (**JVM**)
- Moving beyond the JVM
- Designing Kotlin with best practices in mind
- Checking in on the current state of Kotlin

Technical requirements

In order to download, compile, and execute the samples found in this chapter, you must have the following:

- IntelliJ IDEA 2018.3 Community or Ultimate editions, or newer
- An internet connection
- Git and GitHub (optional)

To download all of the code in this chapter, including the examples and code snippets, please refer to the following GitHub link: https://github.com/PacktPublishing/Mastering-Kotlin/tree/master/Chapter01.

Creating a modern language for the JVM

Kotlin was born out of a desire for a modern programming language that could be run on the JVM while still being fully compatible with Java and existing Java tooling. With these goals in mind, Kotlin has evolved into one of the fastest growing programming languages in the world and continues to carve out space for itself across multiple domains.

 GitHub's 2018 State of the Octoverse report listed Kotlin as the fastest growing language on GitHub: `https://github.blog/2018-11-15-state-of-the-octoverse-top-programming-languages/`.

In this section, we're going to dive into what Kotlin is, how it came to be, and why it's great for developers.

What is Kotlin?

So, what exactly is Kotlin? Kotlin is a statically typed programming language designed to run on the JVM and to be 100% compatible with Java and existing Java tooling. Kotlin combines a modern set of features that gives it unique advantages over other JVM languages.

Kotlin is flexible

Kotlin supports, but does not strictly enforce, multiple programming paradigms. With Kotlin, you can write object-oriented, functional, imperative, and reactive code, both separately and combined. Kotlin also supports modern features such as type inference, allowing the compiler to worry about enforcing strict typing rather than the developer. Kotlin can also be run on a variety of different platforms, from IoT devices and mobile applications to the browser.

Kotlin is expressive and concise

Kotlin is designed to be both expressive and concise. Features such as type inference and default parameter values enable developers to accomplish their goals with less code while features such as `data` classes and `object` classes allow developers to express common patterns such as singletons with a single keyword.

Kotlin is powerful

Although relatively new, Kotlin is a fully featured, powerful programming language ready to tackle the demands of modern software requirements. Features such as higher-order functions, coroutines, and a comprehensive standard library give developers all the tools they need to ship high-quality software.

Hello Kotlin

The following snippet illustrates several interesting features available in Kotlin:

```
fun formatName(name: String?) = name ?: "Fellow Human"

fun greetReader(greeting: String = "Hey", name: String?) =
    println("$greeting ${formatName(name)}")

fun main(args: Array<String>) {
 greetReader("Hello!", "Reader")
 // Hello! Reader
}
```

As you look at these few lines of code, you will notice a few items of interest, which are as follows:

- The use of the `fun` keyword to define a new function
- Functions that exist outside of any enclosing class
- Demonstrations of null and non-null types
- Support for default parameter values and `String` templates

Who created Kotlin?

Kotlin was created by software company JetBrains who are best known for creating excellent development tools such as IntelliJ IDEA. JetBrains has continued to invest in Kotlin over the years and is still a driving force behind the advancement of the language.

Announcing Kotlin

Kotlin was first announced to the world in 2011 at the JVM Language Summit. Having already been in development for a year upon announcement, the first public release came in January 2012. The following month saw the open source release of Kotlin under the Apache License 2.0.

Motivations for Kotlin

According to JetBrains, their motivations for creating an entirely new programming language were threefold:

- They wanted a more productive language for the JVM than was currently available. Existing solutions such as Java or Scala either lacked modern language features or suffered from slow compile times.
- They expected Kotlin's adoption to drive sales of IntelliJ.
- It was hoped that the increased discussion and awareness of the company would lead to greater trust in JetBrains itself and their philosophies around building quality development tools.

Community involvement

From the early days of Kotlin, lead language designer Andrey Breslav made it clear that several things were important in the development of the language such as first-class interoperability and community feedback.

Since the initial announcement of Kotlin, JetBrains has been open about motivations, design decisions, and the development process. This openness has worked in their favor and has contributed to the current success of the Kotlin programming language. Now, let's see what lies beyond all this.

Moving beyond the JVM

Kotlin may owe its origin to JVM interoperability, but it has quickly moved beyond pure JVM applications. One of the early wins for Kotlin was acceptance in the Android development community where most developers were required to use Java 6 or Java 7. Kotlin enabled Android developers to use language features, such as lambdas, which were not available on older versions of Java.

Outside of Android, Kotlin can now be transpiled to JavaScript, used in multiplatform mobile applications, or compiled to run natively on macOS, Windows, and Linux.

Kotlin for Android

To date, Kotlin has received the most popularity in the Android development community. Kotlin starting gaining traction for Android development in 2015, but it was 2017 when Kotlin really came to the forefront. At Google IO 2017, Google announced first-class support for the Kotlin programming language. It was to sit alongside Java and C++ as officially supported languages for the platform and this marked the beginning of the large-scale adoption of the language.

When Android Studio 3.0 was released in October of 2017, there was no longer a major blocker to adopting the language in established projects. Teams that had been concerned about prerelease versions of plugins or IDEs could now try the language on stable tooling with the full, long-term support of Google. This allowed teams and organizations to adopt the language with much more confidence and began the surge in Kotlin's popularity that we see today.

 The official Android documentation now defaults to Kotlin when displaying code snippets. This is just one example of Google's commitment to long-term support for Kotlin on Android.

IntelliJ and Android Studio both make it incredibly easy to integrate Kotlin with existing Android projects, or to start new projects that are 100% Kotlin. Additionally, Google continues to invest in Kotlin with improved tooling and the Core-KTX Jetpack library, which makes building Android applications with Kotlin even more enjoyable.

Chapter 13, *Kotlin on Android*, will dive deeper into the usage of Kotlin for Android application development.

Kotlin for the web

From the beginning, Kotlin has been built with portability in mind. Because it is a JVM language, it can operate anywhere with an existing JVM stack, and with support for transpiling to JavaScript, you can write Kotlin code for a variety of web development needs, such as manipulating the DOM or interacting with Node.js.

Chapter 14, *Kotlin and Web Development*, will further explore the use of Kotlin in JVM and JavaScript web development.

Now, let's see how Kotlin works here.

Server-side Kotlin

Java remains one of the most popular programming languages in the world and much of that use is happening in server-side backend systems. Kotlin can integrate smoothly with any of these JVM supported systems and can be integrated all at once, or bit by bit as developers become more familiar with the language. Kotlin can be used to deploy these applications to any system that supports Java web applications.

Kotlin tooling for server-side work is great as well. IntelliJ IDEA has full support for the language and there are additional plugins for popular frameworks such as Spring. JetBrains has also developed Ktor, an unopinionated framework for developing web applications with Kotlin. These tools aim to make it as easy as possible to use Kotlin for your server-side work.

Kotlin to JavaScript

Not only can Kotlin be used to build JVM-compatible projects for the web, but it can additionally be transpiled to target client-side and server-side JavaScript. The transpiled code currently targets ECMAScript 5.1 and aim to provide as consistent an experience as possible between targeting the JVM and JavaScript.

Native and multiplatform Kotlin

JetBrains continues to work toward Kotlin becoming a more ubiquitous language, and a big part of that effort is in Kotlin/Native. Kotlin/Native enables developers to write Kotlin code that is compiled to native binaries. This enables Kotlin to be run on platforms such as iOS, macOS, Windows, and so on.

Kotlin/Native retains its great interoperability and can be used to integrate with other languages such as C++ or Objective-C. This allows Kotlin to be used in multiplatform projects where common functionality is written in Kotlin and then shared between other targets. A great example of this is in mobile development where Kotlin code can be shared between iOS and Android applications.

In `Chapter 15`, *Introducing Multiplatform Kotlin*, you'll learn more about how Kotlin/Native and multiplatform projects can bring your Kotlin code to additional platforms.

Having an understanding of these concepts, let's now understand some best practices with Kotlin in mind.

Designing Kotlin with best practices in mind

Kotlin has been designed based on decades of experience from working with Java and other programming languages. By building on this experience, JetBrains has worked to improve the developer experience with Kotlin by focusing on things such as first-class tooling support from day one, fast build times, and bringing modern features and best practices to the language design.

Learning from Java

Kotlin is 100% compatible with Java through the bytecode that allows both to target the JVM. Kotlin's origin stems from wanting modern language features and compile speeds that other JVM languages couldn't provide. Because of these, Kotlin is heavily influenced by Java, but can improve areas where deficiencies or best practices have been discovered over the years.

Best practice by design

By examining other languages, and common best practices, Kotlin's designers have been able to provide language features and syntax that make it easier to write safer, cleaner, more concise code by default.

A few examples of this include the following:

- Non-null types
- First-class support for functions and function types
- Invariant arrays
- Language support for singletons
- Data classes

Long considered to be the *billion dollar mistake,* `null`, and how to handle it properly, is one of the most common challenges for Java developers. Kotlin looks to improve on this by making types non-null by default, and it requires developers to explicitly mark something as nullable.

Kotlin includes first-class support for functions and for function types. This makes Kotlin well suited to functional programming and can allow developers to reduce the number of classes in their projects. Features such as data classes, invariant arrays, and final-by-default classes all help enforce immutability in your code base.

By making it easier, or the default behavior, to enforce best practices, it makes it more likely that developers will follow them.

After understanding the best practices for learning Kotlin from Java and by design, we can now check the current state of Kotlin.

Checking in on the current state of Kotlin

Today, Kotlin is one of the fastest growing languages in the world. It has already proven itself for Android development and is now starting to find a home in other domains as well.

Developing Kotlin in the open

Since its public announcement, JetBrains has been very open with the development of Kotlin. This includes a public issue tracker, regular blog posts, conference talks, a yearly Kotlin census, and they even have their own conference now, KotlinConf.

 You can submit your feedback, or leave your own issues and feature requests in the Kotlin issue tracker: `https://youtrack.jetbrains.net/issues/KT`.

Kotlin has seen four major stable releases to date, which are as follows:

- v1.0: February 15, 2016
- v1.1: March 1, 2017
- v1.2: November 28, 2017
- v1.3: October 29, 2018

Each of these releases has brought exciting new functionality to the language. Most recently, Kotlin v1.3 brought coroutine support for asynchronous programming.

Increasing popularity for Kotlin

The popularity of Kotlin can be seen in a number of ways. GitHub's 2018 The State of the Octoverse survey listed Kotlin as the number one fastest growing language by contributors, seeing a 2.6x increase in contributors over the previous year.

JetBrains is currently planning their third KotlinConf, which has welcomed over 1,200 attendees at each of the earlier events. The reception at the first event was so positive, and demand overseas was so high, that in 2018, the event was moved from San Francisco to Amsterdam.

As more and more developers are turning to Kotlin, we are now seeing an increase in learning tools as well. Companies such as Google and Udacity have partnered to develop Kotlin training courses. JetBrains now offers a Kotlin training certification for individuals or companies that want to certify the quality of their Kotlin instruction. Developers are writing and speaking about Kotlin all over the world at meetups, conferences, and on podcasts, webinars, and so on. Much of this is new over the past two years, and all indicators suggest that this will only increase as more and more organizations and individuals start using Kotlin in their projects.

Learning Kotlin

If you've never worked with Kotlin, there are a number of ways to try it out and to begin learning the language.

If you would like to jump right into using Kotlin in your existing code base, Kotlin is supported by a number of popular IDEs:

- Android Studio
- IntelliJ IDEA Community and IntelliJ IDEA Ultimate
- Eclipse

Android Studio and IntelliJ IDEA both provide support for quickly converting Java to Kotlin and for examining the common generated bytecode. Additionally, both IDEs provide a REPL tool and scratch files that allow you to quickly run individual Kotlin commands or functions independently from the rest of the code base. This can make it very easy to start playing with Kotlin within a familiar tool.

If you would prefer to try Kotlin before downloading an IDE, there are several options for hands-on learning in your web browser:

- Playground: `https://play.kotlinlang.org`
- Kotlin examples: `https://play.kotlinlang.org/byExample/overview`
- Koans: `https://play.kotlinlang.org/koans/overview`

Each of these will help you gain an understanding of Kotlin features, and extend from the basics up to more complex coding challenges where you can test your understanding.

In this book, we'll work through examples of many of Kotlin's features. We'll work to understand the features on their own, and then learn how they can be used to cleanly architect your applications and implement familiar design patterns. Additional resources for learning Kotlin can be found at the end of this chapter in the *Further reading* section.

Summary

Kotlin is a modern programming language that can be used to build applications across mobile, the web, and native platforms. Since its inception, JetBrains has developed Kotlin to provide an excellent developer and integration experience so Kotlin can be learned gradually and slowly integrated into existing projects. The design and development of the language has been done very much in the open, and you can view the Kotlin issue tracker and submit your own ideas, issues, and feedback to help contribute to the language. Kotlin's popularity continues to increase rapidly, and its ability to target a variety of platforms makes it likely that the popularity trend will continue.

In this book, you'll learn firsthand why Kotlin is growing so rapidly. We'll start by exploring different application architectures, and how to model data and manage state using Kotlin. We'll then explore how Kotlin can be integrated and tested with existing Java code. Advanced topics such as coroutines and functional programming will be examined, and finally, we'll take a look at how Kotlin can be used on different platforms such as Android and the web.

In `Chapter 2`, *Programmers' Multi-Tool - Flexible, Expressive, and Concise*, we'll dive into the building blocks of the language. You'll learn more about Kotlin's support for multiple programming paradigms, first-class functions, non-null types, and explore Kotlin's extensive standard library.

Questions

1. Which company started the development of the Kotlin programming language?
2. When was Kotlin announced to the world?
3. Who is the lead designer of Kotlin?
4. What platforms did Kotlin initially target?
5. Which platforms are currently supported by Kotlin?
6. For which platform has Kotlin gained the most popularity?
7. List two factors that have contributed to the rapid growth of Kotlin.

Further reading

- *Kotlin Quick Start Guide*, published by Packt (`https://www.packtpub.com/application-development/kotlin-quick-start-guide`)
- *Kotlin Programming By Example*, published by Packt (`https://www.packtpub.com/application-development/kotlin-programming-example`)
- *Learning Kotlin by Building Android Applications*, published by Packt (`https://www.packtpub.com/application-development/learning-kotlin-building-android-applications`)
- *Kotlin Programming By Example*, published by Packt (`https://www.packtpub.com/application-development/kotlin-programming-example`)

2
Programmers' Multi-Tool – Flexible, Expressive, and Concise

This chapter will dive into the building blocks of the language and will provide a foundation upon which the rest of this book can build. It will highlight some of the most popular language features such as first-class functions, non-null types, the Standard library, and support for multiple programming paradigms. You'll begin to develop an understanding of how these features work on their own and how they may impact how you develop your applications.

This chapter is structured as follows:

- Picking your programming paradigm
- Embracing first-class functions
- Fixing the billion-dollar mistake
- Integrating with Java

Technical requirements

To download, compile, and execute the samples found in this chapter, you must have the following:

- IntelliJ IDEA 2018.3 Community or Ultimate editions or newer
- An internet connection
- Git and GitHub (optional)

To download all of the code in this chapter, including the examples and code snippets, please see the following GitHub link: `https://github.com/PacktPublishing/Mastering-Kotlin/tree/master/Chapter02`.

Picking your programming paradigm

When learning about or discussing, a new programming language, it can be useful to understand the programming paradigms that the language can be classified with. A *programming paradigm* can be thought of as a means of classifying languages based on common features.

Object-oriented languages, such as Java and C++, all support some form of modeling data with logical representations such as classes. *Functional* programming languages, such as Common Lisp or JavaScript, perform operations as pure transformations of data without global state or mutable data.

Languages can fall into multiple paradigms at the same time. Kotlin allows developers to write imperative object-oriented code and functional code, as well as asynchronous reactive code. Developers can mix-and-match these methodologies as they see fit because, while Kotlin supports them all, it doesn't enforce any particular programming paradigm.

Object-Oriented Programming

Java developers are used to writing object-oriented code. In Java, everything must happen within a class, so it likely comes as no surprise that Kotlin fully supports Object-Oriented Programming. In fact, Kotlin improves upon Java's support and provides convenient solutions for common Object-Oriented Programming patterns such as defining singletons, creating immutable data classes, and providing getters/setters.

The following code snippet shows a basic example of programming in Kotlin using object-oriented principles. It demonstrates the implementation of a simple class along with accessing the public property of that class:

```
data class Language(val name: String)

fun main(args: Array<String>) {
  val language = Language("Kotlin")
  println(language.name)
}
```

As you likely know, there is much more to Object-Oriented Programming than the simple snippet here. You'll learn more about using Kotlin to write effective object-oriented code in Chapter 4, *First-Class Functions*.

Functional programming

Functional programming languages rely on pure transformations of data to perform work. This approach differs from Object-Oriented Programming rather significantly because functional programming avoids mutable data and a global state.

With Kotlin's support for first-class functions and its large Standard library, it's possible to use it to write highly functional programs as well. The following snippet is a small example of how functional code can be written in Kotlin by chaining multiple function calls together and processing data without side-effects:

```
// Performing multiple filter operations on an input list
studentList
  .filter { student -> student.grade == 11 }
  .filter { student -> student.gpa > 3.5 }
```

In Chapter 12, *Fully Functional – Embracing Functional Programming*, you'll learn more about how to write functional programs in Kotlin as well as some tools that make this easier to accomplish.

Reactive programming

Reactive programming relies on asynchronous streams of data that can be observed, transformed, and responded to. Reactive programming has gained a great deal of popularity recently with the adoption of Redux and ReactiveX across various languages.

For Java developers, RxJava has become quite popular, especially in the Android development domain. Because of Kotlin's strong interoperability with Java, it's also possible to leverage RxJava and RxKotlin to write reactive code.

The following example demonstrates one way in which reactive code can be written in Kotlin:

```
studentsObservable
  .filter { student -> student.grade == 11 }
  .filter { student -> student.gpa > 3.5 }
  .subscribeBy(
    onNext = { displayStudents(it) },
```

```
        onError =  { error -> error.printStackTrace() },
        onComplete = { println("Done!") }
    )
```

Kotlin supports reactive programming via multiple means such as RxJava/RxKotlin and coroutine channels.

In Chapter 3, *Understanding Programming Paradigms in Kotlin*, you'll dive deeper into the specifics of each programming paradigm and how they are influenced and realized in Kotlin.

Now that we understand how to pick a programming paradigm, let's move on to find out about first-class functions and how they fit in.

Embracing first-class functions

Kotlin includes first-class support for functions, which means that functions can be invoked, and entire applications written, without having to rely on classes and methods as in Java. This represents a significant shift in how code is written using Kotlin.

This support for functions enables a variety of useful features in the language:

- Functional programming can be achieved because of Kotlin's functions.
- Extension functions give the ability to modify and adapt APIs to fit our needs.
- Higher-order functions are the backbone of the Standard library.
- First-class functions allow developers to remove entire categories of "helper" and "utility" classes that existed for the sole purpose of containing static methods.

Function types

There are several types of function in Kotlin that all have their unique traits and uses. Understanding these function types and when to use them is an important part of fully embracing Kotlin. By taking advantage of Kotlin's different function types, you'll be able to write cleaner, safer, and more idiomatic code.

Next, you'll see a subset of the function types that will be discussed, including top-level functions, extension functions, and higher-order functions. In Chapter 4, *First-Class Functions*, we will explore in some depth Kotlin's support for functions, their flexibility, and the different variations of functions available.

Top-level functions

In Kotlin, a function can be defined independently of any associated class. If a function is written within a Kotlin file, it will be available as a standalone, callable function within whatever visibility scope has been defined (public, internal, or private). This type of function is what's known as a top-level function.

This differs from other JVM languages such as Java and Scala where all functions are defined as methods of an associated class. This has implications within the Java interop story and will be discussed in more detail in Chapter 4, *First-Class Functions*. The following snippet demonstrates a basic, top-level function available within its declared module:

```
// defined within any *.kt class
fun printHello() = println("Hello!")
```

Extension functions

Similarly to C# or Swift, Kotlin supports extension functions. Extension functions allow you to extend the behavior of an existing type, even if you don't own that type. This can be extremely useful when working with cumbersome APIs or when building custom DSLs. Extension functions can be defined in any Kotlin file, but require special syntax.

The following snippet is taken from the Kotlin Standard library and demonstrates how extension functions can be used to extend common classes as well:

```
// forEach is defined as an extension function CharSequence
inline fun CharSequence.forEach(action: (Char) -> Unit)
```

The forEach function does not exist as a method on CharSequence but can be invoked as if it were a method. This not only gives the language's developers the freedom to extend classes as needed, but any developer is now free to modify existing types as they see fit.

Higher-order functions

Kotlin allows you to write functions that return another function or that take functions as arguments. This is a very powerful feature and is leveraged heavily across the Kotlin ecosystem. One way in which higher-order functions represent a large change from Java is in their ability to replace **Single Abstract Method types** (**SAM-types**) with function arguments and passed lambdas. It's no longer required that you define an interface for simple callbacks that could be treated as a function. You can see one example of this in the following snippet.

In the same example from the Kotlin Standard Library, we see that the `forEach` function takes another function as an argument. That function will define what should happen when each character in `CharSequence` is iterated over:

```
// 'action' is a function that is called for each char
// in the CharSequence
inline fun CharSequence.forEach(action: (Char) -> Unit)
```

Because of Kotlin's support for higher-order functions, it's not necessary to pass any type of class or interface as a callback: instead, pure functions can be used.

Standard library

The Kotlin Standard library provides numerous functions that make working with Kotlin much more idiomatic and enjoyable. These include functions and extension functions for working with strings, collections, and other common JDK classes. The Standard library also includes several functions such as `let` and `apply`, which really encapsulate what people often think of when they consider idiomatic Kotlin.

In `Chapter 12`, *Fully Functional – Embracing Functional Programming*, you'll discover more about Kotlin's rich Standard library of functions and learn about Arrow, a library for fully functional programming with Kotlin.

Let's now move on to understand some improvements to be made and kept in mind before being able to integrate Java with Kotlin.

Fixing the billion-dollar mistake

Many developers quickly learn about the challenges associated with handling null types in a programming language. One of the most common errors for Java developers is `NullPointerException`, which is caused by trying to access an object that is null. In fact, the frustrations attributed to null are so great, it's even been referred to as the *"billion-dollar mistake."*

Seeing, and understanding, the problems that null has caused in Java and other languages, Kotlin was designed to eliminate null as much as possible. In Kotlin, types are non-null by default. To work with a nullable type requires the explicit addition of the `?` symbol. In this section, we'll look at how to define null and non-null types, and a few of the ways we can handle nullable types within our Kotlin code.

Defining null and non-null types

How to best work with, and eliminate, null from Kotlin is a very relevant and important topic, and the presence of non-null types is one of the biggest differences between Java and Kotlin. Having some discussion around this key distinction is important key to learning Kotlin and understanding further concepts around null-safe calls, scoping operators, and so on. Before learning more about working with null, let's look at how we would define a non-null value. In the following snippet, you'll see we create a variable named `language` of the `String` type:

```
fun main(args: Array<String>) {
    var language: String = "Kotlin"
}
```

If we want to assign a `null` value to our `language` variable, we will get a compiler error:

```
fun main(args: Array<String>) {
 var language: String = "Kotlin"
 // Error: Null can not be a value of a non-null type String
 language = null
}
```

This is because types in Kotlin are non-null by default, and so our `language` variable will only accept `String` (non-null) types. To allow a variable to accept a null reference, it must be explicitly declared as accepting nullable values:

```
fun main(args: Array<String>) {
    var language: String = "Kotlin"
    language = null // Error: cannot be null

    var name: String? = "Kotlin"
    name = null // this is okay
}
```

In this case, the `name` variable is defined as the `String?` type. To indicate that a variable should accept null values, you must add `?` after the type.

Working with null

Kotlin aims to eliminate null and `NullPointerException` from your code. This is why types are non-null by default. Unfortunately, it's not always possible to avoid null, especially if working within a mixed Java plus Kotlin code base. There are sometimes scenarios where null might be a reasonable option to represent your data, or you might be working with an API that uses null. For these types of cases, there are several ways in which you can safely work with null types, such as the following ones:

- Safe calls
- Non-null assertion
- Conditionals
- The Elvis operator
- Safe casts

Null-safe calls

With a non-null type, you may safely call methods or access properties on a variable without worrying about `NullPointerException`. In this snippet, `languages` is inferred to be `List<String>`. Because `languages` is of a non-null type, the `isNotEmpty()` method may be called without worrying about `NullPointerException`, as follows:

```
fun main(args: Array<String>) {
    var languages = listOf("Kotlin", "Java", "c++")
    languages.isNotEmpty() // okay
}
```

If the list were defined as `List<String>?`, this would not be the case. In this case, calling `companies.isNotEmpty()` would result in a compiler error. Because the compiler knows the value might be null, it will require you to handle that possibility in some way:

```
fun main(args: Array<String>) {
    var languages = listOf("Kotlin", "Java", "c++")
    languages.isNotEmpty() // okay

    var companies: List<String>? = null
    companies.isNotEmpty() // Error: Only safe (?.)
    // or non-null asserted (!!.) calls are allowed
}
```

Perhaps the simplest way to handle the possible null value is to use a safe call. Safe calls are written using `?.` and allow you to access properties or call methods without fear of `NullPointerException`. In this snippet, `companies?.isNotEmpty()` is a safe call and would return null if `companies` were null:

```
fun main(args: Array<String>) {
    ...

    var companies: List<String>? = null
    companies?.isNotEmpty() // okay
}
```

Safe calls can be chained together as well, making them extremely useful when accessing or assigning nested properties in a nullable type. In the following example, `companies?.get(0)?.toLowerCase()` will safely return null if any part of the expression evaluates to null:

```
fun main(args: Array<String>) {
    ...

    var companies: List<String>? = null
    companies?.get(0)?.toLowerCase() // okay
}
```

In this example, if `student?.favoriteSubject` evaluates to null, `subject[0]` will never be evaluated:

```
fun main(args: Array<String>) {
    val subject = listOf("CS", "Math", "Physics")
    val student: Student? = null
    student?.favoriteSubject = subject[0]
}
```

Non-null assertion

There may be situations in which a null safe call is not how you want to handle null. Another option is to use a non-null assertion call on the nullable variable. This will throw `NullPointerException` if the variable is `null`. This might be desirable if you're parsing input parameters and your program can't run without them. We can see an example of this in the following snippet:

```
fun parseArgs(args: Array<String>?) {
    val argCount = args!!.size // throw NPE if 'args' is null
}
```

In situations like this, it may then be desirable to fail quickly rather than providing a default value.

 If you use a non-null assertion call on a variable and then use that variable again after the call, the compiler will SmartCast the variable to a non-null type and you can omit any further safe or non-null assertion calls.

Conditional checks

It's also completely possible to check for null using standard conditional `if/else` checks. In this snippet, if `args` is `null`, the expression will evaluate to `0`:

```
fun parseArgs(args: Array<String>?) {
    val argCount = if(args != null) args.size else 0
}
```

This type of `if/else` expression makes working with `val` much easier as we can ensure our variable values are assigned only once, adding to the level of immutability within our programs.

The Elvis operator

The use of conditionals is not an uncommon occurrence; however, the syntax is a little verbose for such a common occurrence. For these cases, the Elvis operator, `?:`, can be used to make the code a little more concise. The Elvis operator allows you to return a non-null value in an expression if the left-hand side of the expression evaluates to null. We'll find an example of this in the following snippet:

```
//if args?.size is non null, use args.size, otherwise return 0
fun parseArgs(args: Array<String>?) {
    val argCount2 = args?.size ?: 0 // return 0 if args?.size is null
}
```

In this code, if the null-safe call, `args?.size`, evaluates to null, then the Elvis operator will provide the value specified on the right-hand side, in this case, `0`.

After sorting this mistake, let's finally see how to integrate Kotlin with Java.

Integrating with Java

As we discovered in `Chapter 1`, *A New Challenger Approaches*, seamless interoperability with Java has been a primary goal for Kotlin since its inception. JetBrains started creating Kotlin primarily for themselves and needed the language to work with their extensive existing Java code bases and tooling. Tight integration with Java also would allow Kotlin to be used alongside existing Java code, making the barrier to entry smaller for developers looking to try Kotlin in existing projects.

Using Java from Kotlin

Because Kotlin is the new language on the block and was built to integrate with Java as seamlessly as possible, calling Java code from Kotlin code works out of the box. In this section, we'll take a look at a couple of quick examples of using Java code from Kotlin.

Creating and working with Java classes from Kotlin

The following snippet illustrates a simple Java class with two fields and associated getters:

```java
// basic Java class
public class Developer {
    private String name;
    private String favoriteLanguage;

    public Developer(String name, String favoriteLanguage) {
        this.name = name;
        this.favoriteLanguage = favoriteLanguage;
    }

    public String getName() {
        return name;
    }

    public String getFavoriteLanguage() {
        return favoriteLanguage;
    }
}
```

This `Developer` class is representative of any simple model object representing a person. Even though `Developer` is implemented in Java, we can still use it from Kotlin, as demonstrated in the following snippet:

```
// Kotlin function creating a new Developer object and accessing the 'name'
fun main(args: Array<String>) {
    val kotlinDev = Developer("Your Name", "Kotlin")
    val name = kotlinDev.name
}
```

From Kotlin, we are still able to fully use an existing Java class and all of its methods. This means you don't need to convert existing Java classes into Kotlin before being able to use them in your Kotlin code. This makes Kotlin highly interoperable with existing Java code bases and tooling.

 Notice how, in the preceding snippet, the `name` field was accessed without calling `.getName()`? This is known as the property access syntax and allows you to access a property value directly rather than calling the getter. You'll learn more about this in `Chapter 5`, *Modeling Real-World Data*.

Calling static Java methods from Kotlin

Now let's look at another example of working with Java from Kotlin. In the following snippet, you'll see a simple Java class named `Logger`. This class has a single, static method named `logMessage`:

```
// simple Java class with static method
public class Logger {
    public static void logMessage(String message) {
        System.out.println(message);
    }
}
```

Now see how the Java method can be used from Kotlin to print the name from the `Developer` object created in the previous example:

```
// Kotlin function calling the static Java method Logger.logMessage
fun main(args: Array<String>) {
    val kotlinDev = Developer("Your Name", "Kotlin")
    val name = kotlinDev.getName()

    Logger.logMessage(name)
}
```

The `logMessage` method can be called from Kotlin code the same way as it would be from Java. This is particularly interesting because Kotlin does not have the `static` keyword, and therefore does not have static methods or fields in the same way Java does. You'll learn more about Kotlin's lack of `static`, and its impact on your code, in Chapter 5, *Modeling Real-World Data*, and Chapter 7, *Crossing Over – Working across Java and Kotlin*.

Using Kotlin from Java

Using Kotlin code from Java is possible as well. However, because Kotlin provides a lot of nice syntactic sugar that isn't available from Java, sometimes the resulting Java code does not look quite as concise and readable as it might from Kotlin.

Creating and working with Kotlin classes from Java

The following snippet illustrates our simple `Developer` class written in Kotlin:

```
// simple Kotlin class with 2 properties and associated getters
data class Developer(
    val name: String,
    val favoriteLanguage: String
)
```

In the following, you can see how the `Developer` class written in Kotlin can be used from a Java method:

```
public class KotlinFromJava {
    public static void main(String[] args) {
        Developer developer = new Developer("Your Name", "Kotlin");
        String name = developer.getName();
    }
}
```

The new instance of `Developer` is created like any other Java class, and its properties are available via generated getters even though they weren't defined in the Kotlin code. You'll learn more about how this works in Chapter 5, *Modeling Real-World Data*.

Calling Kotlin functions from Java

Now let's look at how you might use helper functions written in Kotlin from your Java code base. The following snippet shows a top-level function, `logMessage`. This function is defined in a file named `Logger.kt`:

```
// top-level function in Logger.kt
fun logMessage(message: String) = println(message)
```

Now let's see how that top-level function is called from Java:

```
public class KotlinFromJava {
    public static void main(String[] args) {
        Developer developer = new Developer("Your Name", "Kotlin");
        String name = developer.getName();
        LoggerKt.logMessage(name);
    }
}
```

When called from Java, the top-level function cannot be invoked as a standalone function like in Kotlin. In that case, it must call the function as a static method on a generated class corresponding to the filename the top-level function is defined in. This is a good example of syntactic sugar that isn't available from Java, and if it sounds a little confusing right now, that's okay. We will go into much greater detail about this in Chapter 8, *Control the Story*.

Expanding on the interop story

We've just seen several examples of how Kotlin and Java code can be used together in the same project. In Section 3, *Play Nice – Integrating Kotlin With Existing Code*, we'll examine the Kotlin/Java interop story in great detail and learn more about why Java interoperability is so important and how it can be realized.

Summary

As this chapter illustrated, Kotlin is flexible and powerful and aims to improve upon existing languages and provide an enjoyable production-ready programming language. Kotlin allows developers to write code in whatever way makes sense to them. Whether it's object-oriented, reactive, or functional code, Kotlin can support it.

Kotlin's support for first-class functions opens up many possibilities for functional programming and the robust Standard library provides many convenient functions out of the box. If the functionality doesn't exist, you can write your own standalone functions or even extension functions to get the job done.

Years of collective experience and research have been considered in the design of Kotlin. This is fundamental to Kotlin and its interoperability with Java. Kotlin is built to work seamlessly with Java and to improve upon it. One of the biggest, and most popular, differences between the languages is its support for non-null types and the impacts this has on Kotlin code bases.

These elements of Kotlin help form the foundation for how you can use the language to write high-quality software.

In the next chapter, we'll go into much greater detail on how Kotlin can be used to write object-oriented, functional, reactive, and imperative code.

Questions

1. Can you name two programming paradigms that Kotlin supports?
2. Is it true or false that Kotlin requires everything to be contained within classes?
3. What is a top-level function?
4. What are higher-order functions?
5. How do you declare a nullable type in Kotlin?
6. What are the three ways to handle null?
7. Is it true or false that Kotlin code can't be used from Java code?

Further reading

- *Kotlin Quick Start Guide* (`https://www.packtpub.com/application-development/kotlin-quick-start-guide`)
- *Kotlin Programming by Example* (`https://www.packtpub.com/application-development/kotlin-programming-example`)
- *Reactive Programming in Kotlin* (`https://www.packtpub.com/application-development/reactive-programming-kotlin`)
- *Hands-On Object-Oriented Programming with Kotlin* (`https://www.packtpub.com/application-development/hands-object-oriented-programming-kotlin`)

2
Section 2: Putting the Pieces Together – Modeling Data, Managing State, and Application Architecture

This part will teach the reader how Kotlin supports functional, reactive, and imperative programming patterns. The reader will learn how to model data and application state and how to access and manipulate that data using Kotlin functions. Throughout this part, readers will rediscover familiar Java design patterns and how they can be realized in Kotlin.

This section comprises the following chapters:

- Chapter 3, *Understanding Programming Paradigms in Kotlin*
- Chapter 4, *First-Class Functions*
- Chapter 5, *Modeling Real-World Data*

3
Understanding Programming Paradigms in Kotlin

How does Kotlin compare to other programming languages? How is Kotlin similar to, or different from, the programming languages that we are proficient in? These are very reasonable questions. One way you can begin to answer them is to classify languages by the programming paradigms they support.

In this chapter, we will do just that. We will take a look at three programming paradigms that can be used to classify Kotlin, and also clarify that, while Kotlin supports multiple paradigms, it does not enforce any particular coding style.

The following topics will be covered in this chapter:

- Classifying programming languages
- Object-oriented programming
- Functional programming
- Reactive programming

Technical requirements

In order to download, compile, and execute the samples found in this chapter, you must have the following:

- IntelliJ IDEA 2018.3 Community or Ultimate editions, or newer
- An internet connection
- Git and GitHub (optional)

To download all of the code in this chapter, including the examples and code snippets, please see the following GitHub link: https://github.com/PacktPublishing/Mastering-Kotlin/tree/master/Chapter03.

Classifying programming languages

How do you compare programming languages? You might dive right in and examine differences in syntax or idioms. You could compare target platforms or contrast their `Hello World` implementations. All of these can help paint a picture of how two programming languages might differ.

But these approaches are quite specific, and don't work as well for describing groups of related languages. That is where the concept of programming paradigms becomes quite useful. Programming paradigms provide a means of classifying programming languages by common features or patterns. They provide a broad, high-level classification mechanism with which we can quickly group and compare different programming languages.

 Using programming paradigms to classify languages dates back over 40 years. Robert W Floyd is thought to have been the first to use the notion of a programming paradigm in his Turing Award lecture detailing the work of Thomas Kuhn.

While these classifications may not give specific details about language syntax or where the code might run, they allow us immediately to understand key aspects of a language such as how data is modeled or how computation is done.

There are many examples of programming paradigms:

- Declarative
- Imperative
- Object-oriented
- Quantum
- Dynamic
- Functional

All of these represent some set of characteristics than can help you understand how a programming language can be used. In many ways, these high-level characteristics are more useful for language comparison than specific details because they cut straight to the root patterns and conventions present within a language while skipping over their specific syntax and idiosyncrasies.

As many software developers can attest, syntax is often easy to learn from one language to the next. When learning new languages, the more difficult challenge, often, is understanding and adopting new mental models of how to model and structure a program. Robert W Floyd described this challenge well:

> *"To the designer of programming languages, I say: unless you can support the paradigms*
> *I use when I program, or at least support my extending your language into one that does*
> *support my programming methods, I don't need your shiny new languages."*

> *– Robert W Floyd, The Paradigms of Programming, 1978*

These challenges can be mitigated by understanding the programming paradigms embodied by a new language, and then drawing on experience from other similar languages.

In the rest of this section, we'll build up our understanding of common classifications of programming languages to understand better how Kotlin's supported paradigms relate to one another. We'll start with a quick explanation of multi-paradigm languages.

Multi-paradigm languages

Programming paradigms are not mutually exclusive classifications. Within the notion of programming paradigms, there are hierarchies and overlaps. Some classifications such as declarative programming might describe a broad set of characteristics and languages while others such as dynamic programming are quite specific.

Some programming languages, such as Haskell, are designed specifically to conform to a single paradigm (in Haskell's case, functional programming). However, because the definitions and boundaries of the paradigms themselves overlap, it's possible to classify a programming language using multiple programming paradigms concurrently.

Let's take Java, for example. Within Java, there are elements of multiple programming paradigms:

- Imperative programming
- Object-oriented programming
- Structural programming
- Procedural programming
- Generic programming
- Event-driven

Some of these are subtypes of others. For example, object-oriented programming can be considered a subtype of structured programming. Some of the paradigms, such as generic and event-driven programming, can be realized within Java, but aren't necessarily core tenets of the language. In general, understanding a language's supported paradigms can help you quickly understand what is supported and possible with a language, independent of any exact language details.

In the next section, we'll discuss imperative programming languages.

Imperative programming languages

Imperative programming is a programming paradigm in which a program's state is modified by explicit statements.

It focuses on how a problem should be solved. Imperative code defines specific instructions for how a state should be manipulated and transformed to reach the desired outcome.

In the real-world example, tying your shoes, imperative programming instructions might look something like this:

1. Find your shoes.
2. Take your shoes to a location to sit.
3. Sit down.
4. Pick up your right shoe.
5. Ensure the shoe laces are untied.
6. Open up the shoe and so on.

Imperative code is explicitly defined and outlines exactly how to reach a certain outcome. What does this look like in code?

When writing code in Java or in Kotlin, imperative code is very familiar. When implementing functions, methods, or classes, the details and instructions are typically defined using an imperative style. There may be other programming paradigms mixed in, but generally much of the code will follow an imperative style.

The following is globally a simple example in Kotlin:

```
/**
 * @return The sum of the numbers from 1 to n
 */
fun sumNumbersToN(n: Int) : Int {
    var sum = 0
```

```
    for (i in 1..n) {
        sum += i
    }
    return sum
}
```

This example performs a summation from 1 to an input value *N*. The code very explicitly outlines how the desired summation will be performed. It's clear how the state, the `sum` variable, is mutated, and there is a clear flow to the operations performed. OOP comes under this category so let's have a look at that.

Objected-oriented programming languages

Object-oriented programming (**OOP**) languages fall under the larger classification of imperative programming. Object-oriented code implies certain organizational and interaction patterns with the code you write, but much of the code that is written will still probably fall under the definition of imperative programming.

As we'll see later in this section, the logic behind how an object's state is manipulated or how it returns a value from a method is often written in an imperative style where each logical step is clearly defined. Both Java and Kotlin can be considered object-oriented programming languages.

Next, we'll discuss declarative programming languages.

Declarative programming languages

Declarative programming is a programming paradigm in which the goal or outcome is defined without describing the implementation details of how to achieve the outcome.

It is a bit more abstract in its definition and in examples. While imperative code very explicitly defines how to calculate an outcome, declarative code omits those implementation details and instead favors what should be performed or calculated.

Database query languages such as SQL are a good example of this. In the following example SQL snippet, you see the desired outcome is defined by selecting all records from the `ProgrammingLanguages` table where the `Target` field equals `JVM`. The following code shows this:

```sql
/* Selects all programming languages that target the JVM */
SELECT * FROM ProgrammingLanguages WHERE Target="JVM";
```

The details of how that selection will actually be performed are hidden from us, however. There are no explicit instructions defined for how records will be processed or filtered. This illustrates the key distinction between imperative and declarative programming languages.

Domain Specific Languages

An interesting subcategory of *declarative* programming languages is **Domain Specific Languages** (**DSLs**). DSLs are often thought of as mini-languages, specifically crafted to fit the use cases of a specific domain. This makes them very convenient and well suited for a particular problem type, but not for general-purpose computing. A few examples of popular DSLs include:

- HTML
- SQL
- YACC parser language
- MATLAB

In the following snippet, we'll see an example of a typical `Hello World` program written in HTML:

```
<html>
<header><title>This is title</title></header>
  <body>
    Hello world
  </body>
</html>
```

HTML is a great example of a domain-specific language. It's highly optimized and specific to the task of defining how elements should be structured and styled within a web page. Although HTML is highly useful and popular, you wouldn't want to apply HTML to the task of building a scalable backend service, for example.

DSLs exist to make specific tasks easier. Kotlin DSLs exist for testing, the Gradle build system, defining HTML, and for other domains. You'll learn much more about creating your own custom DSLs in `Chapter 11`, *Building Your Own Tools – Domain-Specific Languages (DSLs)*.

Other programming paradigms

So far, we've primarily examined imperative and declarative programming paradigms, but there are many other ways of classifying programming languages or patterns. Some of these, like object-oriented programming, warrant their own sections and chapters in this book, while others are less critical to your overall understanding of Kotlin.

Here, we'll quickly cover event-driven programming and generic programming.

Event-driven programming

Event-driven programming is a programming paradigm in which the logical flow and computation are controlled by events such as user-generated actions.

With event-driven programs, computation is typically only performed in response to some event. That event could be a user clicking a mouse or pressing a key on the keyboard, or it could be a sensor returning a new value. While events are not being processed, the program is idle, probably iterating through a main event loop that continues the operation of the program and regularly checks for new events to process.

The following snippet illustrates what a basic event-driven loop might look like:

```
var isRunning = true
while (isRunning) {
    val newestEvent = events.poll()
    proccessEvent(newestEvent)
}
```

The loop may continually check for events until some event processing indicates that the program should terminate.

Generic programming

Generic programming is a programming paradigm in which code is written without knowing the specific type, which allows the code to be executed by, and to operate on, types to be specified later in the code.

It is not a new concept in Kotlin. Java developers are probably quite familiar with generics and generic programming. In Kotlin, while some of the rules are slightly different, many of the same concepts apply. Much of the Kotlin standard library is built using generics. Collections are a great example of this. Functions for iterating, filtering, and mapping collection values are all written using generic code so they can be applied to collections of any type.

This code snippet is taken from the Kotlin standard library:

```
/**
 * Performs the given [action] on each element.
 */
public inline fun <T> Array<out T>.forEach(action: (T) -> Unit): Unit {
    for (element in this) action(element)
}
```

The implementation of `forEach` shown here is an example of generic code written to work on an `Array` of any `T` type. This allows you to use the same `forEach` function whether using `Array<String>`, `Array<Int>`, or any other array type you need.

Now that we have a basic understanding of some of the broad classifications of programming languages, we're going to go into greater detail about some of the specific programming paradigms supported by Kotlin. We'll start in the next section by exploring object-oriented programming.

Understanding object-oriented programming

Object-oriented programming is a programming paradigm in which data is modeled, stored, and accessed through objects that can extend and inherit properties from other objects.

Object-oriented programming is a popular pattern for organizing state and code into conceptual objects, which often serve as representations of real-world objects or problems. Data formats are defined using *classes* that represent some conceptual model within the problem domain, while objects represent a specific instance of a class.

Many of the most popular programming languages support object-oriented programming:

- C++
- JavaScript
- Python
- Java
- Kotlin

Some languages, such as Java, make everything an object and strictly require object-oriented programming at some level of abstraction. Other languages, such as JavaScript or Python, provide the building blocks for object-oriented programming but don't strictly enforce it.

Key concepts

OOP can take different forms depending on the language, but there are several core principles that are widely applicable:

- Encapsulation of data
- Inheritance
- Polymorphism

We will explore these concepts in the following sections.

Encapsulation

Some data within a class might be considered private implementation details that should not be exposed to anything outside the class. Other data might need to be available, but its access should be controlled. Encapsulation refers to hiding data from outside entities. By carefully considering which data to hide, and which data to expose, class dependencies can be minimized, controlled, and anticipated, which makes refactoring and extension easier.

In the following example, the logic for how the name should be formatted is encapsulated within the getFormattedName method:

```
class Person(val firstName: String, val lastName: String) {
    fun getFormattedName() = "$lastName, $firstName"
}
```

This allows for the logic to be changed without affecting callers of the method. The change would be isolated to, and encapsulated in, the Person class.

Inheritance

Inheritance is the notion that one class can inherit data and methods from another class. This can allow groups of related classes to avoid duplication of critical code or data, and can enforce strict relationships between related things.

Building on the previous example, we see in the following that we can define a `Programmer` class that inherits from `Person`:

```
class Programmer(firstName: String, lastName: String, val favoriteLanguage:
String)
    : Person(firstName, lastName)
```

This makes logical sense as a programmer *is* a person. In this case, `Programmer` adds a `favoriteLanguage` property while inheriting the `firstName` and `lastName` properties from its base class, `Person`.

Polymorphism

Polymorphism is a concept referring to a class's ability to override behavior inherited from a base class. This allows class hierarchies to define similar patterns or behaviors that can be explicitly defined in child classes. The following is globally one way to think of it: animals move, but not all animals move the same way. We define how a dog moves in one way, but we use an entirely different way to define how a bird moves.

Again building on our previous example, the `Programmer` class can override the behavior of `getFormattedName`, which demonstrates the notion of polymorphic behavior, shown as follows:

```
class Programmer(firstName: String, lastName: String, val favoriteLanguage:
String)
    : Person(firstName, lastName) {

    override fun getFormattedName(): String {
        return "$lastName, $firstName - $favoriteLanguage developer"
    }
}
```

Anyone calling `getFormattedName` on either `Person` or `Programmer` won't have any notion of *how* the method is implemented, but they will know to expect that a string will be returned.

Object-oriented programming with Kotlin

Kotlin provides fully featured support for object-oriented programming. As you might expect coming from languages such as Java, in Kotlin you can define classes and interfaces. Additionally, Kotlin provides objects and data classes to make common patterns such as singleton and immutable model classes easier to implement.

In Chapter 5, *Modeling Real-World Data*, we'll fully explore how to realize OOP in Kotlin.

One of the most interesting aspects of Kotlin is that it not only supports OOP but also has first-class support for functions, and can achieve highly functional programming as well. In the next section, we'll discuss functional programming to help understand how it relates to Kotlin.

Functional programming

Functional programming is a programming paradigm in which program structure and control are expressed through pure mathematical functions without global state or mutable data.

Functional programming falls under the umbrella of declarative programming. Rather than writing imperative statements that manipulate application, object, or local state and ultimately come to some final value, functional programs compose expressions, in the form of functions, that operate purely on inputs and outputs.

In functional programming, there is no global or mutable state. When a function is called for a given input X it will always return the same output value. This is in direct contrast with other paradigms such as OOP in which the modeling, saving, and manipulation of the state are key concerns. This absence of state and mutability also means a lack of side-effects. Retrieving an output for a function will only return the specified output; it will not trigger any other global event or modify state in any way.

These traits make functional programs easier to understand because they are mathematically pure. They can be easily traced and reasoned about given any arbitrary input value. These are desirable traits, and, as such, elements of functional programming have made their way into non-functional languages as well.

Modern languages that support functional programming include:

- JavaScript
- C++11
- Java 8
- Kotlin

All of these languages are popular today and allow for the implementation of functional concepts. However, all of these languages also support characteristics of other paradigms, such as object-oriented programming, and are typically not used in a purely functional way in production code bases.

Key concepts

What it means to support functional programming or be a functional programming language is not always clearly defined as many modern languages blur the lines between multiple programming paradigms. Even so, there are several characteristics that must be present to even begin the conversation.

First-class functions

A key pillar of functional programming is first-class functions. These are functions that can be used anywhere other types may be used; they are first-class citizens of the language. Generally, this includes the following:

- Storing functions as variables
- Passing functions as arguments to other functions
- Returning a function from another function
- Storing functions within other data structures

This concept is very similar to that of higher-order functions, which is a more mathematical expression of the idea of functions that operate with/on other functions.

Pure functions

Another defining characteristic of functional programming is that of pure functions. Pure functions are those functions that do not have any side-effects. Calling a pure function will return a consistent output based on any given input. Pure functions will not modify any type of global state or initiate other operations of any kind, which means they do not have any direct or transient dependency on one another.

Functional programming with Kotlin

Is Kotlin a functional programming language?

It can be. Kotlin supports first-class functions and higher-order functions, and has a large standard library filled with useful functions that can be chained together to write highly functional code. Let's look at a few examples of functional code in Kotlin.

In the following snippet, you can see how Kotlin allows you to store a function as a variable:

```
fun main(args: Array<String>) {
    // we can store a function as a variable
    val stringFilter:(String) -> Boolean = { string ->
        string.length > 3
    }
}
```

This variable can then be used to invoke the function, or it can be passed to another function as an argument.

Here's an example of a higher-order function taken from the Kotlin standard library:

```
/**
 * Returns a list containing only elements matching the given [predicate].
 */
public inline fun <T> Iterable<T>.filter(predicate: (T) -> Boolean):
List<T> {
    return filterTo(ArrayList<T>(), predicate)
}
```

The `filter` function takes a function as an argument that is used to filter items from the `Iterable` receiver. The passed argument will be called for each item in `Iterable`, and is used to determine whether or not to include the current item in the `List<T>` output.

In the following code, we can see how the previous two examples can be used together:

```
fun main(args: Array<String>) {
    // we can store a function as a variable
    val stringFilter:(String) -> Boolean = { string ->
        string.length > 3
    }

    val languages = listOf("c++", "php", "java", "kotlin")
    val filteredLanguages = languages.filter(stringFilter)
}
```

We use a standard library function to easily create a list of strings. We then call `filter` on that list, and pass in the function variable that we previously declared.

Finally, we can see how we could achieve the same output by chaining these functions together, as shown in the following code example:

```
val filteredLanguages = listOf("c++", "php", "java", "kotlin")
    .filter { string ->
        string.length > 3
    }
```

In this case, we skip storing a function variable or the original list of strings, and compose a single chain of functional operators that defines our desired output. This functional composition has no side-effects, and produces the same output each time; so it adheres to the properties of functional programming that we discussed previously.

More to learn

In `Chapter 4`, *First-Class Functions*, you will go deeper into understanding Kotlin's support for functions, their flexibility, and the different variations of functions available. In `Chapter 14`, *Kotlin and Web Development*, we'll pull these functional concepts together and see how to write highly functional code with Kotlin. You'll discover more about Kotlin's rich standard library of functions, and learn about Arrow, a library for fully functional programming with Kotlin.

In the next section, we'll continue our exploration of Kotlin-supported programming paradigms and discuss reactive programming.

Reactive programming

Reactive programming is a programming paradigm in which state changes are propagated and reacted to via streams of data

As the name suggests, reactive code is written to react to changes in the underlying data state. State changes are exposed via streams of data that can be subscribed to and manipulated toward achieving the desired output. Changes in the underlying state will propagate new events and update the output state. In practical terms, this means that you can focus on modifying the state and any observers of that state will be notified; the state change is independent of the associated actions.

Reactive code can be used for event-driven programming, and is well suited to applications that must react to events, such as user input or sensor data. It is compatible with other paradigms such as object-oriented and functional programming, and the concepts can generally be translated across implementations.

Reactive programming is quite similar to the observer pattern in that it allows you to write code that responds to changes in some observed state or object. The ReactiveX project incorporates the Observer pattern into its APIs as a means of formalizing the relationship and nomenclature between Observer and Reactive patterns. In the next section, we'll discuss RxJava, the JVM implementation of the ReactiveX project.

RxJava

Reactive programming has gained popularity in large part thanks to the ReactiveX project, which defines a comprehensive set of APIs around common reactive programming concepts. There are ReactiveX (Rx) implementations for many languages, including the following:

- Java—RxJava
- Kotlin—RxKotlin
- C++—RxCpp
- C#(Unity)—RxUni
- RxGroovy—Groovy
- RxDart—Dart

For more information regarding the ReactiveX project, check out `http://reactivex.io/`. There you will find additional resources for understanding reactive programming, as well as links to the full list of Rx implementations. Currently, there are almost 20 languages that have Rx bindings available to them.

RxJava and RxKotlin can both be used to write reactive code in Kotlin, and have gained a lot of popularity in the Android development community.

Key concepts in RxJava

ReactiveX and RxJava, by extension, are built upon several foundational components and concepts. These are the building blocks for all other operators and patterns that make ReactiveX so powerful, popular, and complex.

The following snippet illustrates how Rx `Observables` can be chained together with operators:

```
loadAsyncStudentData()
  .observeOn(Schedulers.io())
  .filter({ student -> return student.getAge() > 17 })
  .sort()
  .first(5)
  .subscribe({
    // handle output
  })
```

By doing so, we make asynchronous programming a much easier task to read, write, and debug.

Observables

ReactiveX builds upon the observer pattern as its conceptual model for handling both synchronous and asynchronous event streams, and introduces `Observable` as the core model of abstraction. Rx observables are flexible and composable, making them a viable solution for many different problems.

Operators

The `Observable` abstraction allows for the existence of operators than can act on `Observable` and be chained together to transform event streams into final output values. These `Observable` chains follow a very functional pattern of programming and can simplify otherwise complex tasks by relying on pure functions to transform data.

RxJava became particularly popular in the Android developer community. In addition to simplifying common threading challenges in Android development, it brought in a functional programming style that could not easily be achieved in older versions of Java that were required by Android at the time.

ReactiveX includes many popular functional operators such as:

- `map`
- `filter`
- `take`
- `first`

It's also possible to create your own operators if you require to. By combining operators and observables, it's possible to compose multiple asynchronous operators, or streams of data, into a single stream. By combining these data sources, it's possible to avoid callback hell (a state in which multiple nested callbacks become difficult to read and understand), and to handle success and error cases at a single point. These traits can greatly reduce the complexity of certain types of computation.

Threading

The Rx observable model is unopinionated when it comes to threading, and yet flexible enough to allow developers to chose a threading model that works best for them. An `Observable` chain can be moved between threads using simple operators, and the handling of `Observable` results can be moved onto any thread just as easily. RxJava provides built-in schedules for common types of async work, including the following:

- `Schedulers.io()`
- `Schedulers.computation()`
- `Schedulers.newThread()`

Ease of threading using Rx is one of its best features as it simplifies an area of computing that is traditionally difficult to get right.

RxKotlin

Since Kotlin has great interoperability with Java, RxJava is fully usable from Kotlin out of the box. RxKotlin provides a set of functions that extend RxJava and make it more idiomatic and easier to use from Kotlin. It takes advantage of Kotlin language features, such as extension functions and named arguments, to make working with RxJava feel more like a native Kotlin library.

Reactive coroutines

ReactiveX isn't the only option available for writing reactive code to handle asynchronous events in Kotlin. Kotlin version 1.3 brought support for coroutines, which is a concept common to other programming languages, designed specifically to write asynchronous code. Coroutines can be thought of as lightweight threads that allow developers to write non-blocking asynchronous code.

Channels and flow

`Channels` are a newer feature in Kotlin that can transfer streams of values similar to how an `Observable` stream might work in RxJava. Using `Channels`, it's possible to create theoretically infinite streams of data and process that data asynchronously in an efficient manner. Consumers can then operate on the results of the asynchronous operations in much the same way that an `Observable` chain is subscribed to.

Flow is also a new feature in Kotlin, built on top of coroutines, and designed to enable cold asynchronous streams of data. This is similar to channels, and yet there is an important distinction. `Flow` will only emit values once something is listening for those values, and `Flow` doesn't necessarily solve any concurrency challenges. It's meant simply to provide asynchronous streams of data.

In this section, we've examined several different threading and concurrency concepts to better understand the tools that are available in the Kotlin ecosystem. You'll learn more about `Coroutines`, `Channels`, and `Flow` in `Chapter 10`, *Practical Concurrency*.

Summary

In this chapter, we explored different programming paradigms that are supported by Kotlin. We compared imperative programming and declarative programming and examined both the object-oriented and functional programming paradigms. Kotlin supports, but does not enforce, all of these programming paradigms along with other models of programming, such as generic and reactive programming. Kotlin aims to provide support and make it convenient to write code in whichever way works best for you.

Kotlin has support for classes, interfaces, and other common OOP language features; in addition to strongly enforcing OOP principles such as encapsulation. Kotlin supports first-class functions and higher-order functions, and provides a rich Standard Library that can be used to write pure functional code. Support for Coroutines, Channels, and RxJava provides multiple options for maintaining asynchronous code.

In the next chapter, we'll dive deeper into Kotlin's support for functions and functional types.

Questions

1. What is a programming paradigm?
2. Can you name three programming paradigms supported by Kotlin?
3. What is the difference between imperative and declarative code?
4. Can you name one declarative programming language?
5. What are the three core principles of object-oriented programming?
6. What are the two core principles of functional programming languages?
7. What is reactive programming?
8. What is the difference between RxJava and RxKotlin?

Further reading

- *Reactive Programming in Kotlin* (`https://www.packtpub.com/application-development/reactive-programming-kotlin`)
- *Functional Kotlin* (`https://www.packtpub.com/application-development/functional-kotlin`)
- *Hands-On Object-Oriented Programming with Kotlin* (`https://www.packtpub.com/application-development/hands-object-oriented-programming-kotlin`)

4
First-Class Functions

In this chapter, we'll dive deeper into Kotlin's support for first-class functions and how that support enables us to rethink how we write our code. You'll learn, in detail, how Kotlin functions are flexible, concise, and powerful by examining different types of functions, such as single expression functions and local functions. Finally, we'll explore how to leverage Kotlin features such as default parameter values, extension functions, and higher-order functions to write expressive, concise, and flexible code that reduces boilerplate and is more convenient to use.

The following topics will be covered in this chapter:

- Understanding Kotlin's first-class support for functions
- Using named arguments and default parameter values to reduce boilerplate and increase the utility of our functions
- Examining different types of functions and how/when to use them

Technical requirements

In order to download, compile, and execute the samples found in this chapter, you must have the following:

- IntelliJ IDEA 2018.3 Community or Ultimate editions, or newer
- An internet connection
- Git and GitHub (optional)

To download all of the code in this chapter, including the examples and code snippets, please see the following GitHub link: `https://github.com/PacktPublishing/Mastering-Kotlin/tree/master/Chapter04`.

Hello functions – first-class support for functions

Functions are first-class citizens of the Kotlin programming language. This means functions can be stored as variables and passed as arguments to other functions. Kotlin has been designed to make functions easy to write and flexible to use. This section will introduce you to functions in Kotlin and help you explore what it means to have first-class support for functions.

Writing a basic function

Let's jump in and look at a basic function written in Kotlin:

```
// Main.kt
fun helloFunctions(greeting: String) {
    println("$greeting Kotlin Functions")
}
```

This snippet demonstrates a fully functional, and quite simple, function written in Kotlin. There are several interesting things to note in this example:

- The `fun` keyword
- Function naming
- Function parameter
- No containing class

A function is written by starting with the `fun` keyword. This tells the compiler that we are writing a new function. The next component is the function name. In the preceding example, the name is `helloFunctions`. Functions in Kotlin follow the same naming conventions as methods in Java. Next, we see that we are defining a `greeting` parameter of the `String` type. This syntax is different than Java method parameters. In Kotlin, parameters are defined by providing the name first, then a colon, then the type.

It's also important to note that the previous snippet does not require an enclosing class. Unlike in Java, functions may exist on their own as top-level functions and can be used as standalone executable functions.

First-class functions

Now that we've seen how to write a simple function with Kotlin, let's talk about how/where functions can be used in Kotlin, and how that relates to the idea of first-class functions.

Functions as variables

In Kotlin, functions may be stored and accessed via variables and properties. This means we can define variables and properties designated to reference a specific function signature, and we can then access and modify those functions as needed. Like any type variable in Kotlin, we can define both read-only and mutable function variables, and we will take a look at both of these variations in the following sections.

Read-only function variables

In this snippet, we've defined the read-only greetingProvider variable to store a function that takes no arguments and returns String:

```
val greetingProvider: () -> String = { "Hello" }
```

Because this is a read-only variable, it must be initialized with a value. In this case, we use the lambda syntax to assign a function that returns the string literal "Hello". We can then use the variable to invoke the function.

Now, consider the following code snippet in which the function assigned to greetingProvider is run twice, but using different syntax for each invocation:

```
fun main(args: Array<String>) {
    var greeting = greetingProvider() // invoke with parentheses
    greeting = greetingProvider.invoke() // use the invoke method
}
```

The first invocation is done by adding parentheses to the variable and calling it as if it were any other function. The second line takes advantage of the invoke() function that is generated by the compiler when defining a function variable.

> The Kotlin compiler will treat a function variable as a generic function class based on the number of arguments it accepts. In the previous example, the greetingProvider function variable would be treated as private static Function0 greetingProvider.

Mutable function variables

We can store functions as mutable variables as well. If we wanted to make the previous example a mutable variable, we could update our variable declaration accordingly by replacing `val` with `var` as in the following code:

```
var greetingProvider: () -> String = { "Hello" }
```

Now, we can reassign the function value being stored within `greetingProvider` as we would with any other variable type:

```
fun main(args: Array<String>) {
  println(greetingProvider())
  greetingProvider = { "Hey" }
  println(greetingProvider())
}
// output: Hello
// output: Hey
```

In this example, we've logged `String` provided by the original `greetingProvider` variable, then assigned a new function to `greetingProvider` and re-logged the resultant function invocation. In the resultant output, we can see that the printed value is updated once the function variable is updated.

Function variables follow the same nullability rules as any other type. This means we can define the nullable function types to use with our variables. The snippet demonstrates how we could update our `greetingProvider` variable to accept a `null` value:

```
var greetingProvider: (() -> String)? = null
```

A nullable function variable might be needed if you don't have a default function that can be assigned, or if the function is only optionally needed as with a click listener. By making the function type nullable, it affects how we can interact with that function variable.

Note that `var greetingProvider: (() -> String)? = null` may be a bit hard to understand. This could be a good place to leverage `typealias` to map the difficult-to-understand type of `() -> String` type to something more readable, such as `GreetingProvider`. The resultant function variable declaration would then be easier to understand and modify: `var greetingProvider: GreetingProvider? = null`.

Since `greetingProvider` is now a nullable type, we can no longer directly invoke the function using parentheses. The following snippet demonstrates the compiler error that results from this change:

```
fun main(args: Array<String>) {
    val greeting = greetingProvider() // error: doesn't compile
}
```

To fix the code, we must now verify that the variable is non-null before invoking the function. The following snippet demonstrates two ways of verifying whether or not the function variable is null before invoking it:

```
fun main(args: Array<String>) {
    greetingProvider?.invoke() // using elvis operator
    greetingProvider?.let { it() } . // using non-null let call
}
```

In both of these cases, the compiler can verify whether or not the function variable is non-null and can safely call the function. This strict typing helps us ensure we don't encounter runtime exceptions, and it forces us to think about how we write our code to better ensure null-safety.

Function properties

We can add function properties to our defined classes as well. These properties follow the same rules as regular function variables, but are scoped to instances of their enclosing class. In the following code, we've defined a `GreetingViewModel` class that has a `greetingProvider` property, which is a function that takes in no arguments and returns a string:

```
class GreetingViewModel {
    var greetingProvider: (() -> String) = { "Hello" }
}
```

We might then modify the class to greet a user in response to some event. We've done this in the following example by adding a `greetUser()` method:

```
class GreetingViewModel {
    var greetingProvider: (() -> String) = { "Hello" }

    private fun greetUser() {
        println(greetingProvider())
    }
}
```

We could then customize the printed greeting by assigning a new function to the greetingProvider property of a given instance of GreetingViewModel as follows:

```
fun main(args: Array<String>) {
    val viewModel = GreetingViewModel()
    viewModel.greetingProvider = { "Hey" }
}
```

In this case, we've reassigned viewModel.greetingProvider to a function that returns "Hey" instead of the "Hello" default.

Functions as arguments

Another important feature of Kotlin functions is the ability to pass functions as arguments to other functions. This is partially what makes up the term higher-order functions, the other component being the ability to return functions from other functions.

A function argument can be added to a function the same way as any other argument type:

```
class GreetingViewModel {
    private val greetings = listOf("Hey", "Hi", "What's up?")

    fun printGreetings(filter: (String) -> Boolean) {
        greetings
            .filter(filter)
            .forEach {  greeting ->
                println(greeting)
            }
    }
}
```

In this example, we've added a printGreetings function to print out all the available greetings. The function takes a function parameter with a signature that takes a String argument and returns Boolean. This function can then be used to filter the available greetings.

The following snippet shows the forEach function from the Kotlin standard library:

```
/**
 * Performs the given [action] on each element.
 */
@kotlin.internal.HidesMembers
public inline fun <T> Iterable<T>.forEach(action: (T) -> Unit): Unit {
    for (element in this) action(element)
}
```

This `forEach` implementation is an extension function on the `Iterable` type, and it takes a generic `action` function as an argument. This `action` argument allows the caller to define the code to be run when each iterable element is visited.

Function arguments enable you to make use of the strategy pattern and encapsulate customizable logic into functions that can be passed around and replaced as needed. This can make code much more flexible, and is used heavily within the Kotlin standard library.

Functions as return values

Another important aspect of higher-order functions is the ability to return functions from other functions. Like defining a function type for a variable or function argument, we can define function return types as well.

One example of where this could be useful would be in writing a factory function that returns a different function for creating values based on some input.

In this example, we've created a `getGreetingProvider` function, which takes a `Boolean` argument and returns a function that returns `List<String>`:

```
fun getGreetingProvider(isFriendly: Boolean) : () -> List<String> {
    return if (isFriendly) {
        { listOf("Hey", "Hi", "Hello") }
    } else {
        { listOf("Go away", "Leave me alone") }
    }
}
```

Within the function block, we can then return a different function depending on the `isFriendly` argument. Both functions must adhere to the defined return type, but they are free to return any function that matches the signature.

Top-level functions

In many of the examples, we've been looking at functions that are not enclosed within any type of class. This is a key feature of functions in Kotlin. Functions may be defined as independent units of execution inside any Kotlin file. Functions defined like this are known as top-level functions and may be fully available to both Kotlin and Java code, depending on their visibility. We'll dive further into top-level functions later in this chapter.

In this section, we introduced Kotlin functions and began exploring how we can work with functions in a variety of ways including as variables, properties, and function arguments. In the next section, we'll dive deeper into how to define Kotlin functions that reduce boilerplate and increase flexibility in how they can be used.

Flexibility by design – reducing boilerplate with effective parameters

One of the most convenient and powerful aspects of functions in Kotlin is the treatment of parameters and arguments. In particular, Kotlin supports both default parameter values and named arguments. These allow developers to write functions with increased flexibility and utility, while reducing boilerplate.

In this section, we'll build up our understanding of working with function arguments and parameters. We'll start by adding simple parameters to our functions, then work our way up to adding default parameter values and working with named arguments.

Adding function parameters

Earlier, we saw a basic example of adding a parameter to a function:

```
fun helloFunctions(greeting: String) {
 println("$greeting Kotlin Functions")
}
```

Parameters can be added after a function name using the Pascal notation of `name: Type`. Passing an argument to a function works the same as in Java:

```
fun main(args: Array<String>) {
    helloFunctions("Hello!")
}
```

Functions with a single parameter would be quite limited, and, thankfully, we can add multiple parameters to our functions as needed.

Multiple function parameters

Like in Java and most other languages, we can define multiple function parameters and then pass the corresponding multiple arguments to a function.

Let's update our `helloFunctions` example to take both a `greeting` and a `name` parameter. To add an additional parameter, we can simply add a comma after the previous parameter and then define the new parameter name and type:

```
fun helloFunctions(greeting: String, name: String) {
    println("$greeting $name")
}
```

In this example, we've added a `name` parameter of the `String` type. Now, to call `helloFunctions`, we must pass both the `greeting` and the `name` parameters as in the following example:

```
fun main(args: Array<String>) {
    helloFunctions("Hello!", "Android")
}
```

With support for multiple function parameters, it's often likely that we will have multiple parameters of a common type. For some of these situations, there is a special syntax Kotlin provides to make working with these functions easier and more flexible.

The vararg modifier

We can define any number of parameters for our functions, but sometimes we may not know how many parameters we need to pass when writing the code. For these situations, it's possible to define a function that takes an unspecified number of parameters of the same type. This is achieved using the `vararg` modifier. Let's see how this is done.

Adding `vararg` to a parameter definition will change that parameter from `Type` to `Array<Type>`, allowing a caller to pass in multiple argument values. In the following code, we've now updated `helloFunctions` to take a variable number of the `name` arguments by adding `vararg` before the name parameter definition:

```
fun helloFunctions(greeting: String, vararg names: String) {
    names.forEach { name ->
        println("$greeting $name")
    }
}
```

Because of this update, `names` is now treated as `Array<String>` rather than `String`. Because of this, the function body has then been updated to iterate over each passed name, and print it out using the passed `greeting` argument.

Now, to invoke `helloFunctions` with any number of passed arguments, we can use it as follows:

```
fun main(args: Array<String>) {
    helloFunctions("Hello!", "Android", "Kotlin")
}
```

When calling a function that uses a `vararg` parameter, you are free to pass 0, 1, or many arguments for the `vararg` parameter, as follows:

```
fun main(args: Array<String>) {
    helloFunctions("Hello!")
    helloFunctions("Hello!", "Android")
    helloFunctions("Hello!", "Android", "Kotlin")
}
```

Here, we are calling `helloFunctions` three times with different numbers of arguments. In the first case, we don't pass any name argument, and so the resultant argument array will be empty and therefore nothing will be printed to the console. In the other cases, a greeting will be output for each input name that is passed. While the `vararg` parameters are useful, they do have their limitations as well.

Limitations of vararg

The `vararg` parameters are convenient, but they have some caveats:

- A function may only have a single `vararg` parameter.
- It's generally a good practice to make a `vararg` parameter the last parameter for a function.

Defining multiple `vararg` parameters will result in a compiler error, as in the following example:

```
// this will not compile
// Error: "Multiple vararg-parameters are prohibited"
fun helloFunctions(vararg nums: Int, greeting: String, vararg names:
String) {
    ...
}
```

It's generally a good idea to make a `vararg` parameter the last parameter in your function, especially if there are other arguments of the same type present. To illustrate why this is important, we can use the following `helloFunctions` example:

```
fun helloFunctions(vararg names: String, greeting: String) {
    names.forEach { name ->
        println("$greeting $name")
    }
}
```

Because the `vararg` parameters are treated as an array once passed, the compiler will attempt to satisfy any `vararg` parameter requirements before single-parameter values. This can lead to trouble if the compiler can't tell which value belongs to the `vararg` parameter and which argument should stand on its own. The following example illustrates this issue by attempting to call `helloFunctions` in various ways that the compiler can't understand:

```
fun main(args: Array<String>) {
    helloFunctions("Hello!")
    // error: no value passed for parameter 'greeting'
    helloFunctions("Hello!", "Android")
    // error: no value passed for parameter 'greeting'
    helloFunctions("Hello!", "Android", "Kotlin")
    // error: no value passed for parameter 'greeting'
}
```

In this case, the compiler is looking for any number of passed `String` arguments, and is then looking for the passed `greeting` parameter. This is simply not possible unless the calling code is making use of named arguments.

If we go back to our previous example usages, we will now see compiler errors in each case. This is because the compiler doesn't know which passed `String` parameter is supposed to be the `greeting` parameter, and therefore treats all `String` instances as the `vararg` parameter, which means no value is ever passed for `greeting`.

We can, however, work around this by making use of named parameters, which we will look at in the next section.

Named parameters

Function parameters have names that we use to access the argument data when passed. In Kotlin, we can make use of parameter names at the function call site to control which parameter an argument value is assigned to.

Let's revisit our previous examples to better understand how to use named parameters. We'll use our `helloFunctions` implementation that has two parameters:

```
fun helloFunctions(greeting: String, name: String) {
 ...
}
```

We see the two parameters, `greeting` and `name`, both of the `String` type. If we want to use this function, it might look something like this:

```
fun main(args: Array<String>) {
    helloFunctions("Hello", "Kotlin")
}
```

This is very straightforward, but because both parameters are the same type, there's always the possibility that we could accidentally mix up the order we pass our arguments in, which may lead to unexpected results.

To help prevent such a case, we could refer to the parameter names when passing the argument values:

```
fun main(args: Array<String>) {
    helloFunctions(greeting = "Hello", name = "Kotlin")
}
```

In this example, you'll notice that we are including a parameter name followed by = and then the argument value. This lets us be very explicit as to which parameter an argument value is assigned to. In fact, by being explicit in this assignment, we are free to pass our argument in any order we like:

```
fun main(args: Array<String>) {
    helloFunctions(name = "Kotlin", greeting = "Hello")
}
```

Here, we've now reversed the passed order of name and greeting, but the compiler understands how to assign the argument values. This flexibility can make APIs easier to work with and refactor.

The compiler can't always determine which arguments to assign to parameters though, especially if we start mixing named and positioned arguments. Let's examine this by first adding another argument to our `helloFunctions` example:

```
fun helloFunctions(greeting: String, name: String, count: Int) {
    println("$greeting $name , you get $count gold stars!")
}
```

Now that we've added an `Int` parameter, `count`, let's see how we can mix named and positioned arguments. If we start by using nothing but positioned arguments, then everything will be fine as long as we are careful about ensuring we pass the arguments in the proper order:

```
fun main(args: Array<String>) {
    helloFunctions("Hello", "Kotlin", 10)
}
```

In this case, we've carefully passed all arguments in an order that makes sense for the underlying implementation of the function.

As another safe alternative, if we use named arguments for everything, we can pass the argument values in any order we wish:

```
fun main(args: Array<String>) {
    helloFunctions(
        count = 10,
        greeting = "Hello",
        name = "Kotlin"
    )
}
```

The challenge comes when we start mixing named and positioned arguments. The following example will result in a compiler error indicating that mixing named and positioned arguments is not allowed:

```
fun main(args: Array<String>) {
    helloFunctions(count = 10, "Hello", "Kotlin") // error
    helloFunctions("Hello", name = "Kotlin", 10) // error
}
```

The error resulting from this code indicates that once we use a named argument, we must use named arguments for all subsequent arguments. We could fix this by updating our sample as follows:

```
fun main(args: Array<String>) {
    helloFunctions("Hello", name = "Kotlin", count = 10)
}
```

Now we've seen how named arguments can be useful when invoking functions with a set number of arguments, but they are also very helpful when working with the `vararg` parameters. Let's revisit one of our previous examples to see how it can be improved with named arguments.

The following snippet includes a `vararg names: String` parameter that allows us to pass an arbitrary number of names to the function:

```
fun helloFunctions(vararg names: String, greeting: String) {
    names.forEach { name ->
        println("$greeting $name")
    }
}
```

Recall that, this function will take any number of `String` instances as part of its `names` parameter, but when calling the function we receive a compiler error because the compiler can't determine which string is the `greeting` parameter:

```
fun main(args: Array<String>) {
    helloFunctions("Hello!")
    // error: no value passed for parameter 'greeting'
    helloFunctions("Hello!", "Android")
    // error: no value passed for parameter 'greeting'
    helloFunctions("Hello!", "Android", "Kotlin")
    // error: no value passed for parameter 'greeting'
}
```

This issue can be solved by using named arguments to specify which string should be the `greeting` parameter:

```
fun main(args: Array<String>) {
    helloFunctions(greeting = "Hello!")
}
```

In this case, even though the `names` parameter is first, the compiler now understands that the passed string is the `greeting` argument, and the code compiles:

```
fun main(args: Array<String>) {
    helloFunctions(greeting = "Hello!", "Android")
    // error: mixing named and positioned arguments is not allowed
}
```

 It's not possible to assign a single value to `vararg` when using named arguments.

If we try to first use a named `greeting` argument and then pass unnamed arguments for the `names` parameter, we will get a compiler error. If we start mixing named and positioned arguments in any order besides the defined parameter order, the compiler doesn't know how to handle it, and we will receive a compiler error.

In this case, if we include the `names` argument first and then use a
named `greeting` argument, the code will compile just fine and work as expected:

```
fun main(args: Array<String>) {
    helloFunctions("Android", "Kotlin", greeting = "Hello")
}
```

This section has demonstrated how to define and work with parameters in our Kotlin
functions. We've looked at basic parameter declarations, the `vararg` parameters, and how
to leverage named arguments to make satisfying these parameter requirements more
flexible. In the next section, we'll look at default parameter values and how they can enable
us to ignore parameters we don't care about.

Default parameter values

Another powerful feature of Kotlin functions are default parameter values. These allow us
to specify a default value when defining any parameter. This value will then be used if the
argument is not passed to the function invocation.

To define a default argument value, add = followed by the desired value after the type
component of your parameter definition:

```
fun helloFunctions(greeting: String, name: String = "Kotlin") {
    println("$greeting $name")
}
```

In this example, we've made `"Kotlin"` the default value for the name parameter. When
`helloFunctions` is called with both arguments, the passed argument values will be used.
However, if only the greeting is passed, then the default value of `"Kotlin"` will be used.
The following snippet shows the use of `helloFunctions` in two ways: one without using
the default parameter value, and one that does use the default value for the `name`
parameter:

```
fun main(args: Array<String>) {
    helloFunctions("Hello", "Kotlin")
    helloFunctions("Hello")
}
```

For both of these example invocations, the resultant output will be the same.

Default argument values are a powerful feature because they can remove the need for overloaded functions. If we update our function to provide a default value for greeting as well, the function can then be called with the 0, 1, or 2 argument values, depending on the desired use case. Consider the following code:

```
fun helloFunctions(greeting: String = "Hello", name: String = "Kotlin") {
    println("$greeting $name")
}
```

Once all of our parameters have default values, we can invoke the function with any number of parameters, making it extremely versatile:

```
fun main(args: Array<String>) {
    helloFunctions("Hello", "Kotlin")
    helloFunctions("Hello")
    helloFunctions()
}
```

This is especially useful when combined with named arguments. It allows us to name any argument we wish, and omit the rest as long as they have default values. In the following example, we combine named arguments and default parameter values to call helloFunctions with any combination of parameters we wish. Named arguments allow us to ignore the defined order of the parameters while default parameter values allow us to avoid passing any arguments we don't care about:

```
fun main(args: Array<String>) {
    helloFunctions(name = "Kotlin")
    helloFunctions(greeting = "Hi")
    helloFunctions(name = "Android", greeting = "Hey")
    helloFunctions()
}
```

Named arguments and default parameter values can make a function extremely flexible. They can remove the need for the Builder pattern or for overloaded methods because we can build that functionality directly into the function definition. Providing default argument values also helps self-document the code by explicitly indicating what the reasonable default values might be.

Now that we've explored the flexibility inherent within basic functions, we'll examine several different types of function variations that provide additional functionality to the language.

A function for every job – understanding function variations

In Kotlin, there are a number of function variations that we can write, and by leveraging these function types we can take advantage more fully of the Kotlin language.

In this section, we'll take a look at a number of the function types, including the following:

- Top-level functions
- Class functions
- Local functions
- Single expression functions
- Infix functions
- Extension functions

Top-level functions

Top-level functions are functions that are not tied to any class instance. These functions can be defined within any Kotlin file as independently callable functions, and can be made publicly available to the rest of your Kotlin code, depending on the defined function visibility.

To demonstrate this, we can define a top-level function named `logMessage`:

```
// Logging.kt
fun logMessage(msg: String) {
    println(msg)
}
```

This `logMessage` function has no association with any class and is defined independently within the `Logging.kt` file. Functions are `public` by default, so this function is publicly available to the rest of the code base—to both Kotlin and Java if using both languages.

If you were to add the `private` visibility modifier, the function would only be callable within the file in which the function was defined:

```
// Logging.kt
private fun logMessage(msg: String) {
    println(msg)
}
```

Because `logMessage` is now private, it can no longer be called from outside its declaration file of `Logging.kt`:

```
// Main.kt

fun main(args: Array<String>) {
 logMessage("Using the log function")
 // error: logMessage is private within a file
}
```

From within `Main.kt`, the `logMessage` function is not available, and the compilation will fail.

Top-level functions allow us to write helper functions without the need for a class to contain them. If you want, you can write functions that are globally available and can be used as if they are more natural components of the language.

Top-level functions provide great freedom in how we define new functions, but we aren't limited to top-level functions. In the next section, we'll see that we can add functions to our class declarations as well.

Class functions

We can add functions to a class to add functionality and to interact with that class. Like in Java, we can refer to a function on a class as a method. Methods are tied to the instance of the class they are associated with.

Defining a method is fundamentally the same as defining a top-level function, with the primary exception being that a method is declared within a class body. In the following example, we've defined a `Person` class that has a single method named `printName()`:

```
class Person(
    val firstName: String,
    val lastName: String) {

    fun printName() {
        println("$firstName $lastName")
    }
}
```

Note that the definition of `printName` doesn't look any different than the other top-level functions we've defined in this chapter.

To invoke the `printName` function, we must first instantiate an instance of `Person` and then reference that instance before calling `printName`:

```
fun main(args: Array<String>) {
 val nate = Person("Nate", "Ebel")
 nate.printName()
}
```

Visibility modifiers for methods are similar to top-level functions, but must also take into account the visibility of the class itself.

If we make the `Person` class `private`, we will no longer be able to call `printName()` even though it is a `public` method:

```
private class Person(
    val firstName: String,
    val lastName: String) {

    fun printName() {
        println("$firstName $lastName")
    }
}
```

Because `Person` was made `private` in the previous snippet, the following code no longer compiles:

```
fun main(args: Array<String>) {
    val nate = Person("Nate", "Ebel")
    nate.printName() // error: class is private in file
}
```

This is just a small look at methods in Kotlin. Methods on classes and objects are covered in more detail in `Chapter 5`, *Modeling Real-World Data*. In the next section, we'll introduce the concept of functions defined within other functions.

Local functions

Kotlin supports the notion of functions defined within other functions. This type of function is known as a local function. Local functions can be defined quite similarly to other functions, with two exceptions:

- A local function must be defined within another function.
- Local functions do not support visibility modifiers.

To better understand local functions, we'll use an example. In this code, we've defined two local functions, `handleSuccess` and `handleError`, within the `handleNetworkResponse` function:

```
fun handleNetworkResponse(response: Response<Person>) {
    fun handleSuccess(person: Person) {
        // handle successful response
    }

    fun handleError(error: Throwable?) {
        // handle error
    }
    when (response.isSuccess) {
        true -> handleSuccess((response.data))
        false -> handleError(response.error)
    }
}
```

These two local functions only exist within the scope of the enclosing `handleNetworkResponse` function. This means they are not callable outside the enclosing function, but they do have access to the arguments and variables of the enclosing function.

To demonstrate how the argument values are accessible within local functions, we've added an `errorMsgPrefix` variable to the top of `handleNetworkResponse`, and then consumed that variable within the implementation of our `handleError` local function:

```
fun handleNetworkResponse(response: Response<Person>) {
    val errorMsgPrefix = "Error occured: "

    fun handleSuccess(person: Person) {
        // handle successful response
    }

    fun handleError(error: Throwable?) {
        println(errorMsgPrefix + " with code ${response.code}"
                + error?.message)
    }

    when (response.isSuccess) {
        true -> handleSuccess((response.data))
        false -> handleError(response.error)
    }
}
```

After adding the additional `errorMsgPrefix` variable and the `response` function argument, both are accessible from within the `handleError` local function, making it possible to share a state between local functions and their enclosing functions.

Local functions can be useful if you want to refactor some code for readability but don't need it to be available to anything else. Rather than writing a separate private function, you could make it a local function instead. This makes it impossible to test the local function in isolation, so the decision to use a local function may depend on whether its implementation needs to be testable on its own, or if it can be considered an implementation detail.

While local functions are somewhat complex when compared to a typical top-level function, Kotlin provides additional mechanisms with which to make the function declarations as concise as possible. In the next section, we'll explore the concept of single expression functions.

Single expression functions

Single expression functions are means of reducing boilerplate when writing functions in Kotlin, by allowing us to remove the curly braces and define a function as a single expression. To demonstrate the usage of single expression functions, we'll start with the following simple `logMessage` function:

```
fun logMessage(msg: String) {
    println(msg)
}
```

This function body is a single simple line. Kotlin allows us to rewrite this function using a single expression function like the following:

```
fun logMessage(msg: String) = println("")
```

To make a function a single expression function, we can add the = operator after the closing parentheses and then define the expression to use as the function implementation. The same is possible for functions that have a non-unit return type. In this example, we've defined a `getPrompt` function that returns `String`:

```
fun getPrompt() : String {
    return "Hello. How are you?"
}
```

This `getPrompt` function can be simplified to a single expression function like so:

```
fun getPrompt() : String = "Hello. How are you?"
```

In this updated implementation, the `String` literal `"Hello, How are you?"` follows the `=` operator and defines what the return value should be. In fact, in cases like this, where the return type can be inferred by the compiler, we can simplify the implementation even further.

In this case, the right-hand side of `=` is `String`, so the compiler can infer the return type of `getPrompt` as a `String` type:

```
fun getPrompt() = "Hello. How are you?"
```

Single expression functions are a common Kotlin idiom as they reduce boilerplate and make simple functions very easy to read and understand. In the next section, we'll explore a more interesting type of function: infix functions.

Infix functions

Infix functions are functions defined with the `infix` keyword, which allows them to be called using the infix notation. Infix notation is best demonstrated using an example. The following example demonstrates the usage of the `to` infix function:

```
"userId" to "1234"
```

The `to` function is part of the Kotlin standard library and returns `Pair`.

The implementation of this type of function is very similar to that of any other function. In the following snippet, we can see the implementation of the `to` function:

```
/**
 * Creates a tuple of type [Pair] from this and [that].
 *
 * This can be useful for creating [Map] literals with less noise, for
example:
 * @sample samples.collections.Maps.Instantiation.mapFromPairs
 */
public infix fun <A, B> A.to(that: B): Pair<A, B> = Pair(this, that)
```

Infix functions must follow several rules:

- They must be associated with a class.
- They must take a single parameter.
- They may not use a `vararg` parameter.
- They may not use a default parameter value.

The reason for these rules lies in the structure of the infix notation. To use the infix notation, the compiler must be able to determine the values on the left and right of the function name. Let's try to understand these rules by writing our own infix function:

1. To start, we'll return to our `Person` class:

   ```
   class Person(val firstName: String, val lastName: String) {
       fun printName() = println("$firstName $lastName")
   }
   ```

2. We'll then add a member function named `addInterest`:

   ```
   class Person(val firstName: String, val lastName: String) {
       ...

       private val interests: MutableList<String> = mutableListOf()

       fun addInterest(interest: String) = interests.add(interest)
   }
   ```

3. Now we can call this function as usual with an instance of the `Person` class:

   ```
   fun main(args: Array<String>) {
       val nate = Person("Nate", "Ebel")
       nate.addInterest("Kotlin")
   }
   ```

4. Now let's make this an infix function by adding the `infix` keyword:

   ```
   class Person(val firstName: String, val lastName: String) {
       ...

       infix fun addInterest(interest: String) =
               interests.add(interest)
   }
   ```

5. We'll then update the usage of `addInterest` to use the infix notation:

```
fun main(args: Array<String>) {
    nate.printName()
    nate addInterest "Kotlin"
}
```

By adding the infix keyword, we were able to remove . and parentheses from the method call. The compiler knows that the instance of `Person` can become the left-hand side of the infix function call, and knows it can treat the right-hand side as the parameter value.

This is why an infix function must have one, and only one, argument value. If there was a default value and no argument was passed, the compiler wouldn't know which value to treat as the argument. Likewise, if a `vararg` parameter was used and multiple arguments were passed, the compiler wouldn't be able to handle any but the first argument value.

Infix functions can be a great way to write human-readable APIs, a useful trait if creating a custom DSL. Here, we've written an infix function named `isEqualTo` to perform an equality check:

```
infix fun <T> T.isEqualTo(other: T): Boolean = this == other
```

As in this snippet, we can then use the `isEqualTo` function to perform equality checks in a very human-readable way:

```
nate isEqualTo person1
nate isEqualTo person2
```

This is an oversimplified example, but it demonstrates how you might design APIs that are easy to read and understand. This type of highly readable code is of great value when writing human-readable tests, or some other type of declarative code.

While infix functions allow us to call methods on a class in new and interesting ways, another type of function allows us to add functions to classes we may not even control. In the next section, we'll explore this concept of extension functions.

Extension functions

Often, we work with classes and APIs we do not control. This can mean we are required to write code based on the style or requirements of those external parties. Extension functions provide a means of extending or modifying code we do not control. For example, we could write an extension function to determine whether or not `String` equals `"Kotlin"`.

In the following snippet, we've written an `isKotlin()` function. This function is an extension function of the `String` type. This means that it's only available to instances of the `String` receiver type. Note that the function name is defined by first specifying the receiver type, in this case `String`, and then adding `.` and then the function name:

```
fun String.isKotlin() = this == "Kotlin"
```

Once the extension function is written, it can be called on instances of the receiver type as if it existed on that type. In this case, `isKotlin()` can be called on any `String` variable or literal:

```
fun main(args: Array<String>) {
    "some string".isKotlin()
}
```

Extension functions are one of the most popular and powerful features of Kotlin. They enable us to extend APIs and classes we don't control, and can even help organize and clean up our own code. Extension functions are a great way to encapsulate helper functions and are a powerful tool in building custom DSLs, as we'll see in Chapter 11, *Building Your Own Tools – Domain-Specific Languages (DSLs)*.

As we've seen in this section, Kotlin functions provide a great deal of functionality and really do empower us to rethink how we write our code.

Summary

Functions are an important feature within Kotlin, and are considered first-class citizens of the language. Kotlin functions can be defined outside of any enclosing class as top-level functions, and can be passed to, and returned from, other functions. These traits make functional programming much more accessible within Kotlin than in other JVM languages. Additionally, functions in Kotlin reduce boilerplate and increase flexibility by providing features such as default parameter values and named arguments, which allow us to reduce the number of overloaded functions we must define.

We can also define a number of different types of functions depending on our current use cases. Extension functions allow us to modify or extend classes and APIs that we may not control, and enable us to decouple low-level components from other helper functions. Top-level functions reduce the need for helper classes that exist only to store static methods. Infix functions can be leveraged to write human-readable APIs that are easy to understand and use. In many ways, the power and flexibility of functions in Kotlin are what make the language so enjoyable to use.

In the next chapter, we'll take a closer look at object-oriented programming in Kotlin and dive deeply into how we can structure and model data in our code bases.

Questions

1. What is the significance of the `fun` keyword?
2. How do you add a parameter to a function?
3. What are named arguments?
4. What are default parameter values?
5. How do you define a local function?
6. What is a top-level function?
7. How do you define an infix function?
8. What are higher-order functions?
9. How do you define an extension function?

Further reading

- *Kotlin Standard Library Cookbook* (https://www.packtpub.com/application-development/kotlin-standard-library-cookbook)
- *Functional Kotlin* (https://www.packtpub.com/application-development/functional-kotlin)

5
Modeling Real-World Data

In this chapter, you'll discover how to apply object-oriented programming principles within your Kotlin code. We'll learn how to write cleaner code by modeling data using classes, interfaces, and the concepts of inheritance and composition. We'll explore different ways of modeling data with classes, enumerations, and sealed classes and learn when to choose one over the other to minimize the amount of code we must write and to enforce best practices such as immutability and strong type safety.

This chapter is structured as follows:

- Discovering how to create a simple class in Kotlin
- Understanding how to realize the concepts of inheritance and composition within your Kotlin code
- Learning how to leverage data classes to reduce boilerplate
- Learning about different types of classes such as object classes, sealed classes, enums, and inline classes

Technical requirements

To download, compile, and execute the samples found in this chapter, you must have the following:

- IntelliJ IDEA 2018.3 Community or Ultimate editions or newer
- An internet connection
- Git and GitHub (optional)

To download all of the code in this chapter, including the examples and code snippets, please see the following GitHub link: `https://github.com/PacktPublishing/Mastering-Kotlin/tree/master/Chapter05`.

Object-oriented programming in Kotlin

As we discussed in Chapter 3, *Understanding Programming Paradigms in Kotlin*, Kotlin fully supports **Object-Oriented Programming** (**OOP**). This probably comes as no surprise, given the popularity of OOP in modern languages and Kotlin's ties to the JVM and other JVM-based languages such as Java.

OOP in Kotlin shares many similarities with Java, but there are important differences as well, as in the following examples:

- Numeric types in Kotlin are all classes, even if they are represented internally as primitive values.
- Classes are closed by default.
- Interfaces may contain properties.

Kotlin also aims to adopt learning and best practices from years of Java to make modeling data easier. Toward this goal, Kotlin provides additional modifiers for creating certain families of classes:

- Sealed classes provide compiler support for defining restricted class hierarchies
- Inline classes provide a minimal-overhead means of declaring simple type classes
- Object declarations provide built-in support for the singleton pattern

As with other aspects of the language, Kotlin also provides mechanisms for reducing the boilerplate required to define and create class instances. Features such as primary constructors, initialization blocks, and secondary constructors provide the flexibility to scale your implementations from very simple class declarations to much more complex cases.

Defining a class

Let's start off by taking a look at how to create a very simple class to represent an online course. The following snippet demonstrates how to define a new class called Course:

```
class Course {
    // empty class body
}
```

This new `Course` class currently contains no user-defined properties or methods but can be instantiated, and common methods such as `toString()` and `hashCode()` can still be invoked from any instance.

The following snippet shows how to instantiate an instance of `Course` from Kotlin:

```
val course = Course()
val displayString = course.toString()
```

Notice that there is no need to use the `new` keyword, or any other keyword, to instantiate the class. We can simply use the class name and provide any required argument values.

Our Kotlin class can be used from Java as well. In the following snippet, we are creating an instance of `Course` from Java:

```
public static void main() {
    // create new instance of Course in Java
    Course course = new Course();
}
```

Notice that, when instantiating `Course` from Java, we do in fact have to use the new keyword as with any class in Java. This is due to the syntax and compiler in Java itself.

Because the `Course` class doesn't contain any user-defined properties or methods, it can actually be simplified to a single-line definition, as in the following snippet:

```
class Course
```

You'll see we were able to remove the `{ }` characters defining the class body of `Course`. Kotlin allows us to omit the curly braces for our class body if it is empty. This is a small convenience that reduces the overall boilerplate required to work with classes in Kotlin.

Now that we understand how to create a simple empty class, let's examine how to store state information within our classes.

Adding properties

Kotlin supports properties as a means of storing the program state within class instances, which is an essential component of OOP. Properties can be added and accessed using very simple and concise syntax but can also be customized to provide more powerful and flexible functionality.

Property basics

We can add properties to our classes in a couple of different ways. Let's start by adding a `title` property to our `Course` class, as follows:

```
class Course(courseTitle: String) {
    val title = courseTitle
}
```

There are a couple of things to note here:

- We've added a primary constructor to pass the `courseTitle` parameter.
- We then define and initialize the `title` property using the value of `courseTitle`.

The primary constructor is defined by the parentheses after the class name. The primary constructor can be considered the default way of creating your class and can often be the only constructor that needs to be defined. We'll explore primary and secondary constructors in more detail later in this section in *Customizing construction*.

Now that we've updated our class definition, we can create a new instance by passing in a title for our course, shown as follows:

```
// create new instance of Course
val course = Course("Mastering Kotlin")
val courseTitle = course.title
```

After passing in `courseTitle` to our constructor and instantiating the class, we can access the `title` property directly by referencing its name.

Any exposed properties which can be accessed from Kotlin may also be accessed when working in Java. This example demonstrates how the properties of Kotlin classes will have getters/setters generated for them when calling from Java:

```
public static void main() {
    Course course = new Course("Mastering Kotlin");
    String courseTitle = course.getTitle();
}
```

 Kotlin supports the property access syntax, which allows callers to access a property by referencing the property name directly without having to define a getter or setter. This reduces the boilerplate needed to access/modify simple properties. These properties are still available from Java via generated getters/setters following standard naming conventions.

You'll notice, in the preceding example, that the `title` property has no visibility modifier applied to it. In Kotlin, properties are public by default and available to any calling code. We'll explore Kotlin's other visibility modifiers later in this chapter.

Now that we've seen a simple example of adding and accessing a class property, let's dive deeper into how properties are treated by the Kotlin compiler.

Working with properties

You might have noticed that, in the previous example, we were able to access the newly added `title` property without having added a getter. This is possible because Kotlin will generate getters and setters for us for properties with simple accessor logic. Let's look more closely at the following code:

In this snippet, we have our `Course` class with a public `title` property:

```
class Course(courseTitle: String) {
    val title = courseTitle
}
```

From Kotlin, we can access that property name directly, as follows:

```
val courseTitle = course.title
```

However, from Java, we must access that property using a generated getter:

```
String courseTitle = course.getTitle();
```

From Kotlin, we can access the property by referencing its name directly without any kind of get/set prefix. This is known as the property access syntax and is syntactic sugar around using getters/setters generated by the compiler. What makes the property access syntax possible is the fact that the Kotlin compiler will generate default getters and setters for any `var` properties on a class and will generate getters for any `val` properties.

In the following code, we can see the decompiled Kotlin bytecode for the `Course` class we've been looking at:

```
public final class Course {
    @NotNull
    private final String title;

    @NotNull
    public final String getTitle() {
        return this.title;
    }
}
```

```
    public Course(@NotNull String courseTitle) {
        Intrinsics.checkParameterIsNotNull(courseTitle, "courseTitle");
        super();
        this.title = courseTitle;
    }
}
```

We'll see here that the public read-only `title` property becomes a private final member and a `getTitle()` method is generated that allows that `title` property to be read.

In this example, we'll add a new read/write property, `description`:

```
class Course(courseTitle: String) {
    val title = courseTitle
    var description = ""
}
```

After adding this additional property, the compiler will add any required getters/setters. The following snippet illustrates the getter that is generated as a result of adding the `description` property:

```
...

@NotNull
public final String getDescription() {
    return this.description;
}

public final void setDescription(@NotNull String var1) {
    Intrinsics.checkParameterIsNotNull(var1, "<set-?>");
    this.description = var1;
}

...
```

By generating getters and setters for simple properties, Kotlin is writing the boilerplate for us, which saves us code and time. However, it's still possible for us to have more control over the *get* and *set* operations for our properties. We'll take a look at how to customize these getters and setters in the following section.

Custom accessors

In some situations, we may not want to rely on the default getter/setter that Kotlin provides. In those cases, we can provide our own custom accessors for any of our defined properties. For mutable variables, we can provide both custom getters and setters, while for read-only variables we can only provide a custom getter. To illustrate this, let's start by adding a custom setter for the `description` property, as follows:

1. We'll start with our existing `Course` class, which exposes a public `description` property:

```
class Course(courseTitle: String) {
    ...
    var description = ""
}
```

2. To add a custom getter to the `description` property, we can then add a `set(field) {}` block immediately following the definition of `description`:

```
class Course(courseTitle: String) {
    ...
    var description = ""
        set(value) {
            field = value
        }
}
```

Within this block, we can then add any custom logic we want. You'll notice, in this example that we assign `value` to `field`. In this case, `field` is the backing property for our custom setter. Without updating `field`, the value for `description` would not be updated.

If we wanted to log the new value when the setter is used, we could add the following line:

```
class Course(courseTitle: String) {
    ...
    var description = ""
        set(value) {
            println("description updated to: $value")
            field = value
        }
}
```

3. Now globally let's add a custom getter as well. The process is very much the same as for the custom setter, except there is no `value` argument passed in:

```
class Course(courseTitle: String) {
    val title = courseTitle
    var description = ""
        set(value) {
            println("description updated to: $value")
            field = value
        }
        get() {
            // add code for getter
            return field
        }
}
```

With custom property accessors, we can control and extend the property access behavior of our classes, giving us greater control over how our classes function. In the next section, we'll explore properties that are defined within a class's primary constructor rather than the class body.

Primary constructor properties

So far, we've been working with a `Course` class that takes in a `courseTitle` argument and then uses it to initialize a `title` property. This matches the pattern of initialization in Java; however, it can be simplified in Kotlin. You might notice that there is a direct 1:1 mapping from the primary constructor argument and eventually a property is assigned. This is not an uncommon occurrence in Java, and so Kotlin was designed to simplify this use case.

To illustrate the use of a primary constructor property, we'll once again start with our simple `Course` class example:

```
class Course(courseTitle: String) {
    val title = courseTitle
}
```

We can then combine the `courseTitle` constructor argument and the `title` property into a single inline property within the primary constructor:

```
class Course(val title: String)
```

This effectively combines the argument and property declaration and assignment and avoids the need to duplicate any constructor arguments and property declarations. Using this form of primary constructor property also still provides the generated default getters/setters so there's no loss of useful generated code from using this simplified form.

The use of primary constructors might bring up the question of when and how this class and property are initialized and ready to consume by calling the code. We're going to dive deep into how class initialization works in the following section.

Initialization

When instantiating a class, the instance and its properties can be initialized in several ways. Those initialization cases and their order are described as follows:

- Primary constructor
- Declaration assignment and initializer blocks
- Secondary constructor

Properties defined within a class's primary constructor are initialized first. Class-level property assignments and initializer blocks are handled next. The last chance to initialize the class and its properties is in the secondary constructors.

Primary constructor initialization

If a property is defined inline within the primary constructor, then its value will be assigned before any other initialization occurs. In this case, the property initialization will be placed at the beginning of the compiler-generated constructor.

In the following code, notice we have two primary constructor parameters—though only `lastName` is defined as a property:

```
class Student(_firstName: String, val lastName: String) {
    val firstName = _firstName
    val id: String
    var nickname = ""

    init {
        id = generateStudentId(firstName, lastName)
    }

    val subjects:MutableList<String> = mutableListOf()
}
```

Even though `lastName` is not the first parameter defined in the primary constructor, it will be the first property to be initialized for the class.

Property assignments and initializer blocks

After any primary constructor properties, the next initialization will occur in class-level property assignments and in initializer blocks. These will occur in the order in which they are defined within the class.

In the following snippet, we are initializing four properties, which we will examine to better understand the initialization sequence:

```
class Student(_firstName: String, val lastName: String) {
    val firstName = _firstName
    val id: String
    var nickname = ""

    init {
        id = generateStudentId(firstName, lastName)
    }

    val subjects:MutableList<String> = mutableListOf()
}
```

In the preceding example, after lastName is initialized, the properties will be initialized in the following order:

- firstName
- nickname
- id
- subjects

It's interesting to note that, while id is defined before nickname, the value of nickname is assigned before id. This is because the actual initialization of id occurs in the initializer block, which doesn't run until after nickname is initialized.

Let's add another initializer block and see how that impacts the initialization order:

```
class Student(_firstName: String, val lastName: String) {
    val firstName = _firstName
    val id: String
    var nickname = ""
    val activities: MutableList<String>

    init {
        id = generateStudentId(firstName, lastName)
    }

    val subjects: MutableList<String> = mutableListOf()
```

```
init {
    activities = mutableListOf()
}
}
```

Now, we've added another property, `activities`, above any of the initializer blocks, but the value of `activities` is not initialized until the second initializer block. This will cause activities to be initialized last after any of these properties.

To understand how the compiler treats this initialization order, we can take a look at the following decompiled Kotlin bytecode to examine the generated code:

```
public Student(@NotNull String _firstName, @NotNull String lastName) {
    ...
    this.lastName = lastName;
    this.firstName = _firstName;
    this.nickname = "";
    this.id = StudentKt.generateStudentId(this.firstName,
                this.lastName);
    List var4 = (List)(new ArrayList());
    this.subjects = var4;
    var4 = (List)(new ArrayList());
    this.activities = var4;
}
```

By viewing this code, we can see how the initialization ordering is handled by the compiler. Notice that the order in which the fields are initialized is not always the same as the order in which they appear in the class declaration. For example, `id` is initialized *after* `nickname`.

Adding methods

Like in Java, and other OOP languages, Kotlin classes can contain member functions (methods). To add a method to a class, we can simply define a function within the class body. Here, we've added a method named `printStudentInfo` to the `Student` class:

```
class Student(_firstName: String, val lastName: String) {
    ...

    fun printStudentInfo() {
        println("id:$id -> $firstName $lastName")
    }
}
```

We can then invoke the `printStudentInfo()` method on an instance of the `Student` class by referencing the instance of `Student`, followed by a `.` and then the method name and any required arguments, as in the following example:

```
fun main(args: Array<String>) {
    val student = Student("Nate", "Ebel")
    student.printStudentInfo()
}
```

To change the visibility of a method, we can add a visibility modifier before the `fun` keyword such as the following:

```
class Student(_firstName: String, val lastName: String) {

    ...

    private fun printStudentInfo() {
        println("id:$id -> $firstName $lastName")
    }
}
```

By adding the `private` modifier, the `printStudentInfo()` method is now private to the `Student` class and inaccessible outside the implementation of `Student`. We'll look at visibility modifiers more closely later in this chapter. In the next section, we're going to look more closely at how we can customize the construction of our class instances.

Customizing construction

So far, we've seen examples that use a primary constructor to initialize a class in Kotlin. While primary constructors are an easy way to instantiate a class, they aren't the only option. There are multiple ways of handling the construction of a class. Through the use of primary constructors, secondary constructors, and various visibility modifiers, Kotlin provides a great deal of freedom in how we choose to instantiate classes, and we'll take a look at those in the following sections.

Primary constructors

Primary constructors are defined inline with the class declaration using the following syntax:

```
class Student public constructor(_firstName: String, val lastName: String)
{
    ...
}
```

If the constructor does not require any visibility modifiers or annotations, the constructor keyword can be omitted to reduce the boilerplate:

```
class Student (_firstName: String, val lastName: String) {
}
```

Within a primary constructor, we can pass arguments and define properties. If the constructor does not require any arguments or properties, then the parentheses can be omitted. In this case, a default empty constructor will be generated by the compiler, allowing the class to be instantiated as if it did have a defined constructor.

The following snippet demonstrates a School class without any declared constructor:

```
class School {
    var name = ""
}
```

Though School has no constructor defined, we can still instantiate it. In the following snippet, we see that we can still instantiate an instance of School using the generated empty constructor:

```
fun main(args: Array<String>) {
    val school = School()
}
```

The existence of a compiler-generated empty constructor ensures that any class we define can be instantiated, even if we don't have to write the boilerplate primary constructor code. In the next section, we'll look at adding multiple constructors to our classes.

Secondary constructors

The primary constructor is considered the default way to instantiate a class, but we can define secondary constructors as well to provide alternative ways to create a class instance. The following code shows how to add a secondary constructor to our School class:

```
class School {
    var name = ""
    constructor(schoolName: String) {
        name = schoolName
    }
}
```

To add a secondary constructor, we can use the `constructor` keyword within the class body to define the new constructor logic. In this example, we've added a secondary constructor that takes a `schoolName` parameter to be assigned to the `name` property.

If a class has a primary constructor, then any secondary constructors must delegate to the primary constructor before any new initialization logic is run. Using our `Student` class as an example, we can see what this looks like:

```
class Student (_firstName: String, val lastName: String) {
    ...
    constructor() : this("", "") {
        // initialization logic
    }


    ...
}
```

We've added a secondary constructor in the same way, but after the constructor's parameter list, we call the class's primary constructor. To do this, we must pass in any required parameter values to satisfy the primary constructor. In the `Student` example, this means a secondary constructor will have to supply values for `_firstName` and `lastName` when calling into the primary constructor.

When calling into the primary constructor, it's possible to access the arguments passed into the newly defined secondary constructor, as follows:

```
class Student (_firstName: String, val lastName: String) {
    ...

    constructor() : this("", "") {
        // initialization logic
    }

    constructor(_firstName: String) : this(_firstName, "") {
        // initialization logic
    }

    ...
}
```

This allows us to control which parameters are exposed in our constructor and to rely on sensible defaults for any primary constructor parameters we don't want to expose directly.

While secondary constructors do provide additional freedom to provide multiple paths towards instantiating a class, you may be able to avoid defining secondary constructors by making use of named arguments and default parameter values. If you commonly use secondary constructors to provide default argument values or reorder parameters, you might consider whether or not you could make use of a single primary constructor with default parameter values and named arguments.

While we can expose as many constructors as we want, sometimes we would prefer not to expose any public constructors to better control how our classes are instantiated. To enable this, we'll explore private constructors in the next section.

Private constructors

It's possible to modify the visibility of a constructor. This is sometimes desirable in order to limit how or what can instantiate a class. A common example of this in Java would be the factory pattern in which the instantiation of a class can only be performed by some factory method.

For example, to make a primary constructor private, we can add the `private` keyword before the constructor keyword when defining the `private` constructor:

```
class School private constructor(val name: String)
```

In this example, `School` can longer be instantiated because its only constructor is `private`. To modify the visibility of a secondary constructor, we once again add the visibility modifier before the `constructor` keyword:

```
class School private constructor(val name: String) {
    private constructor() : this("") {
    }
}
```

It's completely possible to use constructors with different visibilities as well. We could modify the preceding example to make the secondary constructor `internal` while leaving the primary constructor as `private`:

```
class School private constructor(val name: String) {

    internal constructor() : this("") {

    }
}
```

The application of visibility modifiers to our constructors gives us the freedom to choose which parts of our application have access to various constructors. This could allow code within the same internal module to access a specific internal constructor while limiting the public constructors that are available. While private is a very common visibility modifier, it's not the only one. In the next section, we'll examine which visibility modifiers are available in Kotlin.

Controlling visibility

Whether defining a class, property, method, or function, we sometimes want to limit the visibility of that code. Like in Java, Kotlin has multiple visibility modifiers that control how widely a piece of code can be accessed:

- `public`
- `internal`
- `protected`
- `private`

The public modifier

In Kotlin, the default visibility is `public`. If no modifier is specified on a class, function, or so on, it will be `public`. The `public` modifier in Kotlin works the same as in Java. If marked as `public`, or unmarked and defaulting to `public`, then your code will be visible and available to the entire code base.

The internal modifier

Kotlin provides an `internal` visibility modifier that is not available within Java. With `internal`, you can mark a piece of code as being available within a module, but not the entire code base. We'll further discuss modules in the next section.

The protected modifier

In Kotlin, the `protected` modifier is available to classes and interfaces, but not for top-level declarations. Classes, interfaces, methods, and properties marked with `protected` will be visible within their enclosing class and to any available subclasses.

The private modifier

The `private` modifier works similarly to Java. Any `private` property or method in a class will only be visible to the enclosing class. Top-level properties and functions that are `private` will only be available within the file in which they are defined.

Organizing your code

When structuring your Kotlin code base, there are several levels of code organization that can be considered, such as the following:

- Files and classes
- Packages
- Modules

Let's understand each here.

Files and classes

Any Kotlin code will be defined within a file with the `.kt` extension. A Kotlin file can contain top-level function and property definitions, as well as classes or interfaces. Using the private visibility modifier, it's possible to restrict a piece of code to only being visible within its enclosing file.

The following example illustrates a single file with two classes and a top-level property all defined alongside one another:

```
// SingleFileExample.kt

val publicProperty = "hello"

class Shape
class Rectangle : Shape()
```

If a Kotlin file contains only a class definition, it's not required that the class and file share the same name. A single Kotlin file can contain multiple class definitions alongside other top-level properties and functions.

Packages

Like in Java, Kotlin packages are a means of organizing Kotlin code. A package can contain one or more files that will all share a common package name. Packages are generally used to group code by application features or layers. At a high level, they serve to organize code.

Modules

In Kotlin, a module is an executable set of Kotlin files. A module is effectively a self-contained unit of code that can stand on its own or be incorporated alongside other modules in a larger project. A module can contain many packages and Kotlin files. The internal modifier indicates that a piece of code is publicly available within the enclosing module, but not to other project modules. A module may be represented in a variety of ways depending on how the code will be run. A couple of examples include the following:

- IntelliJ IDEA modules
- Gradle source sets

In this section, we were introduced to the basics of OOP with Kotlin. We explored how to declare simple classes, add and access properties, and control the construction of our classes. Finally, we discussed how to use various visibility modifiers and organizational constructs to control who has access to our classes.

In the next section, we're going to build on these concepts and explore inheritance and composition.

Achieving inheritance and composition

When writing object-oriented code, we generally want to leverage inheritance and composition to reuse code, make relationships more flexible, and more efficiently model our data. In this section, we'll explore interfaces, abstract classes, and delegates and how they help us to implement the concepts of inheritance and composition.

Interfaces

Like in Java, we can define interfaces in Kotlin that can be used to define a common functionality or provide class templates. Similar to Java 8, interfaces in Kotlin may define default method definitions. Kotlin also provides the ability to define `interface` properties, which can either be abstract or can include a default implementation.

Defining a simple interface

Defining an interface in Kotlin is quite similar to Java. To declare a new interface, you must add the `interface` keyword followed by the interface name as in the following code:

```
interface GameObject
```

It's not required to provide an interface body or any methods or properties. An empty interface might be used as a simple marker interface.

We can add an `interface` method by defining a method signature to be required by the interface:

```
interface GameObject {
    fun update(currentTime: Long)
}
```

A class or object can them implement this `interface` method. To do this, the class must include `interface` in its declaration and then either implement the required methods or be marked abstract. The following snippet demonstrates a `Player` class, which implements our `GameObject` interface:

```
class Player : GameObject {
    override fun update(currentTime: Long) {
        // add logic
    }
}
```

In Kotlin, the `override` modifier is required by the compiler to indicate that an interface or class method is being overridden. Without the `override` keyword, you will get a compiler error because the method will hide a member from the supertype interface.

Defining an interface property

Kotlin allows us to define `interface` properties as well. An `interface` property can include a value assignment or can include just the property definition, in which case an implementing class is required to either provide a value or to be marked abstract. In the following example, we've added an `id` property to the `GameObject` interface:

```
interface GameObject {
    val id: String
    fun update(currentTime: Long)
}
```

Our `Player` class is now required to either be marked abstract or to override the `id` property. In this case, `id` is overridden using a single expression:

```
class Player : GameObject {

    override val id = "playerId"
    override fun update(currentTime: Long) {
        // add logic
    }
}
```

It's also possible to override an `interface` property using a custom accessor, as in the following code:

```
class Player : GameObject {

    override val id: String
        get() = "playerId"

    override fun update(currentTime: Long) {
        // add logic
    }
}
```

It's possible to provide a default value for the `interface` property. In such a case, it's no longer required to override the property in any implementing class. In the following snippet, we've added a default value for the `id` property:

```
interface GameObject {
    val id: String
        get() = "defaultId"
    fun update(currentTime: Long)
}
```

After adding a default value for `id`, we no longer need to override it in the implementing `Player` class:

```
class Player : GameObject {
    // no longer required to override id

    override fun update(currentTime: Long) {
        // add logic
    }
}
```

In the next section, we'll see that interfaces may inherit from other interfaces to compose a functionality.

Interface inheritance

An interface can inherit from another interface. In this case, we'll define a new interface, `Movable`, that inherits from `GameObject`:

1. We'll start by declaring a new interface, `Movable`, which extends the `GameObject` interface from our previous examples:

   ```
   interface Movable : GameObject
   ```

2. We'll then add a new method to the new `Movable` interface:

   ```
   interface Movable : GameObject {
       fun move(currentTime: Long)
   }
   ```

3. We can then add new methods and properties to the new interface. Any class that then implements `Movable` will be required to implement the methods from both `Movable` and `GameObject` or else will be marked abstract:

   ```
   class Player : Movable {

     override fun update(currentTime: Long) {
           // must implement this GameObject interface method
       }

       override fun move(currentTime: Long) {
           // must implement this Movable interface method
       }
   }
   ```

Because the `Player` class implements `Movable`, it is required to either be abstract or implement the methods found on both `Movable` and `GameObject` since `Movable` extends `GameObject`. This type of interface inheritance provides an additional mechanism with which we can compose behaviors within our classes.

Implementing multiple interfaces

A class can implement multiple interfaces. This is one way in which composition can be achieved in Kotlin. Rather than belonging to strict inheritance hierarchies, all classes can implement interfaces that define specific behaviors.

To add multiple interfaces to the class declaration, separate the interface names by commas, as shown in the following code:

```
class Player : Movable, Drawable {

    override fun update(currentTime: Long) {
        // add logic
    }

    override fun move(currentTime: Long) {
        // add logic
    }

    override fun draw() {
        // add logic
    }
}
```

In this example, we've added a `Drawable` interface to our `Player` class, which already implements `Movable`.

What happens if two interfaces include the same method signature? In that case, the implementing class needs to define a single overridden method, as follows:

1. We'll add a method to the `Drawable` interface, which is identical to a method that already exists in our `GameObject` interface:

```
interface Drawable {
    fun draw()
    fun update(currentTime: Long)
}
```

2. In the following snippet, we'll see that, even though both `Movable` and `Drawable` define an `update()` method, it only needs to be overridden once:

```kotlin
class Player : Movable, Drawable {

    override fun update(currentTime: Long) {
        // add logic
    }

    override fun move(currentTime: Long) {
        // add logic
    }

    override fun draw() {
        // add logic
    }
}
```

After adding an `update()` method to the `Drawable` interface that is identical to the `GameObject` interface, the implementing `Player` class did not need an update to account for the additional method. This changes slightly if the identical methods include default implementations, which we will look at in the next section.

Default methods

Like in Java 8, Kotlin interfaces provide a default implementation for methods. To add a default implementation, we can define a function body within the interface declaration:

```kotlin
interface GameObject {
    val id: String
        get() = "defaultId"
    fun update(currentTime: Long){
        println("id: $id update:")
    }
}
```

In this example, we've added a default implementation for the `GameObject.update` method. If an interface provides a default implementation, it does not need to be overridden in an implementing class:

```kotlin
class Player : Movable {

    override fun move(currentTime: Long) {
        // add logic
    }
}
```

You'll see in this example, that `Player` implements `Movable`, but does not need to override `update`:

```
class Player : Movable {

    override fun move(currentTime: Long) {
        // add logic
    }

    override fun update(currentTime: Long) {
        super.update(currentTime)
    }
}
```

If we want to override `update()` while maintaining the default behavior, we can override the method and call through to the superclass implementation.

What happens if two interfaces both have identical methods with different default implementations? How can we differentiate between superclass implementations or preserve the behavior of multiple superclass implementations? Let's take a look at this with the following example:

```
interface Drawable {
    fun draw()
    fun update(currentTime: Long){
        println("$this drawable update:")
    }
}
```

We'll start by adding an update method with a default implementation to the `Drawable` interface:

```
class Player : Movable, Drawable {

    override fun move(currentTime: Long) {
        // add logic
    }

    override fun draw() {
        // add logic
    }
}
```

Then, we'll make `Player` implement `Drawable` and add the `draw()` method. At this point, the code will not compile even though all methods are either implemented or have a default implementation.

This is because the compiler knows that the update method has two inherited implementations from the superclasses. The compiler will force us to override `update()` to disambiguate which implementation to use, as shown in the following code:

```
class Player : Movable, Drawable {

    ...

    override fun update(currentTime: Long) {
    }
}
```

Once we override `update()`, the code will compile. However, we have lost the superclass implementations. We can preserve them by calling into both of the superclass implementations, as follows:

```
class Player : Movable, Drawable {

    ...

  override fun update(currentTime: Long) {
        super<Movable>.update(currentTime)
        super<Drawable>.update(currentTime)
    }
}
```

This ability to call multiple super implementations of a method is powerful because it provides a means of disambiguating identical method calls that exist on interfaces. In practice, this is likely not a common occurrence, but without this ability features such as default interface method implementations would be far more restricted.

When implementing an interface, we don't always have to implement all of the interface methods. We can define our class as abstract and let a subclass finish the interface implementation. We'll explore this concept in the next section.

Subclasses and abstract classes

In Kotlin, we can define abstract classes and inherit from classes to model data and create class hierarchies. Conceptually, this is the same as in Java, but there are a few differences in how these mechanisms work in Kotlin.

If we want to define a class that implements an interface but doesn't provide implementations for all of the required methods, we can mark the class as abstract:

```
interface Shape {
    fun getArea() : Double
}

abstract class Rectangle : Shape
```

Classes in Kotlin are closed by default. This means that, for a class to be extended, it must use the open keyword. The open keyword will indicate to the compiler that a class is open for extension:

```
open class Rectangle(
    val width: Double,
    val height: Double
) : Shape {
    override fun getArea() = width * height
}
```

After marking Rectangle as open, it can now be extended, as in the following example:

```
class Square(val edgeLength: Double) : Rectangle(edgeLength, edgeLength)
```

Methods are also closed by default. This means that to override a non-interface method, it must be marked as open. Here, we've added a printArea() method to the Rectangle class:

```
open class Rectangle(
    val width: Double,
    val height: Double
) : Shape {
    override fun getArea() = width * height
    fun printArea() = println("Area is ${getArea()}")
}
```

If we wanted to override this method in `Square`, we would have to mark `printArea()` as open:

```
open class Rectangle(
    val width: Double,
    val height: Double
) : Shape {
    override fun getArea() = width * height

    open fun printArea() = println("Area is ${getArea()}")
}

class Square(val edgeLength: Double) : Rectangle(edgeLength, edgeLength) {
    override fun printArea() = println("Square area is ${getArea()}")
}
```

Once a method has been overridden, it is open by default. In our example, this means the getArea() method on the rectangle is open and can be overridden by `Square`:

```
class Square(val edgeLength: Double) : Rectangle(edgeLength, edgeLength) {
    override fun printArea() = println("Square area is ${getArea()}")

    override fun getArea(): Double {
        // override
    }
}
```

We may not want a method to be overridden once an implementation is provided. In the preceding example, it would be desirable to prevent modification of `Rectangle.getArea()` since any subclass will likely have its area calculated the same way. For cases like this, an overridden method can be marked `final` to prevent future modification:

```
open class Rectangle(
    val width: Double,
    val height: Double
) : Shape {
    final override fun getArea() = width * height

    open fun printArea() = println("Area is ${getArea()}")
}
```

By requiring classes and methods to be explicitly marked as open for modification, Kotlin forces classes to be closed for extension by default and forces developers to be very explicit about how a class may be extended and modified.

As we've just seen, we can define inherited class relationships, but we can also define nested class relationships. We'll explore nested classes in the following section.

Nested classes

Nested classes in Kotlin behave a bit differently than in Java. A class defined within another class is not treated as an inner class by default, meaning it does not have an implicit reference to the enclosing class. In the following example, the Nested class cannot access Outer.a because it is not declared as an inner class using the inner keyword:

```
class Outer {
    val a = "a"
    val b = "b"

    class Nested {
        val c = a // error
    }
}
```

If we look at the decompiled bytecode, we see that Nested is a static class, and therefore cannot access members of the enclosing class:

```
public final class Outer {
    @NotNull
    private final String a = "a";
    @NotNull
    private final String b = "b";

    ...

    public static final class Nested {
        @NotNull
        private final String c = "c";

        @NotNull
        public final String getC() {
            return this.c;
        }
    }
}
```

However, if we add the `inner` keyword to `Nested`, it will become a true inner class of `Outer` and will include a reference to the enclosing class:

```
class Outer {
    val a = "a"
    val b = "b"

    inner class Nested {
        val c = a // can now access Outer.a
    }
}
```

In the following we can see the code generated by making the preceding change:

```
public final class Outer {
    @NotNull
    private final String a = "a";
    @NotNull
    private final String b = "b";

    ...

    public final class Nested {
        @NotNull
        private final String c = Outer.this.getA();

        @NotNull
        public final String getC() {
            return this.c;
        }
    }
}
```

If we look at the bytecode after adding the `inner` keyword, we can see that `Nested` is no longer static, and it can reference `Outer`.

Delegation

Delegation is a common design pattern allowing a class to defer the implementation of some behavior to another class; increasing the amount of reusable code in our projects. Kotlin supports delegation natively for both interface implementations and properties, making it easy to apply in our code.

Implementation delegation

A class that implements an interface may implement all required methods by delegating to a specified delegate instance. In the following code, we've defined a `SettingsProvider` interface that is then implemented by a `SettingsManager` object:

```
interface SettingsProvider {
    fun getSetting(key: String) : String
}

object SettingsManager : SettingsProvider {
    private val map = HashMap<String, String>()

    override fun getSetting(key: String)
            = map.getOrDefault(key, "")
}
```

Now, we want to define a `UserManager` class that will implement `SettingsProvider` by delegating to `SettingsManager`:

```
class UserManager : SettingsProvider by SettingsManager
```

We start by declaring the class name and adding the `SettingsProvider` interface, but then we add the `by` keyword and specify a delegate object that implements `SettingsProvider` on behalf of `UserManager`. In this case, because `SettingsManager` implements `SettingsProvider`, it can act as the delegate for `UserManager`.

In this example, we are using an object, `SettingsManager`, to act as the delegate. But what if we want to be able to swap out delegates by passing them through the constructor? In that case, we can define a constructor parameter and then delegate to that parameter instead, as in the following example:

```
object SettingsManager : SettingsProvider {
    private val map = HashMap<String, String>()

    override fun getSetting(key: String)
            = map.getOrDefault(key, "")
}

class UserManager(settingsProvider: SettingsProvider) : SettingsProvider by
settingsProvider
```

After these changes, we can pass different instances of `SettingsProvider` to `UserManager`, and it will continue to delegate to whichever `SettingsProvider` class is passed in.

Type checking

It's often necessary to check the type of a class and take different actions based on that type. Let's take a quick look at how type checking works in Kotlin.

Any

Every class in Kotlin extends `Any`, which is defined like this:

```
open class Any
```

The `Any` class has three member functions:

- `equals`
- `hashCode`
- `toString`

The `Any` class also has several extension functions defined against it. This allows those extension functions to work for any class declared in your project.

Type casting

It's possible to cast a variable of one type to another type. If the types are not compatible, an exception is thrown. To perform a type cast in Kotlin, we use the `as` keyword. We'll explore how to perform a type cast with the following examples:

1. First, we have defined a `SettingsProvider` interface and an implementing `SettingsManager` object:

```
interface SettingsProvider {
    fun getSetting(key: String) : String
}

object SettingsManager : SettingsProvider {
    ...
    fun printSettings() = map.forEach { println(it) }
}
```

2. In this example, we use `as` to cast the `settingsProvider` variable to `SettingsManager` so we can call a specific method on the variable:

```
fun main(args: Array<String>) {
    val settingsProvider: SettingsProvider = SettingsManager
```

```
    (settingsProvider as SettingsManager).printSettings()
}
```

By casting our `settingsProvider` variable to `SettingsManager`, we gain access to a method specific to the `SettingsManager` type. If we were to access `settingsProvider` without the cast, we wouldn't be able to call `printSettings()`.

Smart casting

We can check whether a variable is of a particular type by using the `is` keyword. For example, we could check whether `settingsProvider` is an instance of `SettingsManager` as follows:

```
fun main(args: Array<String>) {
    val settingsProvider: SettingsProvider = SettingsManager
    if (settingsProvider is SettingsManager) {
        // do something
    }
}
```

Conversely, you can check whether a variable is not of a certain type by using `!is`:

```
fun main(args: Array<String>) {
    val settingsProvider: SettingsProvider = SettingsManager
    if (settingsProvider !is SettingsManager) {
        // do something
    }
}
```

The Kotlin compiler can track explicit casts and type checks and can perform smart casting for us. This means that, once the compiler has validated a variable's type, it's no longer necessary to explicitly perform a cast. In this example, once we've checked that `settingsProvider` is an instance of `SettingsManager`, we do not have have to perform an explicit cast within the if block. The compiler performs the cast for us:

```
fun main(args: Array<String>) {
    val settingsProvider: SettingsProvider = SettingsManager
    if (settingsProvider is SettingsManager) {
        settingsProvider.printSettings()
    }
}
```

Smart casting isn't always possible. Mutable variables, whose type may change, cannot be used with smart casts unless we use something like the `let{}` function to freeze the type within the function body.

Kotlin helps to make patterns such as inheritance and composition easier to implement and more explicit in how they operate. The inheritance of interfaces, interface properties, and default method implementations on interfaces all provide a great deal of flexibility in how we model our data. We also have the freedom to create child classes and nested classes and have greater control over how those classes relate to one another through the open, final, and inner keywords. Finally, we explored how the Kotlin compiler handles type casting and smart casting, helping us to ensure strong type safety throughout our code.

In the next section, we're going to continue exploring classes in Kotlin by focusing on a special type of class: data classes.

Understanding data classes

We often create classes that are meant to hold data and nothing else. In these cases, we may often want to override specific methods such as `equals()` and `hashCode()` so these data classes can be compared to one another. In Kotlin, this type of class is supported natively.

Creating a data class

To create a data class, we can add the data keyword to a class declaration as long as the class follows several specific rules:

- It is a primary constructor with at least one property
- It cannot be a sealed class, open, inner, or abstract

In this example, we define a data class, `Article`, which contains two primary constructor properties:

```
data class Article(val title: String, val author: String)
```

Primary constructor properties will be included in the generated implementations of `copy()`, `equals()`, `hashCode()`, and `toString()`.

A data class may also contain properties that are not defined in the primary constructor:

```
data class Article(val title: String, val author: String) {
    var snippet: String = ""
}
```

Data class properties not defined in the primary constructor will not be included in compiler-generated methods, which we will examine in the next section.

Generated code

The best thing about data classes is that they generate `copy()`, `equals()`, `hashCode()`, and `toString()` automatically. This means we can define our data classes with very little code and will still be able to compare and store them in data structures with reliable retrieval and comparison. Let's study each here.

equals()

If an implementation is not provided, the compiler will generate an `equals()` method that considers all primary constructor properties in its comparison. The following code demonstrates the generated implementation of `equals()` for our preceding `Article` example class:

```
public final class Article {
    ...

    public boolean equals(@Nullable Object var1) {
        if (this != var1) {
            if (var1 instanceof Article) {
                Article var2 = (Article)var1;
                if (Intrinsics.areEqual(this.title, var2.title)
                    && Intrinsics.areEqual(this.author, var2.author)) {
                    return true;
                }
            }

            return false;
        } else {
            return true;
        }
    }
}
```

We can see that the implementation compares the `title` and `author` properties of the primary constructor, but does not compare the `snippet` property. This means that, if `title` and `author` are the same but `snippet` is different, a structural comparison of the two objects using `==` will return `true`:

```
fun main(args: Array<String>) {
    val article1 = Article("Kotlin is great", "Nate")
    val article2 = Article("Kotlin is great", "Nate")

    article1.snippet = "an article about Kotlin"
    article2.snippet = "a Kotlin article"

    if (article1 == article2) {
        println("They are the same")
    }
}
```

 To compare whether two objects are structurally the same, the equivalent of calling `.equals()`, use `==`. To check whether two variables point to the same object, use `===`.

If relying on the structural comparison of data classes, it's important to include all relevant properties in the primary constructor, or you'll have to override `equals()` and `hashCode()` as you would for any other class.

hashCode()

If an implementation is not provided, the compiler will generate a `hashCode()` method that considers all primary constructor properties in its comparison. The following code shows the `hashCode()` implementation of our `Article` class example:

```
public final class Article {
    ...

    public int hashCode() {
        String var10000 = this.title;
        int var1 = (var10000 != null ? var10000.hashCode() : 0) * 31;
        String var10001 = this.author;
        return var1 + (var10001 != null ? var10001.hashCode() : 0);
    }
}
```

Once again, we can see that the implementation only takes into account primary constructor properties in its implementation of hashCode().

toString()

A data class will also generate an implementation of toString() if one is not already provided. Once again, the following code shows the generated toString() method for our Article class:

```
public final class Article {
    ...

    @NotNull
    public String toString() {
        return "Article(title=" + this.title + ", author=" + this.author +
")";
    }
}
```

This is useful for debugging or output, but if you require all properties to be included, you will have to ensure that all properties are present in the primary constructor or override toString() on your own.

copy()

Data classes also provide us with a copy() method, which can be used to copy a data class. Additionally, we can use named arguments to modify specific properties on the copied class. In this example, we create an instance of Article named article1 and then copy it into article2. During the copy, we change the title property or article2:

```
fun main(args: Array<String>) {
    val article1 = Article("Kotlin is great", "Nate").apply {
        snippet = "an article about Kotlin"
    }

    val article2 = article1.copy(title = "Kotlin is great part 2")
}
```

After this copy is completed, the two variables will have different titles, but the author and snippet will be the same.

Code generated by data classes is one of the most convenient and useful parts of the Kotlin programming language. It greatly reduces the boilerplate required to implement immutable type classes, making them much more common within Kotlin code bases. Additionally, because they are compiler-generated, they don't require maintenance of `hashCode()`, `equals()`, and `copy()` implementations, which can quickly become out of date when implemented manually.

Destructuring

Data classes will generate component functions for all primary constructor properties. For each primary constructor property, a `componentX` function will be created where `X` is the order of the property. We can illustrate how this works using the following `Article` class:

```
data class Article(var title: String, val author: String) {
    var snippet: String = ""
}
```

For our `Article` example, the compiler will generate `component1()` and `component2()` methods:

```
public final class Article {
    ...

    @NotNull
    public final String component1() {
        return this.title;
    }

    @NotNull
    public final String component2() {
        return this.author;
    }
}
```

These component functions can then be used by the compiler to support destructuring declarations, shown as follows:

```
fun main(args: Array<String>) {
    val article1 = Article("Kotlin is great", "Nate").apply {
        snippet = "an article about Kotlin"
    }

    val (title, author) = article1
}
```

In the final expression of the preceding snippet, we are assigning `article1.title` to the `title` variable and `article1.author` to the `author` variable. Any object can be on the right side of the expression as long as that object has enough component functions to match the number of variables within the parentheses on the left side.

To the compiler, the generated code looks like this:

```
public static final void main(@NotNull String[] args) {
    Intrinsics.checkParameterIsNotNull(args, "args");
    Article var2 = new Article("Kotlin is great", "Nate");
    var2.setSnippet("an article about Kotlin");
    Article var4 = var2;
    String var5 = var2.component1();
    String author = var4.component2();
}
```

In the final lines of this generated code, we see the component functions being called and assigned to new `String` variables.

If you want to skip over a property, you can use _ to tell the compiler to skip that value. In our example, we could skip the title and use a destructuring declaration to only retrieve the author, using the following code:

```
fun main(args: Array<String>) {
    val article1 = Article("Kotlin is great", "Nate").apply {
        snippet = "an article about Kotlin"
    }

    val (_, author) = article1
}
```

Data classes are a powerful feature in Kotlin and rely on the compiler generating and enforcing useful functionality to make developers' lives easier. However, data classes are not the only type of special class in Kotlin that aims to enforce best practices.

In the next section, we'll explore several other types of classes available in Kotlin.

Working with enums, sealed classes, and objects

In addition to classes, abstract classes, and data classes, Kotlin provides several other special types of class that can be utilized in different situations. These special classes can help us to improve explicit type safety in our code, efficiently represent sealed class hierarchies, and even simplify the singleton design pattern. In this section, we will explore the following:

- Enums
- Sealed classes
- Object classes

We will examine each of these class types and how they can improve our Kotlin code.

Enums

Enums in Kotlin are very similar to those in Java. In the following we've defined a basic `enum` class named `ArticleType`:

```
enum class ArticleType {
    Aside,
    Blog,
    Series
}
```

This then can be used as a restricted type anywhere we would use any other existing type. In the following snippet, we've defined a property on `Article` using the new `ArticleType` enum:

```
data class Article(
    var title: String,
    val author: String,
    val type: ArticleType
)
```

When instantiating an instance of `Article`, we can reference the specific values exposed in our `ArticleType` enum:

```
fun main(args: Array<String>) {
    val article1 = Article(
        "Kotlin is great",
```

```
        "Nate",
        ArticleType.Blog
    )
}
```

By limiting the article types to those defined within `ArticleType`, we've provided a clear contract to users of the `Article` class, and it clearly defines what types the developer must account for.

We can add properties to our enum values, as seen in this example:

```
enum class ArticleType(val displayName: String) {
    Aside("Small Post"),
    Blog("Standard Blog Post"),
    Series("Part of a Blog Series")
}
```

We can then access those enum properties like any other property:

```
fun main(args: Array<String>) {
    println(ArticleType.Blog.displayName)
}
```

Enums can be a great way of enforcing a limited set of type options for some value when those types don't require any additional data or state of their own. For cases where we want a restricted set of types, but those types require their own data, we can turn to sealed classes.

Sealed classes

Sealed classes represent restricted type hierarchies. They are similar to enums, but each class in the hierarchy can have its own properties and methods.

In the following example, we've defined a sealed class named `ViewState` by using the `sealed` keyword:

```
sealed class ViewState
object Loading : ViewState()
data class Loaded(val article: Article) : ViewState()
class Error(val error: Throwable?) : ViewState()
```

We've created three classes that extend `ViewState`. This class hierarchy may be defined within the class body or outside it. However, a sealed class may be subclassed only within the same file.

Each of these classes has its own unique properties. You may also notice that we've used object, data, and regular classes when defining our sealed hierarchy:

```
sealed class ViewState
object Loading : ViewState()
data class Loaded(val article: Article) : ViewState()
class Error(val error: Throwable?) : ViewState()
```

By using sealed classes, we can indicate to the compiler all known types for the class. In this function, we are using a `when` statement to return a `String` based on the type of `ViewState`:

```
fun getLogMessage(state: ViewState) : String {
    return when (state) {
        Loading -> "is loading"
        is Loaded -> "is loaded"
        is Error -> "error has occurred"
    }
}
```

Because we are using a `when` expression using a sealed class type, the compiler will enforce that every type is handled, or a default else branch is added. This is useful because it helps us to ensure all states are handled even if we add/remove types in the future.

Object classes

Kotlin introduces the object keyword to handle the creation of anonymous classes and singletons, as well as for companion objects, another Kotlin addition. In this section, we'll take a look at these three concepts.

Singletons

Kotlin makes it easy to implement a singleton. If you aren't familiar with this, a singleton is an object that is only instantiated once for an application. We will explore the singleton pattern specifically in more detail in `Chapter 17`, *Practical Design Patterns*.

To quickly implement a singleton in Kotlin, we can use an object declaration that uses the `object` keyword to define a singleton class. In this code, `SettingsManager` is defined using an object declaration and is a publicly available singleton:

```
object SettingsManager : SettingsProvider {
    val map = HashMap<String, String>()

    fun printSettings() = map.forEach { println(it) }

    override fun getSetting(key: String)
            = map.getOrDefault(key, "default")
}
```

Note that object declarations can implement interfaces or extend other classes. To work with an object declared this way, we can reference the object name directly to access any properties or methods:

```
fun main(args: Array<String>) {
    val setting = SettingsManager.getSetting("key")
}
```

Object declarations are created via thread-safe, lazy instantiation. This means object declarations cannot provide a constructor. Let's take a look at a basic example so we can examine the generated bytecode. We've defined the most basic object declaration we can to create `SimpleSingleton`:

```
object SimpleSingleton
```

Now, let's look at the generated code:

```
public final class SimpleSingleton {
    public static final SimpleSingleton INSTANCE;

    private SimpleSingleton() {
    }

    static {
        SimpleSingleton var0 = new SimpleSingleton();
        INSTANCE = var0;
    }
}
```

We can see here that the compiler generates the standard Java singleton code that you may be used to working with. This is how we can use an object declaration without worrying about manual, thread-safe instantiation.

Object declarations mimic the static functionality available in Java. They allow us to have globally available methods and properties that are available when needed. Sometimes, however, we'd prefer to scope this functionality to some other class. For those situations, we can rely on companion objects, which we'll explore in the following section.

Companion objects

An object declaration within another class can be marked with the `companion` keyword to become a companion object. Companion objects connect the initialization of an object declaration to the instantiation of the enclosing class, and there can be only a single `companion` object for a class. This lets us scope whatever functionality the object declaration provides to the namespace of the enclosing class, cleaning up the global namespace and adding useful semantics in many cases.

In this snippet, we've defined a `companion` object for `SomeClass`:

```
class SomeClass {
    companion object {
        fun foo() {}
    }
}
```

We can access the `companion` object in one of the following two ways:

```
fun main(args: Array<String>) {
    SomeClass.Companion.foo()
    SomeClass.foo()
}
```

You might notice that we didn't provide a name for the companion. By default, the name of a companion object will be `Companion`, but it's possible to provide your own name as well. We could rename our companion object by specifying a name after the object keyword. In this example, we've renamed the companion to `Factory`:

```
class SomeClass {
    companion object Factory {
        fun foo() {}
    }
}
```

After renaming the companion to `Factory`, we can now access it using `.Factory` rather than `.Companion`:

```
fun main(args: Array<String>) {
    SomeClass.Factory.foo()
    SomeClass.foo()
}
```

This flexibility in companion object naming can be really useful when considering the Kotlin-to-Java interop experience and will be explored further in Chapter 8, *Controlling the Story*.

We've seen how to access companion objects, but how, and when, are they actually initialized and ready for use? Companion objects are initialized in two cases:

- When the enclosing class is initialized
- When a function or property on the companion object is referenced

In either of the preceding cases, a companion object is created:

```
fun main(args: Array<String>) {
    SomeClass.foo()
    SomeClass()
}
```

Once the companion object is initialized, it can be treated as any other class. Companion objects may define their own properties and methods and can implement interfaces or even extend other classes:

```
class SomeClass {
    companion object Factory : SomeInterface {
        const val someVal = "val"
        fun foo() {}

        override fun doSomething(foo: String) {
            super.doSomething(foo)
            // do something
        }
    }
}
```

Companion objects have access to private constructors of their enclosing class and can, therefore, be used to implement a factory method if the enclosing class has only private constructors:

```
class SomeClass private constructor() {
    private val id = "id"
    companion object Factory : SomeInterface {
        const val someVal = "val"
        fun foo() {}
        fun createSomeClass() = SomeClass()

        override fun doSomething(foo: String) {
            super.doSomething(foo)
        }
    }
}
```

We'll explore the further use of companion objects and the Factory pattern in Chapter 17, *Practical Design Patterns*. Classes and companion objects are great for defining reusable, named classes. However, sometimes we only need a one-off class that won't be reused. For these cases, we can use object expressions.

Object expressions

To create single, unnamed instances of a class, Kotlin introduces the notion of object expressions. To create an object expression, we use the object keyword followed by : and then any class or interface names we want to use:

```
val someInterface = object : SomeInterface {
    override fun doSomething(foo: String) {
        super.doSomething(foo)
    }
}
```

Object declarations can implement multiple interfaces and have access to the variables defined within the scope in which they were created. It's also possible to use an object expression to create an unnamed class with no supertype. In this example, we assign an object expression to transient, in which we've declared a single property:

```
fun main(args: Array<String>) {
    val transient = object {
        val prop = "foo"
    }
    println(transient.prop)
}
```

That property can then be used within the same scope in which `transient` is available.

One key difference between object expressions and object declarations is that object declarations are instantiated lazily upon first use, whereas object expressions are created and used immediately.

In this section, we've introduced and explored several special types of classes that add to Kotlin's rich typing system. Enums, sealed classes, companion objects, and object expressions all serve specific use cases and can enable developers to write more expressive, safer code with less boilerplate.

Summary

Kotlin includes robust support for a variety of different OOP concepts. It has been designed based on years of research and experience from other languages to make OOP easier. Kotlin natively supports concepts such as delegation and singletons. Kotlin provides rich data types such as data classes to reduce boilerplate and sealed classes to help to model restricted class hierarchies. Interfaces in Kotlin bring features from newer versions of Java as well as new features such as interface properties, which can be used in domains such as Android where newer Java features may not be available. Kotlin's feature set allows you to more easily organize your day in whatever way makes sense to you and enables developers to write concise, flexible, object-oriented code.

In the next chapter, we'll focus on why interoperability between Kotlin and Java is such a big part of the Kotlin programming language.

Questions

1. How do you define a class in Kotlin?
2. How do you define an interface in Kotlin?
3. What are data classes?
4. What are sealed classes?
5. How is a sealed class different from an enum?
6. What is an object expression?
7. What is an object declaration?

8. What is a companion object?
9. What are the four visibility modifiers in Kotlin?
10. What are the differences between a primary and a secondary constructor?

Further reading

- *Hands-On Object-Oriented Programming with Kotlin* (`https://www.packtpub.com/application-development/hands-object-oriented-programming-kotlin`)
- *Kotlin Programming by Example* (`https://www.packtpub.com/application-development/kotlin-programming-example`)

Section 3: Play Nice – Integrating Kotlin With Existing Code

Kotlin's ability to cleanly integrate with Java is one of it's biggest features. The possible or perceived challenges to this integration is also a potential blocker for teams incorporating Kotlin into their code bases. This section will dive into the Java/Kotlin interoperability story and explain how interoperability is achieved, how it can be customized to suit your needs, and how to begin integrating Kotlin into an existing code base.

This section comprises the following chapters:

- Chapter 6, *Interoperability as a Design Goal*
- Chapter 7, *Crossing Over – Working across Java and Kotlin*
- Chapter 8, *Controlling the Story*
- Chapter 9, *Baby Steps – Integration through Testing*

6
Interoperability as a Design Goal

A terrific interop experience has been at the core of the Kotlin programming language since the beginning. The language itself was born out of a desire to have modern features while still leveraging existing JVM tools and infrastructure. Because of this, and because of the developer community's desire to reuse existing Java tools and code, Kotlin has progressed while maintaining excellent interoperability with existing Java code bases and tooling.

In this chapter, we'll learn more about the *why* and *how* of Kotlin/Java interop, and we'll walk through adding Kotlin to an existing Java project to demonstrate how easy it is to start working with both languages within a single project.

The following topics will be covered in this chapter:

- Understanding why Kotlin was designed with Java interoperability in mind
- How to add Kotlin to an existing Java project
- Converting Java into Kotlin

Technical requirements

To download, compile, and execute the samples found in this chapter, you must have the following:

- IntelliJ IDEA 2018.3 Community or Ultimate editions or newer
- An internet connection
- Git and GitHub (optional)

To download all of the code in this chapter, including the examples and code snippets, please see the following GitHub link: `https://github.com/PacktPublishing/Mastering-Kotlin/tree/master/Chapter06`.

Understanding why Kotlin was designed with interop in mind

Kotlin's interop experience has been important from the beginning. The language was born with the requirement of tight integration with existing JVM tooling. In this section, we'll explore why interop has always been integral to the Kotlin story and how it is achieved.

Why is interop so important for Kotlin?

As discussed in `Chapter 1`, *A New Challenger Approaches*, Kotlin was created by JetBrains, best known for creating terrific development tools such as IntelliJ IDEA. JetBrains has explicitly expressed several motivations for creating the language including the following:

- Wanting a more productive language for the JVM than what was then available with Java or Scala
- An expectation that Kotlin's adoption would drive sales of IntelliJ
- A hope that the increased discussion and awareness of the company would lead to greater trust in JetBrains itself

Implicit in these motivations is the need for tight integration with existing Java code and tools. If JetBrains had created a new language that couldn't integrate with their existing JVM code and tools, it's likely their development workflows and efficiency would have been significantly impacted for the worse.

Additionally, adding support for a new JVM language, but not supporting interop between Java, would be seen by the community as a large oversight and might have hindered the adoption of the language and/or IntelliJ. Both of these outcomes would run contrary to the goals JetBrains expressed.

In these ways, interop is important to Kotlin because Kotlin's success was, and is, important to JetBrains. The tight interop experience between Kotlin and Java has contributed greatly to the popularity of Kotlin. Perhaps the best example of this interoperability is in how easy it is to add Kotlin to an existing project and to convert existing Java code into Kotlin.

By simplifying the integration and migration process from Java to Kotlin, JetBrains enabled developers to try the language with minimal risk and effort, both of which are major concerns for any fast development team. Once developers can easily try the language, they can build and understand over time rather than all at once.

How is interop achieved?

Kotlin is primarily a JVM language and therefore is compiled to standard JVM bytecode by the Kotlin compiler. This bytecode is what is actually run by the Java Virtual Machine to execute our programs. Because this resultant bytecode is familiar to JVM developers and tools, it can be integrated and manipulated using known techniques. This is largely how Kotlin can work so seamlessly with Java.

When Kotlin is compiled for the JVM, the underlying bytecode is the same as if you had written Java code. To maintain compatibility with multiple versions of Java, the Kotlin compiler is capable of generating Java 6- and Java 8-compatible versions of JVM bytecode. This means that tools built to support Java through the examination and manipulation of bytecode can also support Kotlin. This also means that classes and methods declared in Java can be understood by Kotlin and worked with from Kotlin files, classes, and functions.

A great example of this tooling interop is the Kotlin Bytecode tool within IntelliJ. With this tool, it's possible to view the bytecode for a Kotlin source file, and then to decompile that bytecode to Java. Through this process, it's very easy to see how the Kotlin we write is understood at a low level in the same way that our Java code would be.

Let's take a quick look at this bytecode examination to illustrate this point:

1. To start, within `Person.kt`, we'll define a simple `Person` class in Kotlin, which we will use to examine the converted bytecode:

   ```
   class Person(var firstName:String, var lastName:String)
   ```

2. Next, ensure `Person.kt` is open, and navigate to **Tools** | **Kotlin** | **View Kotlin Bytecode**. Once this is done, you should see a new tool window open, which displays the bytecode:

```
Kotlin Bytecode                                                          ⋮  —
           DECOMPILE    ☑ Inline ☑ Optimization ☑ Assertions ☐ IR ☐ JVM 8 target
1    // ================Person.class ================
2    // class version 50.0 (50)
3    // access flags 0x31
4    public final class Person {
5
6
7      // access flags 0x2
8      private Ljava/lang/String; firstName
9      @Lorg/jetbrains/annotations/NotNull;() // invisible
10
11     // access flags 0x11
12     public final getFirstName()Ljava/lang/String;
13     @Lorg/jetbrains/annotations/NotNull;() // invisible
14      L0
15       LINENUMBER 1 L0
16       ALOAD 0
17       GETFIELD Person.firstName : Ljava/lang/String;
18       ARETURN
```

3. Once the **Kotlin Bytecode** window is open, we can click the **DECOMPILE** button to view the Java equivalent of our bytecode:

```java
// Person.decompiled.java
public final class Person {
   @NotNull
   private String firstName;
   @NotNull
   private String lastName;
```

```
@NotNull
public final String getFirstName() {
   return this.firstName;
}

public final void setFirstName(@NotNull String var1) {
   Intrinsics.checkParameterIsNotNull(var1, "<set-?>");
   this.firstName = var1;
}

@NotNull
public final String getLastName() {
   return this.lastName;
}

public final void setLastName(@NotNull String var1) {
   Intrinsics.checkParameterIsNotNull(var1, "<set-?>");
   this.lastName = var1;
}

public Person(@NotNull String firstName,
              @NotNull String lastName) {
   Intrinsics.checkParameterIsNotNull(firstName, "firstName");
   Intrinsics.checkParameterIsNotNull(lastName, "lastName");
   super();
   this.firstName = firstName;
   this.lastName = lastName;
}
}
```

This Java class is generated by the decompile tool and represents the Java-equivalent implementation of the Kotlin class we defined previously. You'll likely notice that this class looks very much like what we would implement ourselves if writing our Person class in Java.

This ability to write Kotlin and then decompile the resultant bytecode into human-readable Java demonstrates how well Kotlin is integrated with Java and the IntelliJ tooling. This integration makes it easy to get started and makes it easy to understand what the Kotlin compiler is doing behind the scenes.

In the next section, we'll look at how to add Kotlin support to an existing Java project to start taking advantage of this great interop experience.

Adding Kotlin to an existing Java project

It's often not possible to consider rewriting a project in an entirely new programming language, and therefore, it becomes important for languages to work well together. Java developers that want to take advantage of Kotlin features might want to introduce Kotlin in isolated parts of their code base. As mentioned in the previous section, because Kotlin is well integrated with existing JVM tooling, adding Kotlin to an existing Java project is quick and easy when using IntelliJ or Android Studio.

In this section, we'll walk through how to add Kotlin to an existing IntelliJ project. This will demonstrate how you can start using Kotlin today, even if you're not working on a brand-new project.

Adding Kotlin to an existing IntelliJ project

Let's start by adding Kotlin to an existing Java project. To get started, walk through the following steps:

1. Download or check out the code from the following GitHub link: `https://github.com/PacktPublishing/Mastering-Kotlin/tree/master/Chapter06`.

2. Open the `Chapter06` project with IntelliJ IDEA. Once the project is open in IntelliJ, you should see the following `Main.java` file with a simple `Hello World` example:

3. To verify that it is building correctly, you can click on one of the green arrow icons in the editor and select **Run Main.main().** On clicking, you should see `Hello World!` printed out to the console:

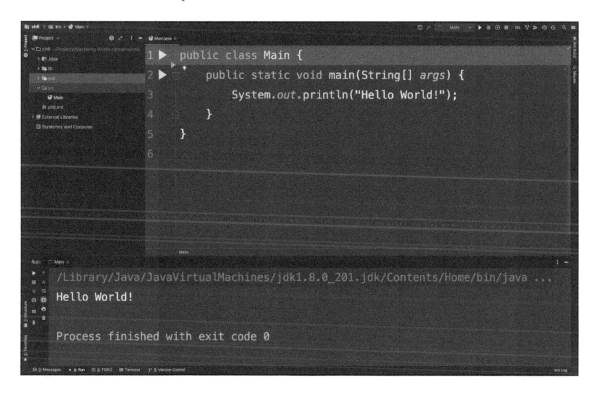

Now, let's add our first Kotlin file to this project:

1. In the project pane on the left-hand side of the IDE, right-click on **src**, then click on **New** | **Kotlin File/Class**:

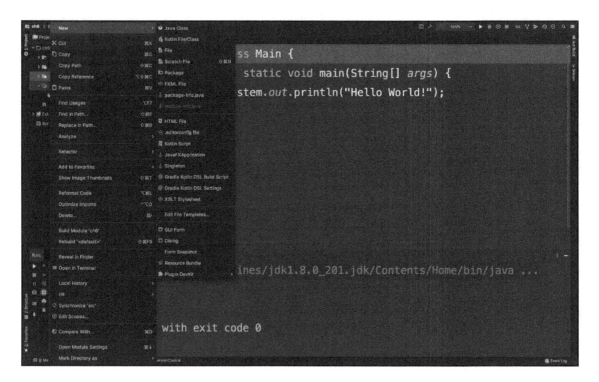

Clicking **Kotlin File/Class** will open the **New Kotlin File/Class** dialog.

2. From here, you can click the **Kind** drop-down menu to select the type of Kotlin file or class you wish to create:

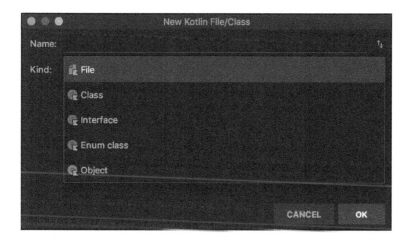

3. Select **File** and enter `Main.kt` as the filename, then click **OK**:

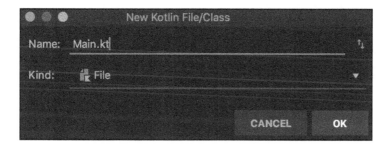

4. After clicking **OK,** the IDE will create a new, empty `Main.kt` file. At this point, we have a Kotlin file and can start writing the Kotlin code, but the project will indicate that Kotlin is not yet configured:

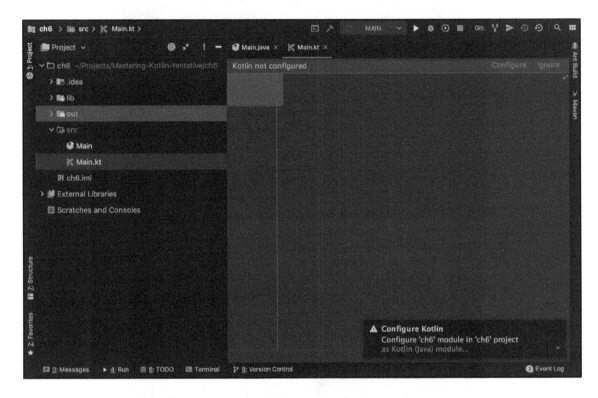

5. To start the configuration process, select **Configure** in the upper-right corner of the editor. In the modal that opens, select **Java**, because we want to work with a mixed Java/Kotlin code base without working with any JavaScript:

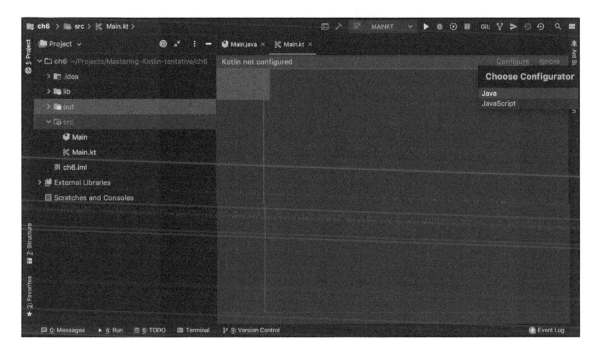

6. After selecting **Java**, you should see a new modal open that says
KotlinJavaRuntime library was added to module ch6:

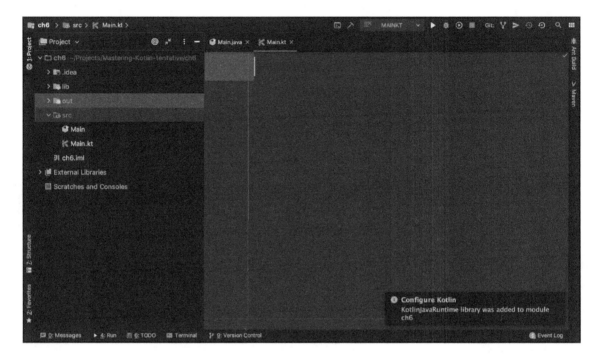

7. If you then open the `ch6.iml` file, you'll find a newly added `<orderEntry />` instance that adds `KotlinJavaRuntime` to the project:

```xml
<?xml version="1.0" encoding="UTF-8"?>
<module type="JAVA_MODULE" version="4">
  <component name="NewModuleRootManager" inherit-compiler-output="true">
    <exclude-output />
    <content url="file://$MODULE_DIR$">
      <sourceFolder url="file://$MODULE_DIR$/src" isTestSource="false" />
    </content>
    <orderEntry type="inheritedJdk" />
    <orderEntry type="sourceFolder" forTests="false" />
    <orderEntry type="library" name="KotlinJavaRuntime" level="project" />
  </component>
</module>
```

When using IntelliJ or Android Studio, you may notice one or more `.iml` files added to your project. This file extension is used by the IDE to store metadata related to a specific project module. This metadata can include elements such as the module path and module dependencies as in the case of the added `KotlinJavaRuntime` dependency we just saw added to our project. While these files are important to the IDE, you'll likely want to avoid checking them into source control and instead let the IDE regenerate them on a local machine when the project is cloned.

Now that Kotlin is configured for the project, we can add and run our Kotlin code:

1. Start by adding a simple `main()` function and a `println` statement.
2. Then, click on the green arrow icon, and select **Run Main.kt**.

This will run the main function and print out `Hello Kotlin` to the console:

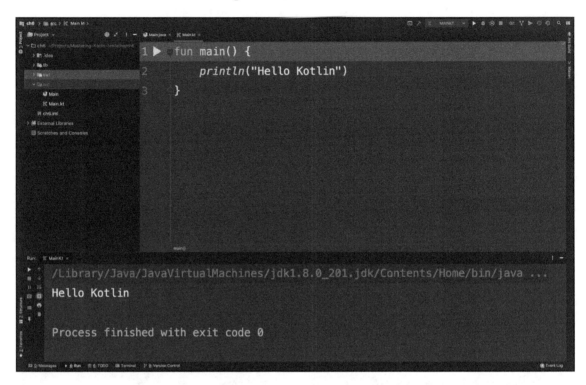

From here, you are free to write in both Java and Kotlin, mixing them as desired. We will dive deeper into the Java/Kotlin interop experience in `Chapter 7`, *Crossing Over – Working across Java and Kotlin*. Before diving deeper into Kotlin and Java interop details, we're going to quickly explore how to easily convert Java into Kotlin in the next section.

Converting Java into Kotlin

Perhaps the easiest example, and one of the most interesting, of interoperability between Java and Kotlin is the ability to quickly convert Java code into Kotlin code with a single IDE command. Technically, this is more of a feature of the IDE, but as powerful tooling is an important aspect of the viability of a language, it's worth exploring how this conversion process works.

By converting existing Java code in this way, you can help to do the following:

- Introduce Kotlin into a Java code base in places where existing tests can validate no regressions
- Understand common Kotlin features and idioms by comparing them to Java code you already understand
- Allow developers to quickly start using Kotlin without a steep learning curve

All of these traits can make the Kotlin learning and adoption process much easier and more enjoyable. In this section, we'll examine two different methods of converting Java into Kotlin.

Converting Java files into Kotlin files

The first method of Java conversion is to convert an existing Java file into a Kotlin file. Let's walk through this conversion process with a simple example. We'll start with this simple Java `ViewModel` class:

```java
public class ViewModel {
    private boolean isLoading = true;
    private boolean hasData = false;

    public boolean isLoading() {
        return isLoading;
    }

    public void setLoading(boolean loading) {
        isLoading = loading;
    }

    public boolean isHasData() {
        return hasData;
    }

    public void setHasData(boolean hasData) {
        this.hasData = hasData;
    }
}
```

We can see that this Java file currently resides within the same source directory as the Main.kt Kotlin file. This illustrates that Java and Kotlin code can exist, side by side, within the same directories. You don't have to concern yourself about isolating one language from the other.

We can convert this ViewModel class into Kotlin using the **Convert Java File to Kotlin File** tool within IntelliJ. To do so, follow these instructions:

1. Navigate to **Code | Convert Java File to Kotlin File**.
2. Use IntelliJ's **Lookup Action** shortcut and search for **Convert Java File to Kotlin File**:

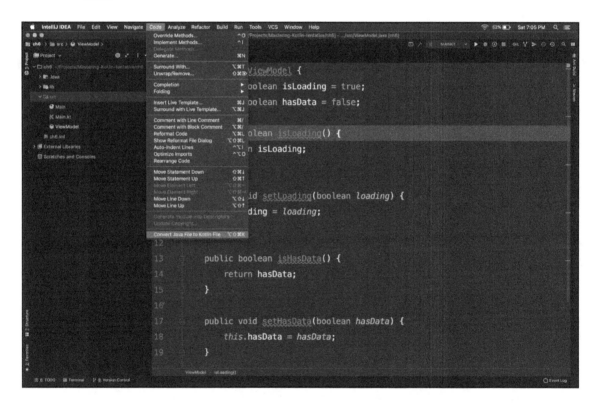

3. The IDE may then present you with the following dialog asking whether you wish to convert usages of the current file or class as well. Clicking **OK** will help to ensure the conversion doesn't break your application:

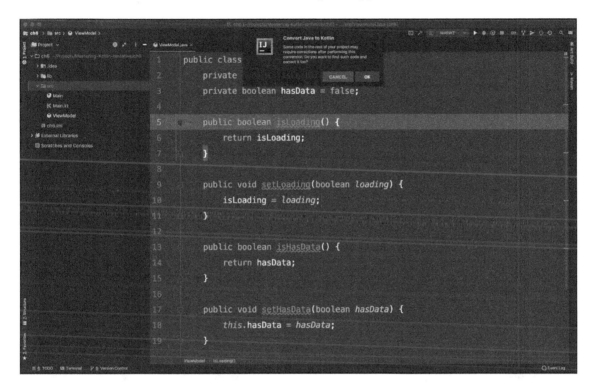

4. Once converted, the file will now have a `.kt` extension and will be 100% Kotlin code. In most cases, this will result in less code that has common Kotlin idioms applied to it:

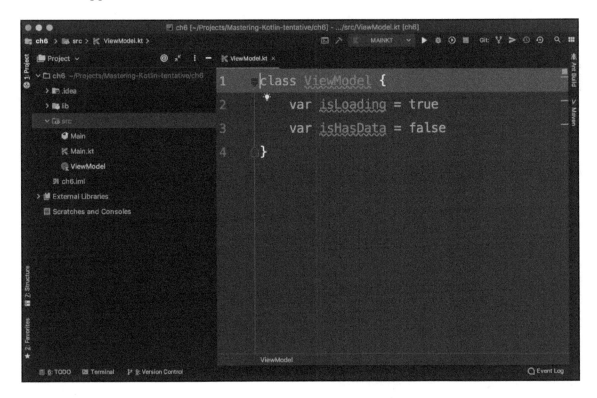

With our `ViewModel` example, the conversion reduces the code from 20 lines to 4. This type of file-by-file conversion from Java into Kotlin can be an effective strategy for migrating an existing code base to Kotlin. Because this conversion can happen at the file level, it gives a lot of flexibility in how the conversion strategy can be implemented. Development teams can migrate a single file, a module, or the whole code base to Kotlin however they see fit.

While migrating existing Java files is very helpful, sometimes, we may also want to convert a snippet of Java code without having to create a new Java file first. We'll take a look at how to manage this situation in the next section.

Converting pasted Java code

It's also worth noting that you can convert Java into Kotlin by simply pasting Java code into a Kotlin file. When Java is pasted into IntelliJ or Android Studio, you'll be presented with the following dialog:

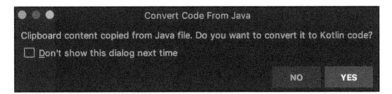

If you click **YES**, a Kotlin implementation of the pasted Java code will be generated and will be available to use. This is one of the easiest ways to start working with Kotlin and to understand how to start writing Kotlin code. The ease with which Java can be converted into Kotlin greatly reduces the barrier to entry for teams and individuals looking to start incorporating the Kotlin language into their project.

Summary

In this chapter, we've delved deeper into why Kotlin is designed to work so closely and seamlessly with existing Java code and tools. From the beginning, JetBrains has strived to make Kotlin work side by side with Java to make adoption easier for outside developers, and so they could use Kotlin with their own existing tools. Because Kotlin compiles to compatible bytecode, it's possible to provide a developer experience that is concise, powerful, and flexible for Kotlin developers while also fully compatible for Java developers. This allows Kotlin to be adopted and integrated incrementally, which has helped to lead to its increased popularity.

We've seen how easy it is to add Kotlin to an existing Java project and how quickly we can convert existing Java code into Kotlin code. Again, both of these features mean you can migrate to Kotlin slowly without major rewrites or refactors, which makes it easier to pitch to managers and engineers that are hesitant to adopt a new programming language.

In the next chapter, we'll explore how to work with both languages at the same time in a single code base.

Questions

- Can you name two reasons why interoperability with Java and Kotlin was important to JetBrains?
- Is it true or false that Kotlin files cannot be in the same source directory as Java files?
- Is it true or false that Java can be quickly converted to Kotlin using IntelliJ?

7
Crossing Over – Working across Java and Kotlin

This chapter will explore the practical ramifications of adding Kotlin to an existing Java code base. Because rewriting an application from scratch in a new language is a risky and rare endeavor, this chapter details how to work with both Java and Kotlin in a single code base. It explores some of the challenges associated with adding Kotlin to an existing Java code base, such as the differences in the null handling and the lack of Kotlin features in Java. Finally, it will examine common Kotlin idioms and how they affect the way you write code with both Kotlin and Java.

The following topics will be covered in this chapter:

- Working with Kotlin from Java
- Working with Java from Kotlin
- Impacts and considerations when working with both Java and Kotlin in the same code base
- Embracing Kotlin idioms

Technical requirements

In order to download, compile, and execute the samples found in this chapter, you must have the following:

- IntelliJ IDEA 2018.3 Community or Ultimate editions, or newer
- An internet connection
- Git and GitHub (optional)

To download all of the code in this chapter, including the examples and code snippets, please refer to the following GitHub link: https://github.com/PacktPublishing/Mastering-Kotlin/tree/master/Chapter07.

Working with Kotlin from Java

Before considering the addition of Kotlin to your existing Java code base, you have to think about how the two languages will work together. While Java and Kotlin can work well together, it's not always possible to take full advantage of Kotlin features from Java. In this section, we'll explore how you can leverage Kotlin code from Java and where the rough edges might be.

Basic interop

At a basic level, working with classes, interfaces, and objects written in Kotlin from Java is seamless. You can instantiate and consume these objects and methods in the same way as you would for any other Java class. We'll take a look at some specific examples in the following sections.

Creating class instances across languages

We can easily instantiate Java classes from Kotlin and Kotlin classes from Java. In this snippet, we've used Kotlin to define a Person class with two public properties:

```
open class Person(val firstName: String, val lastName: String)
```

Here, we can see that we can instantiate an instance of the Person class from Java, like we would any other Java class:

```
public static void main(String[] args) {
    Person person = new Person("John", "Smith");
}
```

Note that when instantiating `Person` from Java, it's still necessary to use the `new` keyword, so even though the class is defined in Kotlin, we must still adhere to the Java syntax rules when consuming `Person` from Java.

Not only can we consume classes across language boundaries, but classes defined in Java can be extended from Kotlin and vice versa. We'll take a look at this in the next section.

Inheritance across languages

We can also use classes and interfaces written in Kotlin to extend and implement new classes in Java. Here, we've defined a new `Programmer` class in Java that inherits from the previously defined `Person` Kotlin class:

```
public class Programmer extends Person {
    private String preferredLanguage;
    public Programmer(String firstName, String lastName,
                      String preferredLanguage) {
        super(firstName, lastName);
        this.preferredLanguage = preferredLanguage;
    }
}
```

From this example, we can see that we can extend `Person` like any other Java class. In fact, to the consuming code it's not obvious whether `Person` is written in Kotlin or Java. Additionally, because both languages are being compiled to common JVM bytecode, there is no underlying performance penalty in declaring a class using a different language than its base class.

Property access

The accessing of properties is an interesting example of the differences inherent in using a Kotlin class from either Kotlin or Java. To illustrate this, we'll once again define the following `Person` class:

```
open class Person(val firstName: String, val lastName: String)
```

As we discussed previously in Chapter 5, *Modeling Real-World Data*, Kotlin properties do not require explicit getters and setters as they will be generated automatically by the compiler. When accessing properties from Kotlin, it's a general convention to use property access syntax and reference the property names directly. But how does this work from Java?

When consuming a Kotlin class from Java, we cannot use property access syntax. However, we can make use of the generated getters and setters. In the `Person` example, we have getters available to us for each of the defined properties. In the following snippet, we can see how properties in the `Person` class can be accessed from Java:

```
public static void main(String[] args) {
    Person person = new Person("John", "Smith");
    person.getFirstName();
    person.getLastName();
}
```

The getters available when consuming `Person` from Java are generated by the Kotlin compiler. Unless otherwise specified, the compiler will generate getters from any `var` or `val` property in our class.

The lack of property access in Java is an important interop difference when working with Kotlin and Java. Another important difference in the languages is in how to handle null when crossing language boundaries, which we will explore in the next section.

Handling null

One of the biggest differences between Kotlin and Java is the handling of null types. Because of this, it is one part of the interop story that must be given careful thought. Thankfully, our tools can help make this easier.

To explore the handling of null across language boundaries, we'll, once again, return to the `Person` class. In our `Person` example, both properties are defined as non-null `String` types:

```
open class Person(val firstName: String, val lastName: String)
```

Because the Kotlin compiler knows these values will not be null, we can safely reference them without any type of null check, as shown in the following snippet:

```
person.firstName.length
```

However, when we access those properties from Java, we must store them as nullable types, because that's all that Java has:

```
// firstName is now a nullable type
String firstName = person.getFirstName();
```

At this point, we can't be sure that the value returned from `getFirstName()` is non-null, because there's no way for Java to enforce that. In the following code, we access the `firstName` variable without any type of `null` check, which could lead to potential issues:

```
String firstName = person.getFirstName();
firstName.length();
```

To protect properly against null access in Java, we must rely on traditional strategies of Java development, such as checking for null before accessing a variable:

```
String firstName = person.getFirstName();
if (firstName != null) {
    // handle non-null value
}
```

While the Java type system might result in the loss of strict typing information present in Kotlin, the available tooling can help us understand whether a variable might be nullable. IntelliJ-based IDEs can analyze the code in an attempt to understand when Java fields and variables may be non-null. In this example, IntelliJ is able to inform us that the `firstName` variable will not be null since `Person.firstName` is a non-null property:

```
// firstName is now a nullable type
String firstName = person.getFirstName();
if (firstName != null) { // condition is always true
    // handle non-null value
}
```

While the inspection warning is useful, it's not something strictly enforced by the compiler, so you need to be aware of when and where you can correctly infer nullability across the languages, and where you still need to perform explicit type checks.

Another example of this is passing parameters to constructors or functions written in Kotlin. This snippet illustrates the issue:

```
// Passing a null value when instantiating from Java
new Person(null, "Smith"); // compiles but will result in error
```

This code will compile even though both properties of the `Person` class are non-null. From Java, there isn't any way to strictly enforce the rule that the passed values should be non-null. In this case, `IllegalArgumentException` will be thrown indicating that the passed parameter must be non-null. The IDE can help in these situations as well by providing inspections that warn if a potentially null value is passed where a non-null value is expected, but it's up to you to ensure that the code handles these situations correctly since the compiler can't enforce it.

Another area of Kotlin where interop code from Java becomes potentially more verbose is function arguments. In the next section, we'll take a look at how Kotlin features such as named arguments and default parameter values can and can not be used from Java.

Function arguments

Two of the most interesting and convenient features of Kotlin are default parameter values and named arguments. However, these features are not always available to us by default in Java.

To illustrate this, we'll start by updating the `Person` example to use default values for each parameter:

```
open class Person(val firstName: String = "", val lastName: String = "")
```

Now, we can instantiate `Person` from Kotlin without passing any parameters, like this:

```
val person = Person()
```

In this case, we can do the same thing from Java because the compiler will generate an empty default constructor that provides the default values:

```
Person person2 = new Person();
```

However, the same is not true if we add a method to the `Person` class:

```
open class Person(val firstName: String = "", val lastName: String = "") {
    fun foo(name: String = "") { }
}
```

With a default value defined for this method parameter, we can call the method from Kotlin without passing any arguments:

```
val person = Person()
person.foo()
```

But from Java, we *must* pass the argument value when invoking the function:

```
Person person2 = new Person();
person2.foo(); // wont compile
```

This difference highlights how convenient Kotlin features, such as default parameter values, may not be available from Java by default. In the next chapter, we'll take a look at how we can improve this behavior.

Lack of static

Kotlin doesn't have a `static` keyword, so what should you do if you want your code to be written in Kotlin, but still adhere to patterns and conventions that require `static`, or at least the appearance of `static`? There are a few different options for these cases.

One of the more common uses of static methods and fields is for things such as helper functions and constants. In Java, it's common to have classes that exist for the sole purpose of containing static methods or fields. In Kotlin, these types of static methods/fields, and their associated classes, can be replaced with things such as top-level functions and properties, extension functions, or companion objects. We'll look at these in depth later in the chapter.

The Kotlin alternatives don't always translate to the same bytecode as their static Java counterparts. If you need true JVM static properties or methods, you can leverage the `@JVMStatic` annotation. Let's explore this annotation with an example.

Here, we've defined a `Foo` class with a companion object that contains a single `const val` property:

```
class Foo {
    companion object {
        const val ID = "123"
    }
}
```

From Java, we can access the `const` property directly, like this:

```
String id = Foo.ID;
```

If we wanted to enforce the rule that the value should be accessed through a static getter, we could use the `@JVMStatic` annotation like this:

```
class Foo {
    companion object {
        @JvmStatic
        val ID = "123"
    }
}
```

By doing so, it would then force us to access the property using the generated getter:

```
String id = Foo.getID();
```

This annotation will force the compiler to generate static methods and/or getters/setters for the annotated target. By using this annotation, you can instruct the API to behave similarly with Java.

In this section, we've seen several examples of how to work with Kotlin from Java and some of the limitations that includes. In the next section, we'll explore how to work with Java code from Kotlin.

Working with Java from Kotlin

Working with Java code from Kotlin comes with fewer limitations and drawbacks. Existing Java code and libraries should generally be completely compatible with your Kotlin code, allowing you to start integrating Kotlin while leveraging existing code.

Using existing code

We can easily instantiate and manipulate Java classes from Kotlin. Let's revisit the Programmer class written in Java:

```java
public class Programmer extends Person {
    private String preferredLanguage;

    public Programmer(String firstName, String lastName,
                      String preferredLanguage) {
        super(firstName, lastName);
        this.preferredLanguage = preferredLanguage;
    }

    public String getPreferredLanguage() {
        return preferredLanguage;
    }
}
```

We can instantiate this from Kotlin like so:

```kotlin
val programmer = Programmer("John", "Smith", "Kotlin")
```

An interesting side effect of using a Java class from Kotlin is that we can take advantage of property access syntax to access fields exposed via getters/setters without having to actually call the getters and setters.

Note that in this snippet, we can access all the properties of `Programmer` using property access syntax, regardless of whether they were originally defined in Kotlin or Java:

```
val programmer = Programmer("John", "Smith", "Kotlin")
programmer.preferredLanguage
programmer.firstName
```

In this code snippet, we are only able to access `preferredLanguage` because we exposed a `getPreferredLanguage()` method. The field itself is private, but the Kotlin compiler will generate a synthetic accessor based on a getter if it detects one, thereby allowing us to use property access syntax.

Synthetic accessors are just one area where the Kotlin compiler does a lot of work behind the scenes to make our code more concise and convenient. Another such area is in the strict enforcement of nullability; however, when working across both Kotlin and Java, some of this strict type information can be lost. In the next section, we'll shed some more light on this occurrence.

Enforcing null safety

When calling from Kotlin into Java, there is less to consider regarding `null` safety. Because Kotlin has the more strict type system, the Kotlin code will generally have more information available regarding properties and variables. This does mean that once we make a call over into Java, we may lose some of that type information, but, like we saw before, there are things we can do in Java to help preserve that type information in some situations, such as making use of the `@Nullable` and `@NonNull` annotations.

As we've seen in this section, we can easily work with existing Java code from within our Kotlin code base. Existing Java classes may not have as much syntactic sugar available within the project as Kotlin code, but functionally they work side by side with little issue. In the next section, we'll look at moving beyond both Java and Kotlin coexisting in a single project, and will look at how to embrace common Kotlin idioms.

Embracing Kotlin idioms

When introducing Kotlin to an existing code base, it's beneficial to be aware of common Kotlin idioms. Many of these common idioms can be used without a direct impact on interoperability; however, there are some common patterns in Kotlin that can impact interop, and you should be aware of them.

Goodbye helpers – embracing top-level and extension functions and properties

A common pattern in Java is to have the helper and `util` classes that exist solely for the purpose of storing static methods and data that needs to be accessible to the code base. These are classes such as `StringUtils`, `DateUtils`, and `ViewHelpers`. In Kotlin, we have another option.

Top-level functions and properties allow us to replace these types of helper and `util` classes with globally available functions and/or extension functions. This can not only remove the classes, but make our APIs cleaner by making these types of helper functions feel like first-class parts of the language.

Top-level functions

Let's take a look at an example of how we can leverage top-level functions. In this snippet, we define a top-level function to print a greeting:

```
// Helpers.kt
fun printGreeting(name: String) {
    println("Hello $name")
}
```

This function can then be used anywhere within our Kotlin code base as follows:

```
printGreeting("Nate")
```

Calling top-level functions from Kotlin is very fluent, and has a very friendly syntax. However, calling these from Java takes a little more work. To call the top-level function from Java, we must invoke it as a static method on a generated class:

```
HelpersKt.printGreeting("Nate");
```

By default, the generated class will be named as `<kotlin filename>Kt`. So in this case, the function was defined in `Helpers.kt` and the generated class is named `HelpersKt`.

Extension functions

In Java, it's common to define helper classes/methods that all act on a common type. An example of this might be a `StringUtils` class that contains a number of helper methods that all act on `String`. In Kotlin, we could define top-level functions for this that might all take a `String` parameter, but we could also solve this with extension functions.

Let's first imagine a `StringHelpers` class in Java:

```
public class StringHelpers {
    public static void log(String msg) {
        System.out.println("log: " + msg);
    }
}
```

We could call this from both Java and Kotlin by passing a string into each invocation. With extension functions, we can define a function that, from Kotlin, will appear to be a method on the `String` type itself, and, from Java, will not require the enclosing class:

```
// extension function on String
fun String.log() {
    println("log: $this")
}
```

From Kotlin, we can call this function like this:

```
"message to log".log()
```

It will be treated like any other method in the receiver class.

From Java, we can still use this function like we would any other top-level function, but the first parameter will be the receiver type. In this case, the receiver is `String`, so we pass the message into the function like any other parameter:

```
HelpersKt.log("message to log");
```

This ensures that we can make use of our extension functions from both Java and Kotlin.

Top-level properties

Kotlin supports top-level and extension properties in addition to top-level functions and extension functions. Top-level properties allow us to define scoped constants or other values independent of any enclosing class.

Top-level constant properties

The following snippet demonstrates a publicly available top-level property:

```
// Constants.kt
const val KEY_ID = "id"
```

Within the specified scope of the property, it can be accessed from Kotlin directly by name:

```
println(KEY_ID)
```

From Java, it can be accessed as a static field on the associated generated class:

```
System.out.println(ConstantsKt.KEY_ID);
```

Not only can we work with immutable top-level properties from both Kotlin and Java, but we can access mutable top-level properties as well, as we'll see in the next section.

Top-level mutable properties

You can also define mutable top-level properties if you need to track some type of global state. The following snippet shows an example of such a property:

```
var screenCount = 0
```

We've defined an integer variable that can be accessed and modified from anywhere in the defined scope:

```
screenCount++
```

In this case, it's public, so it can be accessed from anywhere within the code base. In the next section, we'll look at using companion objects as a means of scoping this kind of top-level property.

Companion objects

You may not want to rely on top-level functions and properties in cases where you would ideally like to scope, or associate, a function or value with a particularl class. This might be the case for things such as factory methods or scoped constants. For these situations, we can rely on companion objects to achieve that type of relationship.

Let's say that we want to provide constants to represent the result state of a page. We could achieve this using companion objects, like so:

```
class AuthScreen {
    companion object {
        const val RESULT_AUTHENTICATED = 0
        const val RESULT_ERROR = 1
    }
}
```

By defining the constants within the companion object, we avoid polluting the global namespace with top-level properties. We will then be able to access the values, in the same way as we would when working with static fields in Java:

```
val result = AuthScreen.RESULT_AUTHENTICATED
```

In this case, working with the properties is very similar in Java as well. In the following snippet, we can see that from Java, we can access and store the property in the same way:

```
int result = AuthScreen.RESULT_AUTHENTICATED;
```

In Chapter 8, *Controlling the Story*, we'll examine some additional edge cases to be aware of when working with companion object properties.

As mentioned earlier, we can also define methods within our companion objects to replicate the functionality of static methods in Java. This may be useful when trying to avoid polluting the global namespace with a method specific to another class.

In this example, we've defined a factory method that allows us to instantiate AuthScreen, even though it has a private constructor:

```
class AuthScreen private constructor(){
    companion object {
        const val RESULT_AUTHENTICATED = 0
        const val RESULT_ERROR = 1
        fun create(): AuthScreen {
            return create()
        }
    }
}
```

By adding this method to the companion object, we have to reference the enclosing class name directly before invoking the function that allows us to follow the same naming conventions for other classes without conflict:

```
val authScreen = AuthScreen() // wont compile
val screen = AuthScreen.create()
```

This syntax doesn't work quite as well from Java, however. The following snippet demonstrates the more verbose syntax required to access the method from Java:

```
AuthScreen authScreen = AuthScreen.Companion.create();
```

You'll notice that, in Java, to call the method on the companion object, you must reference the companion object directly. In Chapter 8, *Controlling the Story*, we'll explore how you can improve this.

In the next section, we will see why two languages exist and how they help us while writing code.

Are two languages better than one?

We've seen that Kotlin and Java can exist, side by side, within the same code base. It's possible to work between the two languages without issue, but there are costs associated with having multiple languages within a single project. In this section, we'll explore a few of these costs.

Project structure

Your Kotlin and Java files can exist within the same source directories inside your project. You do not need to separate Kotlin and Java into homogeneous packages, modules, and so on. In general, your Kotlin and Java files will follow similar conventions for package naming and imports; however, Kotlin files can specify an arbitrary package name. This means that even though two files may exist within the same directory, they may have different declared packages, and therefore might require an explicit import.

Let's revisit the `AuthScreen` example:

```
internal class AuthScreen private constructor(){
    ...
}
```

Both `AuthScreen.kt` and `Main.kt` are within the same folder, and exist within the default global package, so `AuthScreen` can be used from `Main.kt` without any explicit import statement:

```
val screen = AuthScreen.create()
```

However, we can specify a custom package name for `AuthScreen.kt`, as shown in the following code:

```
package authscreen

internal class AuthScreen private constructor(){
    ...
}
```

But specifying a package name for the existing code within `Main.kt` will cause it to break:

```
val screen = AuthScreen.create() // won't compile
```

We must now add an explicit import to `Main.kt`:

```
import authscreen.AuthScreen
val screen = AuthScreen.create()
```

Specifying custom package names can help you organize your code exactly how you see fit, but it adds complexity, and is something to be aware of as a difference between Java and Kotlin when you start to integrate Kotlin into an existing project.

Increased build size and speed

Adding Kotlin and the Kotlin standard library to your project does come with an additional size cost. It's minimal, but it will potentially increase the size of your executable and increase your method count. The extent of this increase can be mitigated by making use of tools, such as ProGuard, which will optimize your code and remove any unused methods added by Kotlin or the Kotlin standard library.

The addition of Kotlin may also slow down your build speeds by requiring additional build steps to compile the new Kotlin code. The amount of slowdown generally depends on how your project is built, how many modules you have, and how much mixing of Java and Kotlin you are doing. It's hard to know the exact impact, but profiling your build process can illuminate the impact and whether the change in build speed is acceptable or not.

Annotation processing

Kotlin supports JSR 269 standard annotations via the Kotlin annotation processing tool (`kapt`) compiler plugin. If you're relying on the annotations and annotation processors, you'll need to use `kapt` to properly handle the annotations from Kotlin. Unfortunately, the Kotlin annotation processor is not as well optimized as the Java annotation processor, and therefore annotation processing in Kotlin is slower than in Java. This is improving, but it can still impact your build times.

Performance

A common question about using both Kotlin and Java is whether there are performance impacts that come with using two languages. Thankfully, this is not a problem. Because both Kotlin and Java compile down to common JVM bytecode, the JVM doesn't really see them as separate languages. This means there are no interop layers or other bridging that might slow down the runtime performance. At runtime, Kotlin should be just as efficient as Java.

Complexity

When working with both languages in a single project, there is an increase in the overall complexity of the project. It requires a developer to be comfortable with two languages to understand the entirety of the code base. There is increased complexity in having to consider multiple typing models, and also in having to consider how code can be consumed from each language.

Having multiple languages could be seen as a risk to management, or as an additional challenge to new developers. This can impact on hiring or resource allocation as well. You may have to consider how to integrate, refactor, or rewrite your app using Kotlin, and the ramifications this has on your time and resources.

All of these questions have answers, and have been dealt with by many teams and developers, but you'll have to evaluate them for your specific situation if you are considering adding Kotlin to your existing code base. Here are a few common questions for you to consider:

1. Which language will the new code be written in?
2. Will you migrate your entire code base to Kotlin, or only new developments?
3. Do you want to start adding Kotlin in production, or start with tests?
4. Are there people on your team who are comfortable with the language and willing to mentor others?

By thinking through these questions, you may start to form a foundation on which to answer other questions that come up around the complexities of using both languages in a single project.

Summary

In this chapter, we've taken a deeper look at the implications of adding Kotlin to an existing Java code base and managing interop between the two languages. We explored how Kotlin code can be used from Java, and examined some of the associated challenges, such as differences in type safety and the lack of static.

We also examined how existing Java code can be used easily from Kotlin. We looked at some common Kotlin idioms, such as favoring top-level functions and extension functions, and the impact they can have on how you write and consume helper classes/methods. Lastly, we examined some of the practical impacts of having multiple languages in a single project, such as project structure and increased complexity.

This has provided a solid background for interop between Kotlin and Java, but there's more to the story. In the next chapter, we'll look at how we can improve some of the pain points discussed in this chapter.

Questions

1. Is it true or false that it's possible to call Kotlin code from Java?
2. Is it true or false that it's possible to call Java code from Kotlin?
3. Is it true or false that Kotlin's strict null typing is persisted when calling into Java?
4. What are the two ways of managing the lack of static methods in Kotlin?
5. How are top-level functions accessed from Java?
6. How are extension functions accessed from Java?
7. Is it true or false that default parameter values can be used from Java?

Further reading

- *Mastering Android Development with Kotlin* (https://www.packtpub.com/application-development/mastering-android-development-kotlin)
- *Mastering High Performance Kotlin* (https://www.packtpub.com/application-development/mastering-high-performance-kotlin)

8
Controlling the Story

While Kotlin/Java interop works well out of the box, the experience can be modified to suit the needs of each individual project, thereby making Kotlin code feel more integrating with existing code and team conventions.

This chapter will detail how Kotlin code can be modified to provide a better interop experience with Java and help us understand how to work with objects to write better working statics.

In this chapter, we'll explore the following topics:

- Modifying the naming conventions of generated classes
- Leveraging default values and named parameters from Java
- Tips for working with companion objects
- How to write true JVM statics in Kotlin

Technical requirements

In order to download, compile, and execute the samples found in this chapter, the following is required:

- IntelliJ IDEA 2018.3 Community or Ultimate edition, or newer
- An internet connection
- Git and GitHub (optional)

To download all of the code in this chapter, including the examples and code snippets, please refer to the following GitHub link: `https://github.com/PacktPublishing/Mastering-Kotlin/tree/master/Chapter08`.

Improving generated class names

As we saw in the previous chapters, Kotlin features, such as top-level functions, top-level properties, and extension functions, can all be used from our existing Java code. This is important when working in a mixed code base using both Java and Kotlin. However, by default, the syntax for working with these features from Java may not be as clean or meaningful as we would like them to be.

To improve this aspect of interoperability, it's possible to modify the name of a class that's generated by the Kotlin compiler. By controlling how these generated classes are named, we can make it easier to consume Kotlin features, such as top-level and extension functions, when working in Java. Let's explore this by looking at a simple top-level function example.

How are class names generated?

To understand how to control generated class naming, we'll explore how these class names are generated by the Kotlin compiler by default. In this snippet, we've defined a new top-level function named `sayHello()`:

```
// GreetingFunctions.kt
fun sayHello(name: String) = println("Hello $name!")
```

This function prints a simple greeting and can be used freely from the rest of our Kotlin code, like this:

```
// Main.kt
fun main() {
    sayHello("Nate")
}
```

In this Kotlin case, calling the top-level function feels like a natural part of the language because the function is freely available, and is not associated with any class. However, from Java's perspective, that's not the case. To invoke the `sayHello()` function from Java, we must reference the function as a static method on a generated class:

```
// Main.java
public class Main {
    public static void main(String[] args) {
        GreetingFunctionsKt.sayHello("Nate");
    }
}
```

To understand how this works, and ultimately how we can control this behavior, we can turn to the decompiled Kotlin bytecode for the top-level function:

```
public final class GreetingFunctionsKt {
    public static final void sayHello(@NotNull String name) {
        Intrinsics.checkParameterIsNotNull(name, "name");
        String var1 = "Hello " + name + '!';
        System.out.println(var1);
    }
}
```

In this decompiled bytecode, we can see that the compiler has generated the `GreetingFunctionsKt` class for us with our top-level function as a static method on the class.

By default, the Kotlin compiler-generated class name is defined using the following format: `<kotlin file name>Kt`. In our example, `sayHello()` was declared within `GreetingFunctions.kt`, so the class name that's generated becomes `GreetingFunctionsKt`.

Now that we understand that the generated class name is derived from the filename in which the top-level function was declared, we can take a look at how to customize this class name with the `@JvmName` annotation.

Renaming the generated class

The `@JvmName` annotation is part of the Kotlin `stdlib`. Its purpose is to specify the name of any Java class or method that's generated from the target element. When used at the file level, it can be used to specify the name of the class that's generated for top-level functions and properties in the Kotlin file. In the case of our `sayHello()` function example, this means we can modify the name of the `GreetingFunctionsKt` class that's generated.

Renaming a generated class name for top-level functions

To demonstrate the renaming of a generated class, we'll make use of the `@JvmName` annotation within our `GreetingFunctions.kt` file. Here, we've added the `@JvmName` annotation to our `GreetingFunctions.kt` file using the `@file` use-site target (we'll talk more about use-site targets later on in this chapter):

```
@file:JvmName("GreetingsHelper")

// GreetingFunctions.kt
fun sayHello(name: String) = println("Hello $name!")
```

Within the `@JvmName` annotation, we've specified the `"GreetingsHelper"` string as the name we'd like to use for the compiler-generated class. After this addition, calling the `sayHello()` function from Kotlin is unchanged:

```
// Main.kt
fun main() {
    sayHello("Nate")
}
```

But now, when calling the `sayHello()` function from Java, we have a different enclosing class to reference; `GreetingsHelper`:

```
// Main.java
public class Main {
    public static void main(String[] args) {
        GreetingsHelper.sayHello("Nate");
    }
}
```

Now, the generated class directly matches the name that's passed to the `@JvmName` annotation. Changing this name allows us to hide any indication of Kotlin from the name of the class. By removing the `Kt` suffix from the class name, it's no longer obvious to the caller that the class or method is written in Kotlin. This improves the interop experience by hiding that implementation detail.

This process of generated class naming not only works for top-level functions, but for top-level properties as well, as we will examine in the next section.

Renaming a generated class name for top-level properties

Using the @JvmName annotation to control how generated classes are named works for features such as top-level properties and extension functions as well. In the following code snippet, we've declared a top-level property named screenCount:

```
// Constants.kt
var screenCount = 0
```

We can then reference screenCount from Java by referencing the default class name that's generated; in this case, this is ConstantsKt:

```
// Main.java
public class Main {
    public static void main(String[] args) {
        GreetingsHelper.sayHello("Nate");
        ConstantsKt.getScreenCount();
    }
}
```

By adding the @JvmName annotation, we can change the generated class name from ConstantsKt to Constants:

```
@file:JvmName("Constants")

// Constants.kt
var screenCount = 0
```

Once we've added the annotation, our call sites can use the updated, simplified name:

```
// Main.java
public class Main {
    public static void main(String[] args) {
        GreetingsHelper.sayHello("Nate");
        Constants.getScreenCount();
    }
}
```

By modifying the class names that are generated, we can improve how our APIs are used from Java. We can remove any hint of Kotlin from the class names, thereby making the code more transparent and easier to refactor in the future.

Hiding any indication that code is written in Kotlin can help make the Java/Kotlin interop experience more seamless, but what about exposing Kotlin features to Java as well? One example of this is making default parameter values from Java usable. We'll explore this in the next section.

Leveraging default values in Java

Default values are a powerful feature of Kotlin. They allow us to write fewer overloaded functions and can even help us replace the builder pattern. Unfortunately, we can't leverage this feature from Java. Because of this, we have to think carefully about how to write functions if they will be used from both Kotlin and Java. If a class written in Kotlin will be used from Java, you may have to consider whether or not you can make heavy use of default values.

To help make this decision, we can consider making use of the `@JvmOverloads` annotation to generate Java method overloads, which will make use of our defined default values.

In this snippet, we've defined a class, `Student`, that includes a primary constructor. This constructor includes four properties that all contain a default value:

```kotlin
class Student(
        val firstName:String = "",
        val lastName: String = "",
        val grade: Int = 10,
        val classes:List<String> = listOf("Home Room", "Math")
)
```

With this class declaration, we can instantiate instances of `Student` in Kotlin using 0-4 argument values in the constructor:

```kotlin
// Main.kt
fun main() {
    val defaultStudent = Student()
    val student = Student(
            "John",
            "Smith",
            12,
            listOf("Home Room", "Math", "Science", "Music")
    )
}
```

From Java, however, we are required to pass all the argument values to the constructor:

```
// Main.java
public class Main {
    public static void main(String[] args) {
        Student student = new Student(
                "John",
                "Smith",
                11,
                Arrays.asList("Home Room", "Math", "Science", "Music")
        );
    }
}
```

To improve this, we can add the `@JvmOverloads` annotation to the constructor of our `Student` class:

```
class Student @JvmOverloads constructor(
        val firstName:String - "",
        val lastName: String = "",
        val grade: Int = 10,
        val classes:List<String> = listOf("Home Room", "Math")
)
```

Adding this annotation will tell the compiler to generate constructor overloads that use the default values. After adding this annotation, it's then possible for us to invoke the `Student` constructor from Java without having to include each argument value:

```
// Main.java
public class Main {
    public static void main(String[] args) {
        Student student = new Student(
                "John",
                "Smith",
                11,
                Arrays.asList("Home Room", "Math", "Science", "Music")
        );

        Student defaultStudent = new Student();
    }
}
```

How does this work? It works because the Kotlin compiler generates multiple constructors that all call through to each other and include the defined default values. The following code demonstrates what the Kotlin compiler generates for our `Student` class once the `@JvmOverloads` annotation has been added:

```
public final class Student {
    ...
    @JvmOverloads
    public Student(@NotNull String firstName,
                   @NotNull String lastName,
                   int grade, @NotNull List classes) {
        ...
    }

    @JvmOverloads
    public Student(@NotNull String firstName,
                   @NotNull String lastName,
                   int grade) {
        this(firstName, lastName, grade, (List)null, 8,
            (DefaultConstructorMarker)null);
    }

    @JvmOverloads
    public Student(@NotNull String firstName,
                   @NotNull String lastName) {
        this(firstName, lastName, 0, (List)null, 12,
            (DefaultConstructorMarker)null);
    }

    @JvmOverloads
    public Student(@NotNull String firstName) {
        this(firstName, (String)null, 0, (List)null, 14,
            (DefaultConstructorMarker)null);
    }

    @JvmOverloads
    public Student() {
        this((String)null, (String)null, 0, (List)null, 15,
            (DefaultConstructorMarker)null);
    }
}
```

In cases where your function or constructor arguments are generally called sequentially, this solution might work well for you. The limitation of not being able to use named arguments to explicitly control the order of passed arguments means that even the generated overloads may not provide the same level of convenience as the Kotlin version of the function.

Using the @JvmOverloads annotation allows you to write concise, flexible APIs in Kotlin, and allows the compiler to generate the appropriate overloads for Java clients. This reduces the amount of code you must write, and can allow you to focus on writing idiomatic Kotlin code. In the next section, we'll examine how to make companion objects easier to work with from Java.

Better companions

Companion objects are an effective way to scope properties and methods to an enclosing class and to mimic the behavior of static properties and methods from Java. Unfortunately, the syntax for working with companion objects can be cumbersome when used from Java. In this section, we'll take a look at how to work effectively with companion objects.

How do companion objects work?

When a companion object is declared within a Kotlin class, the compiler will generate an inner class named Companion during compilation. Here, we've defined an empty companion object on a Widget class:

```
class Widget {
    companion object { }
}
```

From the preceding code snippet, the following Java code is generated by the compiler:

```
public final class Widget {
    public static final Widget.Companion Companion = new
Widget.Companion((DefaultConstructorMarker)null);

    ...
    public static final class Companion {
        private Companion() {
        }

        ...
    }
}
```

As you can see here, any time an instance of the enclosing `Widget` class is instantiated, an associated instance of the inner `Companion` class will also be instantiated. From Java, properties and methods of the `Companion` class can then be referenced via that instance:

```java
// Main.java
public class Main {
    public static void main(String[] args) {
        Widget.Companion.goo();
    }
}
```

Defining `companion` objects in this way provides a Java syntax that looks very similar to `static` methods. However, these `companion` objects are, in fact, real objects that must be instantiated to be used. We will discuss how to modify the definition and usage of companion objects later in this chapter.

When should we use a companion object?

You may be wondering when you may want to use a `companion` object. A few examples of when to use a `companion` object include the following:

- Writing factory methods for classes with private constructors
- Providing static constants and methods
- Scoping top-level properties and functions

Companion objects have access to the private properties, methods, and constructors of the enclosing class. This means that if a class has a private constructor, its companion object can still instantiate instances of the enclosing class. This allows you to write factory methods on a companion object to control how a class is created.

While Kotlin generally prefers top-level functions and properties, it's possible to leverage companion objects to scope those properties and functions to an enclosing class. This can help avoid pollution of the global namespace.

Modifying companion object names

Using companion objects from Java can be cumbersome because of the need to reference the instance of the `Companion` class. This can lead to Java code that very clearly looks like it's referencing Kotlin code. We can improve this by providing an alternative name for the `companion` object.

In the following snippet, we've specified `Factory` as the name of our companion object by adding the desired name after the `object` keyword:

```
class Widget {
    companion object Factory {
        fun create() {}
    }
}
```

With an alternative name specified, the generated class will have the newly specified name. We can then use that new name, `Factory`, in this case, to reference our `companion` object and any associated methods or properties:

```
// Main.java
public class Main {
    public static void main(String[] args) {
        Widget.Factory.create();
    }
}
```

This allows you to provide greater semantic meaning to your `companion` objects. If it's being used for factory methods, you may use a name such as `Factory`. If the companion object will primarily be used for constants, you could name it `Constants`.

By providing more meaningful names to your `companion` objects, you can provide greater semantic meaning to your calling code. Additionally, more semantic names can also make it feel more natural to use compared to Java because it hides the companion name, which is an indicator that the code is written in Kotlin.

Bringing static to Kotlin

Kotlin doesn't have a `static` keyword like Java does. Kotlin idioms rely on concepts such as top-level functions and properties, extension functions, and compile-time constants to achieve the same functionality without the need for an explicit `static` keyword. If you're working strictly within a Kotlin code base, this doesn't pose much of a problem, but if you're working across both Java and Kotlin, there may be times when you want to expose properties or methods as static so they can be used more naturally from Java. In this section, we'll learn how to expose Kotlin elements as true JVM static elements so they can be used more naturally from Java.

Where can we use JvmStatic?

To generate JVM static elements from our Kotlin code, we'll make use of the `@JvmStatic` annotation. The `@JvmStatic` annotation can be applied to properties and methods in named objects and companion objects.

@JvmStatic properties

Let's examine the impact of `@JvmStatic` on a `companion` object property. Let's start out with the following snippet, which defines a `companion` object on a `Widget` class:

```
class Widget {
    companion object {
        val foo = "foo"
    }
}
```

The `foo` property we defined earlier can be used from Java, as shown in the following code:

```
// Main.java
public class Main {
    public static void main(String[] args) {
        Widget.Companion.getFoo();
    }
}
```

There is a possible issue with this code, though. The `foo` property is an instance on an actual class. This means that an instance of the `companion` object has to be instantiated to access `foo`:

```
public final class Widget {
    @NotNull
    private static final String foo = "foo";
    ...
    public static final class Companion {
        @NotNull
        public final String getFoo() {
            return Widget.foo;
        }
        ...
    }
}
```

If we would like to access `foo` with a true static method on the `Widget` class, we can add `@JvmStatic` to the property definition on the `companion` object:

```
class Widget {
    companion object {
        @JvmStatic val foo = "foo"
    }
}
```

Once the annotation has been added, the compiler will generate a true JVM static getter for `foo`, as shown in the following code:

```
public final class Widget {
    @NotNull
    private static final String foo = "foo";
    ...

    @NotNull
    public static final String getFoo() {
        Widget.Companion var10000 = Companion;
        return foo;
    }

    public static final class Companion {
        ...
    }
}
```

With this generated getter available, we can access `foo` without an instance of the companion object:

```
// Main.java
public class Main {
    public static void main(String[] args) {
        ...
        Widget.getFoo();
    }
}
```

Not only is this new syntax less verbose and more Java idiomatic, but it's more efficient as well as we don't have to generate a new instance of a class to access the constant, `foo`. This usage of `@JvmStatic` can be applied to more than just properties. In the next section, we'll look at using `@JvmStatic` with companion object methods.

@JvmStatic methods

Similarly to properties, we can apply @JvmStatic to methods defined on companion objects or named objects. Let's examine this by adding a method to our existing companion object:

```
class Widget {
    companion object {
        ...

        fun goo() { }
    }
}
```

From Java, we can then use this method by once again using an instance of the companion object:

```
// Main.java
public class Main {
    public static void main(String[] args) {
        Widget.Companion.goo();
    }
}
```

In this example, we must reference the companion object instance because the goo() method is a member of the companion object itself, as seen in the following generated code:

```
public final class Widget {
    ...
    public static final class Companion {
        ...

        public final void goo() {
        }

        ...
    }
}
```

To move this generated goo() method to the Widget class itself, we can once again apply the @JvmStatic annotation:

```
class Widget {
    companion object {
        ...

        @JvmStatic
```

```
        fun goo() { }
    }
}
```

Adding the @JvmStatic annotation to the companion object declaration of goo() will indicate to the compiler that it should generate a static method, goo(), on the Widget class itself:

```
public final class Widget {
    ...

    @JvmStatic
    public static final void goo() {
        Companion.goo();
    }

    public static final class Companion {
        ...
    }
}
```

Once the compiler has generated the true JVM static method, it can be accessed from Java without needing to reference, or know about, the companion object:

```
// Main.java
public class Main {
    public static void main(String[] args) {
        Widget.goo();
    }
}
```

By writing your function with @JvmStatic, the code can be used from Java like any other static method in your Java code base. If you're working in a code base with a lot of Java and Kotlin code, this familiar syntax and usage might be a desirable trait.

When should we use the @JvmStatic annotation?

When should you consider using the @JvmStatic annotation? You may consider it for a few different reasons:

- You want to improve the syntax of referencing companion object properties and methods from Java.

- You want to avoid requiring an instance of the `companion` object to work with constants or static methods.
- You want to have constants that aren't tied to a class instance, but can't leverage the `const` keyword.

Use-site annotation targets

We've already seen several examples of how annotations can be used to control how code is generated, and how that generated code can improve the interop between Java and Kotlin. Sometimes, we need to have greater control over how annotations are applied to the Java elements generated. For these situations, we can specify a user-site target for the annotation.

What are use-site targets?

Use-site targets give us control over how annotations are applied to the Java code that's generated by the Kotlin compiler. They can help us indicate whether an annotation should be applied to a generated field, a generated getter/setter, or a number of other Java targets. In most situations, these use-sites will be used when annotating properties or constructor parameters.

The following is a full list of use-site targets:

- `file`
- `property`
- `field`
- `get`
- `set`
- `receiver`
- `param`
- `setparam`
- `delegate`

Specifying a use-site target

Let's look at how specifying different use-site targets impacts the generated Java code. We'll start by defining a simple `ViewModel` class:

```
class ViewModel( @param:ColorRes val resId:Int )
```

In this code snippet, we've added a `@ColorRes` annotation with a use-site of `param`. By adding this, the `ColorRes` annotation will be applied to the constructor parameter in the generated Java class:

```
public final class ViewModel {
    private final int resId;

    public final int getResId() {
        return this.resId;
    }

    public ViewModel(@ColorRes int resId) {
        this.resId = resId;
    }
}
```

The `@ColorRes` annotation is an annotation from the Android support library. It can be used to specify that an integer value represents a resource identifier.

Next, we'll change the use-site to `field`:

```
class ViewModel( @field:ColorRes val resId:Int )
```

Now, we can see that the `ColorRes` annotation is then applied to the `resId` field of the generated `ViewModel` class:

```
public final class ViewModel {
    @ColorRes
    private final int resId;

    public final int getResId() {
        return this.resId;
    }

    public ViewModel(int resId) {
        this.resId = resId;
    }
}
```

We can use the `get` target to add the annotation to the generated getter:

```
class ViewModel( @get:ColorRes val resId:Int )
```

Once we do that, we can see that the Java getter now has the `ColorRes` annotation:

```
public final class ViewModel {
    private final int resId;

    @ColorRes
    public final int getResId() {
        return this.resId;
    }

    public ViewModel(int resId) {
        this.resId = resId;
    }
}
```

We can also specify multiple use-site targets if we want to add the annotation to multiple generated elements:

```
class ViewModel( @get:ColorRes @param:ColorRes val resId:Int )
```

In this case, the getter and the constructor parameter will both have the `ColorRes` annotation applied to them in the generated code:

```
public final class ViewModel {
    private final int resId;

    @ColorRes
    public final int getResId() {
        return this.resId;
    }

    public ViewModel(@ColorRes int resId) {
        this.resId = resId;
    }
}
```

By specifying use-site targets, we can ensure that our annotated parameters and properties are annotated as expected and work correctly across both Kotlin and Java.

Default targets

If a use-site is not specified for an added annotation, the target will be chosen based on the targets specified on the annotation.

Let's look at the following custom annotation:

```
@Target(AnnotationTarget.PROPERTY_GETTER)
annotation class ColorRes
```

This annotation can be applied to property getters, but not other targets. Therefore, in this example, the code will not compile:

```
class ViewModel( @ColorRes val resId:Int ) . // will not compile
```

However, if we specify the `get` use-site, then the code will compile just fine:

```
class ViewModel( @get:ColorRes val resId:Int )
```

If an annotation declaration doesn't include the `@Target` annotation, the following targets will be applicable:

- `class`
- `property`
- `field`
- `local_variable`
- `value_parameter`
- `constructor`
- `function`
- `property_getter`
- `property_setter`

By leveraging these targets for your custom annotations, you can improve how the annotations are recognized and used across both Kotlin and Java.

Summary

Interoperability between Java and Kotlin is very strong by default. However, there are a number of options available to us so that we can improve how we can use Kotlin from Java. We can use the `@JvmName` annotation to control the name Java classes that are generated from our Kotlin code. By using the `@JvmOverloads` annotation, we can generate method overloads to help us take advantage of default parameter values that are not supported in Java. While Kotlin does not have a static keyword, we can use the `@JvmStatic` annotation to mark properties and methods of companion objects. By doing this, the compiler will generate true JVM static methods for accessing these properties and methods with a syntax that feels much more natural from Java.

We also saw how we can provide alternative names for our `companion` objects to improve the call-site syntax in Java and to provide increased semantic meaning to our code.

Lastly, we saw how we can specify use-site targets for our annotations so that we have greater control over how the Kotlin compiler annotates generated Java elements. These tools allow us to write Kotlin code that can be used from Java in a manner that feels very natural.

In the next chapter, we'll explore how to start introducing Kotlin through testing.

Questions

1. What is the `@JvmName` annotation used for?
2. What is the `@JvmStatic` annotation used for?
3. What does the `@JvmOverloads` annotation do when applied to a Kotlin function?
4. What are use-site targets used for?
5. Is it true or false that companion objects can be given more meaningful names?
6. What are two uses for companion objects?

Further reading

- *Mastering Android Development with Kotlin* (`https://www.packtpub.com/application-development/mastering-android-development-kotlin`)
- *Mastering High Performance with Kotlin* (`https://www.packtpub.com/application-development/mastering-high-performance-kotlin`)

Baby Steps – Integration through Testing

9

When choosing to integrate Kotlin into an existing code base, there are generally two approaches. The first is the *jump right in and write production code using Kotlin* approach. The other is to start integrating Kotlin through test code. In this chapter, we'll explore the pros and cons of a test-first integration plan, examine how testing with multiple languages can improve interop, and see how Kotlin DSLs can actually make testing easier.

This chapter is structured as follows:

1. Understanding the pros and cons of integrating Kotlin via a testing-first approach
2. How writing production code and tests in different languages can improve the overall interop experience
3. Exploring how the available testing DSLs make testing easy in Kotlin

Technical requirements

In order to download, compile, and execute the samples found in this chapter, the following is required:

- IntelliJ IDEA 2018.3 Community or Ultimate edition, or newer
- An internet connection
- Git and GitHub (optional)

To download all of the code in this chapter, including the examples and code snippets, please refer to the following GitHub link: `https://github.com/PacktPublishing/Mastering-Kotlin/tree/master/Chapter09`.

Test-first integration

When developers start looking at using Kotlin, most development teams will be integrating Kotlin into an existing project rather than starting from scratch on greenfield development. Before beginning this kind of integration, your team may debate the best way to go about this. Typically, there are two common schools of thought regarding how to approach this:

- Start with feature development.
- Start with tests.

In this section, we're going to discuss these two approaches, as well as their advantages and disadvantages.

Feature integration

First off, let's examine a feature-first integration of Kotlin. What exactly does *feature-first integration* mean? This refers to an integration strategy where Kotlin is immediately adopted for production code. This could mean that new features are written using Kotlin, or it could mean migrating existing code over to Kotlin. In either case, Kotlin code will be shipped to production. Like most decisions in software development, there are advantages and disadvantages associated with this approach.

Advantages

There are several main advantages to adopting a feature-first integration of Kotlin:

- This is more likely to take full advantage of language features.
- It gives us the opportunity to test and monitor the impact of Kotlin in production.
- It has a minimal impact on the development process.

When writing production-ready feature code, you will encounter a variety of scenarios that lend themselves to different patterns and approaches to solve. These scenarios provide a perfect opportunity so that we can fully explore Kotlin and the features we've been exploring in this book. By exploring the language more fully, developers can more quickly learn Kotlin and better leverage it to improve the quality of their code base. This greater exploration of the entirety of Kotlin is not present when writing test code, where code often falls into the same setup | exercise | validate pattern.

Another possible benefit to integrating Kotlin into production code from the beginning is that you can quickly determine whether there are any issues with shipping Kotlin to your production users. If, for some reason, you discover a compatibility issue, or find that an applied programming pattern breaks in the field, you will discover this sooner rather than later. This can help ensure that your development team finds these issues before they grow and before bad habits develop.

If your team is not in the practice of writing tests, then starting with feature-first integration will have less impact on your development process. If your team doesn't test, then starting with a test-first approach also requires becoming comfortable with the concept of testing as a whole, and you may find yourself evaluating your new development process as much as the language. However, this may increase overhead and reduce productivity too much in the short term.

Disadvantages

Integrating Kotlin via a feature-first approach is not without its drawbacks. For example, if new features are being developed with a new language, there may be a temporary decrease in developer productivity as they learn the language and get comfortable with new idioms and features. Anecdotally, this dip in productivity is generally considered to be minimal, but it will absolutely depend on the individual developer experience and team dynamics.

While shipping a new development language to your production users can be exciting, it also comes with some risks. You may need to closely monitor your first Kotlin releases to verify that features such as `lateinit` or non-null properties are being used correctly across the entirety of your user space.

Test integration

Now, let's explore the pros and cons of integrating Kotlin via a test-first approach. In this approach, Kotlin is added to your project specifically for test code that will not be shipped to production.

Advantages

Perhaps the biggest advantage of integrating Kotlin using a test-first approach is that it's safe. You're not slowing down feature development through migration or refactoring and you're not shipping a new language to production users; it frees your team so that they're able to try the language without much impact on what is actually shipped.

One benefit of writing tests with Kotlin is that it can help expose stability and interop issues in your Java and Kotlin code. By exercising your code through tests, you can ensure you're using language features correctly and examine how they work from both Java and Kotlin. This can illuminate where you want to modify and how you write your code based on whichever level of interop support you need.

Kotlin can be largely beneficial for testing, irrespective of whether it's your first choice. The ability to write DSLs in Kotlin means we can write test code that is very fluent and expressive, making it easier to write, read, and validate. By reducing boilerplate and increasing readability, we can encourage developers to write tests with a lower barrier to entry.

Disadvantages

The disadvantages to starting with a test-first approach are minimal. Test code is often repetitive, so it might not expose developers to the entire scope of language features if that's all you're using Kotlin for. If your code is not shipped to production, you won't see how it behaves on different deployment targets. And finally, if you're not already testing, then starting with test-first integration also requires you to rethink your development workflows to take testing into account.

It's likely that none of these disadvantages are deal breakers. For many teams, test-first integration is the easiest, lowest risk way to introduce Kotlin to a project.

General impact of integration

When adding Kotlin to an existing code base, regardless of whether you start with a test-first or feature-first integration of Kotlin, there are certain impacts that will be incurred, including the following:

- Additional complexity
- Additional tooling
- Increased artifact size
- Possibly increased build speed

By adding a new development language to your project, you've increased the number of languages you have to understand in order to be able to work on the entirety of the code base. While this might be a minor cost, it does increase the overall complexity of the project.

Adding Kotlin to your project will likely require additional tooling and dependencies. Again, these increase the complexity of your project. In particular, you may have to pay close attention to make sure that your version of Kotlin and any associated plugins are compatible with your existing tools.

Including Kotlin and the Kotlin standard library will likely increase the size of your output artifact. This is typically a minimal size increase, but if you're working on a project where every byte counts, you may have to consider this cost and how to mitigate it.

Lastly, adding Kotlin to an existing Java project will increase your build time. This increase is even worse if you're using annotation processors. When adding Kotlin to your project for the first time, it may be worth your time to profile your build and determine whether the impacts on build performance are acceptable or not. Now, let's take a step ahead and see how the testing of interop works.

Testing interop

In the previous chapters, we explored the interop experience between Java and Kotlin. We've examined some of the pain points and saw how we can improve the interop experience through the use of things such as annotations and companion objects. Understanding where your code base's interop experience can be improved relies heavily on actually using APIs from different languages.

Using your APIs is typically dependent on whatever task you're currently working on, and it might not make sense to exercise a particular Kotlin API from Java, or vice versa. This is where testing can be really useful. We can make an explicit effort to write tests that explore how our code works from one language to the next.

In this section, we'll explore how we can improve the interop experience in our code base through writing tests.

Exercising your Kotlin code

To begin exploring how testing can improve the integration and interop experience of our Kotlin code base, we'll start by writing a basic test using Kotlin.

For this example, we'll imagine we're testing how a view model is formatting data so that it can be presented in our UI. We'll test the following function, which takes in `String` as name and returns that `name` prepended with `Hello`:

```
fun formatGreeting(name: String) : String {
    return "Hello $name"
}
```

We can then write a simple JUnit4 test with Kotlin to test the behavior of our new function:

```
import org.junit.Assert.*

class UtilitiesKtTest {

    @org.junit.Test
    fun test_formatGreeting() {
        val formattedName = formatGreeting("Nate")
        assertEquals("Hello Nate", formattedName)
    }
}
```

At this point, this should look similar to how we write a simple test in Java.

One interesting thing about writing tests in Kotlin is that the naming rules for functions are modified slightly. For test sources, Kotlin allows function names to have spaces in them as long as the full name is wrapped with ` ... `. With this, we can update the name of our test function to something a little less restrictive:

```
@org.junit.Test
fun `test the formatGreeting function`() {
    val formattedName = formatGreeting("Nate")
    assertEquals("Hello Nate", formattedName)
}
```

We also have access to other common testing frameworks, such as Mockito, that you may be familiar with from Java code bases. To demonstrate the use of Mockito, we're going to refactor our `formatGreeting()` function so that it closely matches a real-world scenario. Let's imagine we don't want to hardcode the greeting string within the implementation of `formatGreeting()`. Instead, we want to define an interface that will provide a greeting so that we can easily customize and test the behavior of `formatGreeting()`.

To do this, we'll start by defining a new interface, `GreetingProvider`:

```
interface GreetingProvider {
    fun getGreeting(): String
}
```

Now, we'll update our `formatGreeting()` function to take in this `GreetingProvider` interface and use it to customize the output `String`:

```
fun formatGreeting(greetingProvider: GreetingProvider, name: String) :
String {
    return "${greetingProvider.getGreeting()} $name"
}
```

Now, we can test this more realistic function by using Mockito to mock out a `GreetingProvider` interface and control the return value of the `getGreeting()` function:

```
@org.junit.Test
fun `test foo`() {
    val mockProvider = Mockito.mock(GreetingProvider::class.java)
    Mockito.`when`(mockProvider.getGreeting()).thenReturn("Hello")

    val formattedName = formatGreeting(mockProvider, "Nate")

    assertEquals("Hello Nate", formattedName)
}
```

These examples have illustrated that testing in Kotlin is not much different than in Java. We can use familiar tools, such as JUnit and Mockito, and apply the same common testing patterns you may be familiar with.

Testing closed classes

There is one small challenge associated with mocking in Kotlin. As you may remember, classes in Kotlin are closed by default, meaning they cannot be inherited from without explicitly being marked as `open`. This is incompatible with common mocking frameworks, such as Mockito. However, there are several ways to work around this issue, and we will take a look at both in the following sections.

Using Mockito

To demonstrate the challenge associated with testing closed classes in Kotlin, we can walk through a simple, but common, example. In this code snippet, we've defined a class, `SimpleGreeter`, that implements the `GreetingProvider` interface:

```
class SimpleGreeter() : GreetingProvider {
    override fun getGreeting(): String {
        return "Hi"
    }
}
```

Now, we can try to mock this `SimpleGreeter` class with Mockito:

```
val mockProvider = Mockito.mock(SimpleGreeter::class.java) // Runtime error
```

However, mocking `SimpleGreeter` in this way will result in an error. That error will look something like this:

```
org.mockito.exceptions.base.MockitoException:
Cannot mock/spy class SimpleGreeter
Mockito cannot mock/spy because :
 - final class
```

Essentially, what the error is indicating is that Mockito can't mock final classes, and because all classes in Kotlin are final by default, this prevents us from using Mockito. So, how do we mock our Kotlin classes without marking everything as `open`?

In the case of Mockito, thankfully, this is quite easy to solve. We can simply add the `mockito-inline` dependency alongside our existing Mockito2 dependency:

```
// https://mvnrepository.com/artifact/org.mockito/mockito-inline
testCompile group: 'org.mockito', name: 'mockito-inline', version: '2.27.0'
```

After adding the `mockito-inline` dependency, the mocking of final classes will work without marking them as `open`.

Using the compiler plugin

If you're using a framework other than Mockito, or as an alternative to the `mockito-inline` approach that we described in the previous section, it's also possible to solve this problem using the `allOpen` compiler plugin. This plugin allows developers to make classes open for mocking/testing without having to actually mark each class as `open`.

To add the plugin to your Gradle project, you can modify your buildscript dependencies or use the plugins block like this:

```
plugins {
  id "org.jetbrains.kotlin.plugin.allopen" version "1.3.31"
}
```

Once the `allOpen` plugin dependency has been added to your project via Gradle, Maven, and so on, the next step is to configure the plugin to recognize a custom annotation. This annotation will be used to indicate that a class should be open for testing. With Gradle, you can specify the custom annotation like this:

```
allOpen {
  annotation("com.yourpackagename.OpenForTesting")
}
```

In this case, we've configured the `allOpen` plugin to look for an annotation named `OpenForTesting`. We would then define this custom annotation as follows:

```
annotation class OpenForTesting
```

Once the annotation has been created and the plugin has been configured, we can mark our classes with the annotation, and the compiler will take care of modifying those classes for us so that they can be mocked and tested as needed. Both of the approaches in this section allow developers to take advantage of testing frameworks such as Mockito, while maintaining the Kotlin characteristic of classes that are closed by default.

Exercising Java code from Kotlin

Another means of using tests to exercise and improve interop between Java and Kotlin is to use Kotlin code to test our Java code and vice versa. By using Kotlin to test Java, we can test more efficiently by taking advantage of Kotlin features such as data classes and the Kotlin standard library.

To explore this testing interplay between Java and Kotlin, let's walk through an example. Here, we've created a simple Java class called `StudentPresenter`:

```java
public class StudentPresenter {

    private List<Student> students;

    public StudentPresenter(List<Student> students) {
        students.sort(Comparator.comparing(Student::getLastName));

        this.students = students;
    }

    public List<Student> getStudents() {
        return students;
    }
}
```

We can write a test in Kotlin to validate that the `students` field is properly sorted:

```kotlin
@Test
fun `test students are sorted correctly`() {
    val presenter = StudentPresenter(
            listOf(
                    Student("Nate", "Ebel"),
                    Student("Jane", "Doe"),
                    Student("John", "Smith")
            )
    )

    val sortedStudents = presenter.students

    assertEquals(sortedStudents[0], Student("Jane", "Doe"))
}
```

With this test written in Kotlin, we are able to quickly pass in our list of `Student` objects by using the `listOf()` function. We can quickly validate our expected value by taking advantage of the `Student` data class that has the `equals()` function generated for us, thereby making comparisons easy.

Testing this same code from Java would have required a good deal more boilerplate code. By leveraging helper functions such as `listOf()` and language features such as data classes, our test code starts to become more concise, easier to read, and easier to maintain.

Exercising Kotlin code from Java

By testing our Kotlin code from Java, we can gain a better understanding of how the interop works between the two languages. This can shed some light on where and how we may want to modify our Kotlin APIs to be more friendly vis-à-vis Java clients.

Let's look at one example. In this code snippet, we've added a factory method to our `Student` class via a `companion` object:

```kotlin
data class Student(val firstName: String, val lastName: String) {

    companion object {
        fun createDefaultStudent() = Student("Jane", "Doe")
    }
}
```

Then, we can validate the behavior of that factory method using tests written in Java or Kotlin. In the following code, we've written a test in Java to validate the behavior of `createDefaultStudent()`:

```
public class StudentTest {

    @Test
    public void testCreateDefaultStudent() {
        Student defaultStudent =
            Student.Companion.createDefaultStudent();

        assertEquals(defaultStudent.getLastName(), "Doe");
        assertEquals(defaultStudent.getFirstName(), "Jane");
    }

}
```

By writing this test in Java, we are able to examine how the use of the `companion` object impacts our API design. We can see that in order to use the `createDefaultStudent()` function, we must first reference the `Companion` class, which makes for a verbose and cumbersome API call. This is something we may not have noticed if we were only testing our Kotlin code using Kotlin itself.

In a code base using both Java and Kotlin, we may want to improve the syntax required when calling `createDefaultStudent()` from Java. In this case, we could modify the companion object to be named `Factory`. After doing so, our test looks something more like this:

```
@Test
public void testCreateDefaultStudent() {
    Student defaultStudent = Student.Factory.createDefaultStudent();

    assertEquals(defaultStudent.getLastName(), "Doe");
    assertEquals(defaultStudent.getFirstName(), "Jane");
}
```

At the time of writing, if you're working in a code base with a lot of interplay between Java and Kotlin, then testing your Kotlin from Java can be an effective way of improving your APIs, rather than down the line when they are being used. Let's see how that works next!

Improved testing with Kotlin

While writing tests in Kotlin, we can leverage the same tools and APIs that we are familiar with from testing Java. However, like other aspects of working with Kotlin, we can make use of Kotlin language features to improve the testing experience. More concretely, there are annotations and libraries specific to Kotlin that enable us to write more fluent, expressive, Kotlin-idiomatic tests, thereby improving the overall testing experience. We'll examine these in the following sections.

The kotlin.test library

The `kotlin.test` library is a core library provided by Kotlin. Its aim is to provide helper functions and annotations to be used in a test framework-independent fashion. These annotations and top-level functions are abstracted away from individual supported test frameworks using a set of library modules, including the following:

- `kotlin-test-junit`
- `kotlin-test-junit5`
- `kotlin-test-testng`
- `kotlin-test-js`

These tools and abstractions allow you to annotate and assert your tests in a consistent way, irrespective of which testing framework you are using.

Annotations

Within `kotlin.test`, there are a number of annotations that can be used to mark our test classes and functions in a test framework-independent fashion. Examples of these annotations include the following:

- `@AfterClass`: Indicates that a function should be run after a test suite
- `@AfterTest`: Indicates that a function should be run after each test
- `@BeforeTest`: Indicates that a function should be run before each test
- `@Test`: Marks a function as a test

These annotations may look familiar if you've used other test frameworks in the past. These annotations are meant to provide similar functionality in a more native way. The specific meaning of each annotation can then be customized for whichever test framework you're targeting.

In this example, we're targeting `kotlin-test-junit` and using the `@BeforeTest` annotation to create a function that will run before any of our defined Junit tests:

```
class UtilitiesKtTest {

    @BeforeTest
    fun runBeforeAnyTest() {
        println("before test")
    }

    . . .

}
```

Once the annotation has been added, you can then swap out the underlying `kotlin-test` target if you need to switch to a different testing framework, or if you need to target a different framework when working in a multi-platform project.

Helper functions

Many testing frameworks include common functions for validating the state of your tests. These types of functions may include things such as the following:

- `assert`
- `assertTrue`
- `assertNotNull`

The `kotlin.test` package includes a variety of top-level functions aimed to provide similar functionality, independent of any specific testing framework. A few examples of these `kotlin.test` functions include the following:

- `assert`
- `assertEquals`
- `assertFailsWith`
- `containsAll`

These functions aim to provide common default functionality as a first-class supported aspect of the Kotlin core libraries.

Mockito-Kotlin

Mockito-Kotlin is an interesting example of a testing library that makes use of Kotlin features to provide a custom testing DSL that makes mocking and testing feel very fluent and readable.

In the following code snippet, you can see an example of using Mockito-Kotlin to mock the behavior of the GreetingProvider class:

```
@Test
fun `test with mockito-kotlin`() {
    val mockGreeter = mock<SimpleGreeter> {
        on { getGreeting() } doReturn "Hey there!"
        on { getMessage() } doReturn  "You're great!"
    }
}
```

Notice that this test code is making heavy use of lambdas and higher-order functions.

The mock() function is passed a lambda within which that mocked object can have its behavior configured. This configuration becomes very human readable when using functions such as on() and doReturn(), which allow us to define which values should be returned when specific methods are invoked. This allows us to write test code that reads very similarly to how we might verbally describe the testing behavior.

Once your mock has been configured, you are then free to confirm any state and behavior you wish to verify. In this example, we can invoke the getGreeting() method and then verify that getGreeting() was called on one occasion:

```
@Test
fun `test with mockito-kotlin`() {
    val mockGreeter = mock<SimpleGreeter> {
        on { getGreeting() } doReturn "Hey there!"
        on { getMessage() } doReturn  "You're great!"
    }

    mockGreeter.getGreeting()

    verify(mockGreeter, times(1)).getGreeting()
}
```

With Mockito-Kotlin, you can write fluent Kotlin test code that is easy to read and observes common Kotlin idioms. This is possible thanks to the custom DSL that Mockito-Kotlin provides, which enables the Kotlin-idiomatic creation and configuration of mocked objects. If you're writing test code in Kotlin, Mockito-Kotlin is potentially a very useful tool to explore.

Summary

Adding Kotlin to your code base via a test-first approach can be a safe way of integrating and experimenting with the language. By starting with tests, development teams can incorporate the language into their projects with minimal impact on their production artifacts. This can be a good way to convince reluctant management to try Kotlin.

Writing test code in multiple languages can also help improve the interop experience between existing Java code and Kotlin. It demonstrates how easily the two languages can be used together, and it can illustrate areas where Kotlin features or APIs are more cumbersome than Java.

Writing tests in Kotlin can also be highly efficient and expressive, if you use the available testing libraries that make use of Kotlin DSLs. All of these add up to an enjoyable testing experience with Kotlin and a viable path forward toward adding Kotlin to your project.

In the next chapter, we'll begin to explore the more advanced features of Kotlin, starting with coroutines.

Questions

1. What are two common approaches for integrating Kotlin into an existing project?
2. What are two advantages of incorporating Kotlin via a test-first approach?
3. What is one drawback of incorporating Kotlin via a test-first approach?
4. How does writing tests with multiple languages improve interop between Java and Kotlin?
5. What is one way we can handle the testing of Kotlin classes that are final by default?
6. What is the purpose of the `kotlin.test` package?
7. Can you name one Kotlin-focused testing library?

Further reading

- *Hands-On Data Structures and Algorithms with Kotlin* (`https://www.packtpub.com/application-development/hands-data-structures-and-algorithms-kotlin`)
- *Learning Android Application Testing* (`https://www.packtpub.com/application-development/learning-android-application-testing`)
- *Mockito Essentials* (`https://www.packtpub.com/application-development/mockito-essentials`)

4

Section 4: Go Beyond – Exploring Advanced and Experimental Language Features

This part will explore advanced Kotlin features and concepts that are applicable over multiple domains.

This section comprises the following chapters:

10
Practical Concurrency

In this chapter, we will explore options for writing asynchronous code in Kotlin. We'll start with common threading primitives you may be familiar with from Java, and then work our way up to more Kotlin-idiomatic approaches to writing asynchronous code.

The following topics will be covered in this chapter:

- Async primitives, such as threads and executors
- Fundamentals of coroutines
- Coroutines in practice

Technical requirements

In order to download, compile, and execute the samples found in this chapter, the following is required:

- IntelliJ IDEA 2018.3 Community or Ultimate edition, or newer
- An internet connection
- Git and GitHub (optional)

To download all of the code in this chapter, including the examples and code snippets, please refer to the following GitHub link: `https://github.com/PacktPublishing/Mastering-Kotlin/tree/master/Chapter10`.

Understanding async patterns

To write asynchronous code in both Java and Kotlin, there are a number of different primitives, libraries, and patterns at our disposal. Choosing the correct way to model async code for your project will depend on your specific needs, but understanding which options are available can improve the selection process. In this section, we will examine a number of primitives and patterns for writing asynchronous code across both Kotlin and Java.

Threading primitives

Kotlin and Java share a number of lower-level primitives for writing async code. These primitives can be used for simple, one-off operations, or can be combined with more complex systems so that you can manage asynchronous code in your project. This section will examine several of these primitives, including the following:

- Thread/ThreadPool
- ExecutorService
- CompletableFuture

Thread

The Thread class maps directly to the programming concept of a thread of execution within a programming language. Multiple threads can be run at the same time. Therefore, we can create new threads to run code in a non-blocking way. Let's look at a simple example.

To start, we'll define a function called threadExample():

```
fun threadExample() {
    println("Running threadExample()")
    println("Finished threadExample()")
}
```

Within that function, we've added log statements for when the function begins and ends. These are to help illustrate the non-blocking nature of the eventual Thread usage.

Next, we'll create, and start, a new Thread class:

```
fun threadExample() {
    println("Running threadExample()")
    val thread = Thread {
        Thread.sleep(1000)
```

```
        println("Thread finished after 1 second")
    }
    thread.start()
    println("Finished threadExample()")
}
```

Within the lambda of the `Thread` initialization, we have called `Thread.sleep(1000)`, which will delay the finish of that `Thread` by 1 second. Once the `Thread` has been declared, we call `start()` to begin execution of that `Thread`.

If we invoke `threadExample()` from our main function, we can examine the output:

```
fun main() {
    println("Hello Chapter 10")
    threadExample()
}
```

After running the preceding code, we'll receive the following output:

```
Hello Chapter 10
Running threadExample()
Finished threadExample()
Thread finished after 1 second
```

From this output, we can see that the log statement from our new `Thread` is the last thing printed out to the console. This is because that `Thread` was delayed, while the initial `Thread` continued with its execution.

While quite simple, this example demonstrates one of the core challenges in asynchronous programming. With our `threadExample()` function, our `Thread` was created and started before the `Finished threadExample()` log message was executed. However, `println("Finished threadExample()")` is run before the thread has finished executing. To ensure that our original thread doesn't complete until our new `Thread` has finished executing, we would require additional blocking mechanisms, which become challenging to write, test, and maintain.

Threads provide a means of executing an independent piece of code without blocking the current thread of execution. There are challenges associated with using threads, however. Creating a new `Thread` is a relatively expensive operation when executing your program, and having too many threads can potentially strain system resources. We'll explore one possible solution to this challenge in the next section.

ExecutorService

Creating a new `Thread` for every task is not an ideal approach for managing asynchronous work. The number of threads and associated resources can quickly get out of hand. One way to improve upon this is to make use of `ExecutorService`. With `ExecutorService`, we can submit tasks to be run asynchronously and let `ExecutorService` make decisions about how to manage which threads the tasks are run on.

We can define a specific number of threads to create and reuse for `ExecutorService`. This limits the amount of resources used, and makes it easier to understand the potential performance impacts of our code.

Creating `ExecutorService` with a fixed `Thread` count can be done quite simply, as shown in the following snippet:

```
val executor = Executors.newFixedThreadPool(3)
```

We can leverage the `newFixedThreadPool()` factory method to create `ExecutorService` with a specific thread count, in this case, 3.

Once we have an executor available, we can use that `Executor` to submit our tasks to be run in the background:

```
fun threadPoolExample() {
    executor.submit {
        Thread.sleep(500) // simulate network request
        println("Runnable 1")
    }
    executor.submit {
        Thread.sleep(200) // simulate db access
        println("Runnable 2")
    }
    executor.submit {
        Thread.sleep(300) // simulate network request
        println("Runnable 3")
    }
}
```

In this example, the executor will use its available thread pool to schedule the submitted `Runnable` tasks and execute the work. Upon execution of this code, we should see the following output:

```
Runnable 2
Runnable 3
Runnable 1
```

In this case, the first `Runnable` we submit to the `Executor` completes last because it delays its `Thread` for the longest duration. This simulates a long-running task such as a network request.

Because we've created this `Executor` with a thread pool of size 3, we can be sure that no more than three threads will be created and running at any given time, thereby limiting the amount of system resources available to run our async code.

Advanced threading

In addition to the lower-level async constructs such as `Thread` and `ExecutorService`, there are several more advanced mechanisms for writing non-blocking code across both Kotlin and Java. In this section, we'll take a look at several of those options, including the following:

- `CompletableFuture`
- RxJava
- Coroutines

CompletableFuture

`CompletableFuture` was a new addition in Java 8. It provides a future that can be explicitly completed. We can then respond to the completion of the future using a variety of callbacks to transform and respond to our data in a variety of ways.

Here's a basic example of a `CompletableFuture` that waits for 5 seconds before emitting a `String` value:

```
CompletableFuture.supplyAsync {
    Thread.sleep(5000)
    "Future is done"
}
```

We can retrieve this value in a blocking fashion like so:

```
val returnedValue = future.get()
```

It's more likely that we'll want to run the code in an asynchronous manner and then respond once the value is returned. The following snippet shows one way in which we could do this, that is, by using the `thenAccept()` method:

```
CompletableFuture.supplyAsync {
    Thread.sleep(5000)
    "Future is done"
}.thenAccept {
    println(it)
}
```

The `thenAccept()` method is a terminal method that allows us to respond to the completion of this future. When using `thenAccept()` to respond to completion, we have access to the final value. However, if we don't require the final value, we could use `thenRun()` to run an arbitrary code in response to completion:

```
CompletableFuture.supplyAsync {
    Thread.sleep(5000)
    "Future is done"
}.thenRun {
    println("The future completed")
}
```

When using `CompletableFuture`, we can also transform our data stream using a variety of operators. In the following code snippet, we can map the returned `String` to a new `String` value using `thenApply()`:

```
CompletableFuture.supplyAsync {
    Thread.sleep(5000)
    "Future is done"
}.thenApply {
    "The supplied value was: $it"
}.thenAccept {
    println(it)
}
```

`CompletableFuture` is a useful API for composing, transforming, and responding to asynchronous operations if you're targeting Java 8 or newer.

RxJava

RxJava is a library for writing event-based, asynchronous code using observable streams. RxJava provides a lot of functionality and is quite powerful. However, it can also be used for simple asynchronous code as well.

A simple example of using RxJava to run some work on a background thread can be seen in the following code snippet:

```
Single.fromCallable {
    Thread.sleep(5000)
    "Single is done"
}
.observeOn(Schedulers.io())
.subscribe { value -> println(value) }
```

With RxJava, we can define how our events will be emitted, which schedules should be used to run the work, and then manage the completion of that work. This is quite similar to the `CompletableFuture` API we looked at previously.

With RxJava, we can also perform more advanced operations such as transforming our streams of data:

```
Single.fromCallable {
    Thread.sleep(5000)
    "Single is done"
}
.map { RequestResult(it) }
.observeOn(Schedulers.io())
.subscribe { value -> println(value) }
```

In this example, we've applied the `map()` method to transform the emitted `String` value into an instance of a `RequestResult` class. This type of transformation of asynchronous streams of data is one reason why RxJava is such a popular library.

It should be noted that while RxJava can be used for writing simple asynchronous code that isn't necessarily event-driven, it might be overkill for such a use case. RxJava is a large dependency that provides many different operators to address a number of use cases. For simpler cases, something like `CompletableFuture` or coroutines might be a more lightweight solution.

Coroutines

Coroutines allow us to write asynchronous code in a sequential fashion without the use of callbacks. They are a part of the Kotlin language, and are now the default, Kotlin-idomatic way to write non-blocking code.

The following snippet demonstrates a basic example of using coroutines:

```
fun main() {
    GlobalScope.launch {
        delay(500)
        println("Coroutines")
    }
    println("Hello")
    Thread.sleep(1000)
}
```

In this example, a new coroutine is started by calling `GlobalScope.launch { }`. This code will be run in the background without blocking the starting thread. This code will produce the following output:

```
Hello
Coroutines
```

Because the launched coroutine doesn't block, `Hello` will be printed before the `Coroutines` line is printed within the coroutine.

Now that we've understood these async patterns, in the next section, we will see how we can build on our understanding of coroutines by looking at what they are and how they can be used.

The foundations of coroutines

Before taking a closer look at the practical applications of coroutines, it may be beneficial to understand more about the foundations of coroutines as a concept. This section will explore the history of coroutines and look at how and why they have been added to Kotlin. Additionally, we'll learn about what problems coroutines solve and why they are a beneficial tool to take advantage of.

What are coroutines?

Coroutines, as a concept, date back to 1958 when Melvin Conway used the term to describe the construction of an assembly program. Coroutines are a means of achieving concurrent programming. They are similar to a thread, but generally more lightweight, as multiple coroutines can actually be run, suspended, and resumed on the same thread using the same resources.

Unlike threads, coroutines don't run in parallel. They employ cooperative multitasking. This means that the operating system can move from coroutine to coroutine without context switching. Each coroutine will suspend execution at some point, at which point the OS can resume the execution of other routines. This removes some of the complexities associated with true parallelism in multithreaded environments. Because only a single coroutine is typically running at a time, the need for mechanisms such as a mutex is eliminated.

The concept of coroutines has been applied to a variety of programming languages, and today, many languages have support for coroutines, including the following:

- Python
- Ruby
- C++20
- Go
- JavaScript

Coroutines are well suited for use cases including generators/streams and communication sequential processes, which may rely on asynchronous operations. Because today's problems continue to require more and more asynchronous code, coroutines were brought to Kotlin.

Coroutines with Kotlin

Coroutine support for Kotlin was first available as an experimental feature with the 1.1 release. The 1.3 release of Kotlin brought stable support for coroutines.

Kotlin's coroutines are implemented as a first-party library, `kotlinx.coroutines`, rather than being built into the language directly. This keeps the surface area of the core language smaller, and allows for the faster iteration of coroutines. To begin working with Kotlin coroutines, you must import the `kotlinx-coroutines-core` module as a project dependency.

Coroutines in practice

Now that we understand the foundations of coroutines, let's learn how to leverage coroutines with a view to handling async operations.

In this section, we'll explore the practical usage of coroutines in Kotlin. We'll examine the available primitives and we'll work through several examples. Finally, we'll examine some more advanced concepts, such as proper error handling and controlling coroutine scope.

Coroutine primitives

There are several fundamental concepts to understand when working with Kotlin coroutines. To highlight these, we can look at our example from the previous section:

```
fun main() {
    GlobalScope.launch {
        delay(500)
        println("Coroutines")
    }

    println("Hello")
    Thread.sleep(1000)
}
```

Within the preceding snippet, there are examples of three key concepts:

- Coroutine scopes
- Coroutine builders
- Suspending functions

Let's examine each of these in detail in the coming sections.

Coroutine scopes

In our simple working example, `GlobalScope` is the coroutine scope for the launched coroutine:

```
fun main() {
    GlobalScope.launch {
        delay(500)
        println("Coroutines")
    }
```

```
    println("Hello")
    Thread.sleep(1000)
}
```

A coroutine scope defines the lifetime of a coroutine. Coroutines within `GlobalScope` can exist for the lifetime of our application. This is similar to threads that will exist for the lifetime of the application if not cleaned up properly. The concept of coroutine scope allows us to restrict our coroutines so that we can specify contexts and life cycles within our application. This concept is known as **structured concurrency**.

We can create our own coroutine scope that ties into our applications' existing life cycles. For example, if we're working on an Android app, we might want a coroutine scope bound to the `Activity` life cycle. We can accomplish that by writing something like this:

```
class ViewModel {
    private val mainScope = MainScope()
    init {
        mainScope.launch {
            // fetch data
        }
    }

    fun destroy() {
        mainScope.cancel()
    }
}
```

With this code, we've created our own scope, named `mainScope`, that is tied to the lifetime of the enclosing `ViewModel` class. As long as we clean up our scope in the `destroy()` method, any running coroutines will be cleaned properly and the resources will be released.

By leveraging `CoroutineScope`, we can help ensure that our coroutines are cleaned up correctly and run as efficiently as possible.

Coroutine builders

Coroutine builders are extension functions of the `CoroutineScope` class that can be used to launch coroutines with different characteristics. If we look back at our working example, we can see an example of the `launch()` builder:

```
fun main() {
    GlobalScope.launch {
        delay(500)
        println("Coroutines")
```

```
    }
    println("Hello")
    Thread.sleep(1000)
}
```

By calling `launch()`, we can start a new coroutine without blocking the current thread. There are a variety of other coroutine builders available to us, including the following:

- `async`: Creates a coroutine and returns a future result as deferred
- `produce`: Creates a coroutine that returns a stream of values via `ReceiveChannel`
- `broadcast`: Creates a coroutine that returns a stream of values via `BroadcastChannel`
- `runBlocking`: Runs a new coroutine and blocks the current thread until it returns

By using `launch()` and other builders, we can control how we want to interact with the results of our coroutines.

Suspending functions

Coroutines in Kotlin include the notion of suspending functions. Suspending functions are denoted by adding the suspend modifier to a function definition. There are two key things to remember regarding suspending functions:

- They can be called from within a coroutine in the same way as a regular function.
- They can call other suspending functions.

If we return to our working example, we can see an example of the suspend function, `delay()`:

```
fun main() {
    GlobalScope.launch {
        delay(500) // simulate network request
        println("Coroutines")
    }
    println("Hello")
    Thread.sleep(1000)
}
```

`delay()` is a suspending function that will suspend the current coroutine for a specified amount of time. Suspending functions is the primary mechanism by means of which we can suspend our current coroutine, go and do some other work, and then resume the coroutine once that work is finished.

Working with blocking code

Coroutines work well together to achieve non-blocking code. At some point, however, it's likely that the code will need to interact with traditional, sequential blocking code. We can illustrate this by revisiting out working example:

```
fun main() {
    GlobalScope.launch {
        delay(500)
        println("Coroutines")
    }
    println("Hello")
    Thread.sleep(1000)
}
```

In the preceding code, we are launching our coroutine from our standard `main()` function. However, the `main()` function isn't aware of any coroutines, so we have to call `Thread.sleep()` to prevent the termination of that function before our coroutine finishes. This mirrors the simple examples given at the beginning of this chapter using `Thread` and a short delay. However, for a non-trivial example such as loading network data, relying on some predefined delay is not feasible.

For uses cases such as network requests or database operations, we could use the `runBlocking()` coroutine builder we mentioned previously:

```
fun main() = runBlocking {
    GlobalScope.launch {
        delay(500) // simulate network request
        println("Coroutines")
    }
    println("Hello")
}
```

With this change, our `main()` function will not complete until all the coroutines within the scope of `runBlocking()` complete. If we run this code right now, we will get the following output:

Hello

Notice that we aren't seeing the result of our coroutine, which should be printing out
Coroutines. This is because that coroutine is launched using GlobalScope rather than the
scope of runBlocking(). Because our coroutine is scoped within GlobalScope, the scope
associated with runBlocking() completes because it has no active coroutines, which is
why we aren't seeing the result from our launched coroutine.

Let's change that behavior in the following snippet:

```
fun main() = runBlocking {
    launch {
        delay(500)
        println("Coroutines")
    }
    println("Hello")
}
```

Now that we are launching our coroutine within the same scope that our main() function
is associated with, we can see the following correct output:

```
Hello
Coroutines
```

By making use of the runBlocking() coroutine builder, we can connect our blocking and
non-blocking code with minimal changes.

Fetching data

One practical example of using coroutines for a production application is in loading data
from separate data sources. With other approaches or frameworks, this might require
multiple callbacks or the use of something along the lines of reactive streams. These
approaches can be difficult to read and follow. Coroutines can make this type of use case
much simpler:

1. First, let's define a new main() function that simulates the initialization of a
   screen in our application:

   ```
   fun main() = runBlocking {
       println("show loading....")
       launch {
           println("loaded data = ${loadData()}")
       }
       println("called loadData()")
   }
   ```

2. We are launching a new coroutine that calls `loadData()` and then prints out its output. Because this is done within a coroutine, the execution of `loadData()` does not delay the remainder of our initialization:

```
show loading....
called loadData()
loaded data = 9
```

3. Now, let's see how `loadData()` is implemented:

```
suspend fun loadData() : Int {
    return loadFromSource1() + loadFromSource2()
}
```

4. The `loadData()` function is very straightforward. It is simply returning the added values of `loadFromSource1()` and `loadFromSource2()`:

```
suspend fun loadFromSource1() : Int {
    delay(1000)
    return 3
}

suspend fun loadFromSource2() : Int {
    delay(4000)
    return 6
}
```

In this case, `loadFromSource1()` and `loadFromSource2()` delay for some period of time and return an integer. However, this could easily be a blocking network request or database operation. In any of these cases, the calling code does not know how long the function will take to return, which is why they've been implemented as suspending functions.

Because both of our loading functions are suspending functions, `loadData()` must also be a suspending function. By leveraging coroutines for this type of code, the result is sequential, efficient, and easy-to-follow asynchronous code.

Summary

Modern applications increasingly require asynchronous, multithreaded code to deliver adequate performance and quality user experiences.

Kotlin applications have a variety of tools available for writing async code. As in Java, we can make use of `Threads`, `ThreadPools`, and `Executors` to control our applications' threading model. There are more advanced tools at our disposal, such as RxJava, that can be leveraged to simplify writing these asynchronous operations across both Java and Kotlin. In this chapter, we examined how Kotlin supports coroutines as a first-party solution for writing non-blocking, asynchronous code. Coroutines allow developers to write async code in an imperative manner that is easy to read and follow, while also being highly performant and efficient. They can be used anywhere that Kotlin can, which makes them available for platforms such as Android, iOS, and the web—anywhere that can be targeted by Kotlin Native.

In the next chapter, we will explore additional advanced language features as we look into creating our own custom domain-specific languages.

Questions

1. Can you name two mechanisms for executing code in the background for JVM applications?
2. When was `CompleteableFuture` introduced to Java?
3. What is RxJava?
4. What are coroutines?
5. What is structural concurrency?
6. Why are different coroutine builders useful?
7. What are suspending functions?

Further reading

- *Learning Concurrency in Kotlin* (https://www.packtpub.com/application-development/learning-concurrency-kotlin)
- *Mastering Concurrency Programming with Java 8* (https://www.packtpub.com/application-development/mastering-concurrency-programming-java-8)

11
Building Your Own Tools – Domain-Specific Languages (DSLs)

This chapter will introduce you to the concept of custom **domain-specific languages** (**DSLs**) written in Kotlin and how they can be used as a powerful tool for building expressive and convenient declarative APIs.

We'll explore how DSLs can be applied to different problem types and create our very own DSL. As the chapter progresses, you will be able to build your own DSL tools.

The following topics will be covered in this chapter:

- What is a DSL?
- The building blocks of a DSL in Kotlin
- Creating your first Kotlin DSL

Technical requirements

In order to download, compile, and execute the samples found in this chapter, the following is required:

- IntelliJ IDEA 2018.3 Community or Ultimate edition, or newer
- An internet connection
- Git and GitHub (optional)

To download all of the code in this chapter, including the examples and code snippets, please refer to the following GitHub link: `https://github.com/PacktPublishing/Mastering-Kotlin/tree/master/Chapter11`.

What is a DSL?

In this section, we're going to explore the fundamentals of DSLs. We'll discuss what they are and why they can be useful, and finally, we'll briefly explore several examples of Kotlin-based DSLs for different domains.

Domain-specific languages

So, what is a DSL? A DSL is a computer language targeting a specific problem or domain space. This is in contrast to general-purpose programming languages that are meant to be capable of solving general computing problems. HTML is an example of a domain-specific programming language as it's meant to be used for a very specific problem.

The distinction between general-purpose programming languages and domain-specific languages can be fuzzy at times. For example, HTML has a very clear and focused purpose, whereas Kotlin can be used for general computing problems as well as for building custom DSLs for specific problems.

Where are DSLs used?

Domain-specific languages can crop up in a variety of different computing domains. A few common examples include the following:

- **HTML**: For defining web-based content
- **SQL**: For working with relational data
- **YACC**: For creating grammar and lexical parsers

While these examples are likely quite familiar to you, DSLs are available in many other domains that may be less familiar:

- **Matlab**: For mathematical programming
- **GraphViz**: For defining graph layouts
- **Gradle DSL**: For a configuration build using Gradle

As you can see, the use cases for DSLs are many and varied, and with these different DSLs come different languages, syntax, and conventions.

This is where the concept of Kotlin-based, domain-specific languages becomes very appealing. If you're already familiar with Kotlin, you can create your own DSL for these same types of problem spaces using a language you already know. This can empower you to create new tools for any problem area you see fit.

Now, let's take a look at several examples of Kotlin-based DSLs.

HTML

The official Kotlin documentation includes an example of a DSL for working with HTML. The example includes a playground to work with the DSL to see how the different functions work.

 The Kotlin documentation for DSLs and type-safe builders can be found here: https://kotlinlang.org/docs/reference/type-safe-builders. html.

The following code snippet demonstrates the usage of this Kotlin DSL to declare valid HTML code via Kotlin syntax:

```kotlin
fun main() {
    val result = html {
        head {
            title { +"HTML encoding with Kotlin" }
        }
        body {
            h1 { +"HTML encoding with Kotlin" }
            p {
                +"this format can be used as an"
                +"alternative markup to HTML"
            }

            // an element with attributes and text content
            a(href = "http://jetbrains.com/kotlin") { +"Kotlin" }

            // mixed content
            p {
                +"This is some"
                b { +"mixed" }
                +"text. For more see the"
                a(href = "http://jetbrains.com/kotlin") {
                    +"Kotlin"
                }
                +"project"
```

```
                    }

            p {
                +"Can even leverage loops and control flow"
                ul {
                    for (i in 1..3)
                        li { +"${i}*2 = ${i*2}" }
                }
            }
        }
    }

    println(result.toString())
}
```

The preceding code makes use of various functions as well as control flow structures. It's a good example of how you can develop a DSL to abstract away details of a problem space. In this case, you don't need to remember the exact syntax for each HTML element, and instead can rely on statically typed functions to build your document definition.

The previous code snippet will generate the follow result when printed to the screen:

```
<html>
  <head>
    <title>
      HTML encoding with Kotlin
    </title>
  </head>
  <body>
    <h1>
      HTML encoding with Kotlin
    </h1>
    <p>
      this format can be used as an
      alternative markup to HTML
    </p>
    <a href="http://jetbrains.com/kotlin">
      Kotlin
    </a>
    <p>
      This is some
      <b>
        mixed
      </b>
      text. For more see the
      <a href="http://jetbrains.com/kotlin">
        Kotlin
      </a>
```

```
      project
    </p>
    <p>
      Can even leverage loops and control flow
      <ul>
        <li>
          1*2 = 2
        </li>
        <li>
          2*2 = 4
        </li>
        <li>
          3*2 = 6
        </li>
      </ul>
    </p>
  </body>
</html>
```

This approach for building a DSL for HTML is similar to the approach being taken in the development of the Jetpack Compose library for Android development, which is a Kotlin-based DSL for building a declarative UI.

Testing

There are several testing frameworks that provide Kotlin-based DSLs for writing tests. One such example is MockitoKotlin, which is a small library that was built to provide Kotlin-friendly convenience functions for working with Mockito when writing JUnit tests.

With MockitoKotlin, we can write very readable, Kotlin-idomatic mocking code, as shown in the following code snippet:

```
val mockGreetingProvider = mock<GreetingProvider> {
    on { greeting } doReturn "Hello"
    on { friendlyGreeting } doReturn "Hi! How are you?"
}
```

In this example, we can call a mock() function and pass a lambda that can then be used to mock out the behavior of each property or method on the interface. The on and doReturn functions help us write mocking code that is very human readable and fluent to write.

Dependency injection

Another domain where Kotlin DSLs have cropped up is that of dependency injection, or dependency retrieval. `Koin` and `Kodein` are libraries that allow you to get your application dependencies through a type of object graph.

Using `Kodein`, we can develop our object graph using a variety of functions, as demonstrated in the following example:

```
val kodein = Kodein {
    bind<GreetingProvider>() with provider { FriendlyGreetingProvider() }
    bind<Repository>() with singleton { NetworkRepository() }
}

class ViewModel(private kodein: Kodein) {
    private val repo: Repository by kodein.instance()
}
```

Now that we understand what DSLs are, in the next section, we'll start to explore how DSLs are built using Kotlin.

The building blocks of a DSL in Kotlin

Now that we have an understanding of what domain-specific languages are in a general sense, let's dive into the building blocks of DSLs in Kotlin. At its core, a Kotlin-based DSL is comprised of functions and function literals with a receiver that can be leveraged to configure and build components via a human-readable, statically typed syntax. Beyond basic functions, we will examine several other features of Kotlin that can enable us to build custom DSLs:

- Top-level and extension functions
- Function types with receivers
- Custom scope annotations

Let's look at each of these in turn.

Top-level and extension functions

Writing a domain-specific language in Kotlin largely boils down to using well-named functions. These functions can often be composed together to create highly readable and fluent code. To start using any DSL, there needs to be some type of starting point. That starting point is going to be either a top-level function or an extension function.

Let's revisit the previous HTML example to examine these function types.

Top-level functions

In our previous HTML example, we began building our HTML definition by calling a function called `html`:

```
val result = html {
  ...
}
```

That `html` function is a top-level function that is available in the global namespace:

```
fun html(init: HTML.() -> Unit): HTML {
    val html = HTML()
    html.init()
    return html
}
```

Notice that the name of the function corresponds to the name of the type that it returns in HTML. This is a common pattern when creating a declarative DSL as it makes the function call match the type that will be returned. This makes it easy to understand what the code is doing.

Extension functions

In the previous example, the `html` function was called and its internal implementation was left to provide an initial instance of the HTML class that we can use with the passed `init` function. This is convenient when we're beginning a new HTML construction from scratch.

In some cases, you may want to leverage your DSL with an existing object. For those cases, you could use an extension function to provide an alternative entry point to your declarative DSL. The following code shows this:

```
val result = html {
    ...
}

result.html {
    body {
        p {+"add on to existing HTML"}
    }
}
```

To enable this extension of an existing HTML object, we can create a simple extension function like the following:

```
fun HTML.html(init: HTML.() -> Unit): HTML {
    init()
    return this
}
```

This takes the same type of receiver argument but relies on the implicit HTML receiver of the extension function for configuration, thereby allowing us to add to what is already configured in the existing HTML.

Function types with receivers

Much of the power of DSLs in Kotlin comes from their type safety. When we call the html function we've been examining, we pass in a function argument with an HTML receiver. Because of Kotlin's lambda syntax, we can then move the passed function outside of the parentheses, thereby making the code easier to read and write:

```
val result = html {
    ...
}
```

In the following snippet, we can see how the init argument is defined as a function type with a receiver of the HTML type. To indicate a function type with a receiver, we must first reference the type and then add a .(). So, in this case, HTML.() indicates a function type returning Unit with an HTML receiver:

```
fun html(init: HTML.() -> Unit): HTML {
    val html = HTML()
    html.init()
```

```
        return html
    }
```

We can then pass that `init` argument to the function using lambda syntax. Within that passed lambda, we can access properties and call methods from the HTML receiver, as follows:

```
val result = html {
    head {
        . . .
    }
    body {
        . . .
    }
```

In this case, the `head` and `body` function calls are methods on the HTML class:

```
class HTML : TagWithText("html") {
    fun head(init: Head.() -> Unit) = initTag(Head(), init)

    fun body(init: Body.() -> Unit) = initTag(Body(), init)
}
```

Within the lambda block, the implicit reference to the HTML receiver will reference the new HTML instance that was created within the HTML function:

```
fun html(init: HTML.() -> Unit): HTML {
    val html = HTML()
    html.init()
    return html
}
```

However, any HTML instance can be used, as in the case of the extension function we looked at previously. In this case, instead of creating a new instance of HTML, we can use the implicit reference of the extension function to access an instance of HTML:

```
fun HTML.html(init: HTML.() -> Unit): HTML {
    this.init()
    return this
}
```

By leveraging function types with receivers, we can make our functions composable and configurable with static type safety.

Scope control

As we start to nest function calls, we may end up with multiple receiver contexts available to us. This can start to get confusing or even incorrect. For example, in the HTML example, creating a HEAD element inside another HEAD is probably not the desired behavior.

To help avoid this situation, we can make use of the `DslMarker` annotations. The use of these annotations can tell the Kotlin compiler when to limit the scope of a given function so that outer scopes are no longer available.

To create a `DslMarker`, we can create a custom annotation, as shown in the HTML DSL example:

```
@DslMarker
annotation class HtmlTagMarker
```

By adding that annotation to the parent class, `Tag`, we can indicate which receivers are available within a given scope:

```
@HtmlTagMarker
abstract class Tag(val name: String) : Element {
    ...
}
```

Once we've applied `DslMarker`, the following code becomes invalid:

```
html {
    head {
        // error: can't be called in this context by implicit receiver
        head { }
    }
}
```

This extra layer of control can help ensure that the methods that are available by default in any scope within the DSL are the most relevant to the current context, thereby making the DSL easier to work with. Armed with this knowledge, we can create our first DSL and understand it with the help of an example.

Creating your first Kotlin DSL

Now that we know which tools are at our disposal and understand how they can work together, let's put all the pieces together and build our own custom DSL for ordering a meal from a pizza restaurant.

What problem are you trying to solve?

When thinking about how to create our DSL, we'll want to consider what syntax we would like to have, as well as what our solution would look like without a DSL. Let's start by imagining what our code might look like without using any kind of DSL.

Without a DSL, we might write code that looks something like this:

```
val order = Order("123")
order.items.put(Sprite, 1)
order.items.put(Coke, 1)

val pizza1 = HawaiianPizza()
pizza1.toppings.add(Pepperoni)

val pizza2 = BuildYourOwn()
pizza2.toppings.add(Pepperoni)
pizza2.toppings.add(Olive)

order.items.put(pizza1, 1)
order.items.put(pizza2, 1)
```

In this code, we're able to create all of our items in a very ordered, imperative way. It's pretty easy to follow, but there is a fair bit of repetition in the code.

We could simplify this code a bit without using a DSL as follows:

```
val order = Order("123").apply {
    items.put(Sprite, 1)
    items.put(Coke, 1)
}

val pizza1 = HawaiianPizza().apply {
    toppings.add(Pepperoni)
}

val pizza2 = BuildYourOwn().apply {
    toppings.add(Pepperoni)
    toppings.add(Olive)
}

order.apply {
    items.put(pizza1, 1)
    items.put(pizza2, 1)
}
```

This version of the code starts to avoid some of the repetition by making use of the scoped apply calls.

What we would like to be able to do is something much more natural and human readable—something that looks more like this:

```
create new order

add coke
add 2 sprite

add pizza {
    pepperoni
    pineapple
    olive
}
```

This code is not much more than pseudocode, but it's easy to read and understand and gives us a goal that we can target when designing our pizza shop DSL.

Creating your starting point

Following the outline of our target DSL syntax, our first step is to create some type of order object that can then be configured:

1. To do this, we'll start by creating an `Order` class to hold our order of pizza:

   ```
   class Order(val id: String)
   ```

   We've created this as a simple class with a single `id` property so that orders can be unique.

2. Next, we'll create an `Item` class that can be added to an `Order` class:

   ```
   abstract class Item(val name: String)
   ```

3. Now, we'll add a map of `Item` and counts to our `Order` class:

   ```
   class Order(val id: String) : Item("Order")  {
       val items: MutableMap<Item, Int> = mutableMapOf()
   }
   ```

4. With our `Item` map in place, we're ready to create an order. To do this, we'll create a top-level function:

```
fun order(init: Order.() -> Unit): Order {
    val order = Order(UUID.randomUUID().toString())
    order.init()
    return order
}
```

The following two interesting elements should be observed in relation to this function:

- The function name mirrors the return type.
- We pass a function argument with an `Order` receiver.

These two characteristics allow us to call the function and understand that we are creating a new order, which helps enforce the declarative nature of the DSL. This also allows us to configure the `Order` instance within a passed lambda:

```
val order = order {
    println(this.id)
}
```

Now, we're ready to start adding items to our order.

Adding elements

Now we'll now take a look at adding `Items` to the order. Specifically, we'll examine adding non-configurable `Soda` items and then look at adding configurable `Pizza` items.

Adding sodas

Let's start by adding support for adding a soda to our order:

1. To do this, we'll define `Soda` as a sealed class with several options to choose from:

```
sealed class Soda(name: String) : Item(name)
object Coke : Soda("Coke")
object Sprite : Soda("Sprite")
object Dr_Pepper : Soda("Dr Pepper")
```

2. With our `Soda` class in place, we can add a soda to our order by accessing `Order.items` directly:

```
val order = order {
    this.items[Coke] = this.items.getOrDefault(Coke, 0) + 1
}
```

This works, but is verbose and requires direct interaction with the underlying data structure. Let's improve this by making the syntax more natural and by hiding the data structure.

There are a couple of ways in which we can do this, as follows:

1. First, let's refactor the previous code into a simple method so that we can add a soda to the map:

```
fun soda(soda: Soda) = items.put(soda, items.getOrDefault(soda, 0) + 1)
```

2. Now, we can add a soda with much less code and without leaking implementation details:

```
val order = order {
    soda(Coke)
}
```

3. We can also implement the `unaryPlus` operator for our `Soda` class to help provide a more fluent syntax for adding a soda to the order. We can do this by making use of the previous method's implementation:

```
operator fun Soda.unaryPlus() = soda(this)
```

4. With this new `add` operator, we can add a soda to the order like this:

```
val order = order {
    soda(Coke)
    +Sprite
}
```

What if we wanted to add multiple sodas to our order? We could manually add the soda each time we wanted it, or we could provide a mechanism for updating the quantity at the same time as declaring the item.

To implement this, we'll add a new infix function to the `Soda` class:

```
infix fun Soda.quantity(quantity: Int) {
    items.put(this, items.getOrDefault(this, 0) + quantity)
}
```

Now, we can add a soda and specify a quantity in a very human-readable way:

```
val order = order {
    soda(Coke)
    +Sprite
    Coke quantity 2
}
```

Adding pizzas

Now, let's add the ability to add a pizza to our order, as well as configure it:

1. First, we'll create a `Topping` class, which will be contained within our `Pizza` class:

   ```
   sealed class Topping(name: String): Item(name)
   object Pepperoni : Topping("Pepperoni")
   object Olive : Topping("Olive")
   object Pineapple : Topping("Pineapple")
   ```

2. Now, we'll add a `Pizza` class:

   ```
   sealed class Pizza(name: String) : Item(name) {
       val toppings: MutableList<Topping> = mutableListOf()
   }
   ```

   This `Pizza` class extends `Item` and has a field, `MutableList<Topping>`, for storing our pizza toppings.

3. Next, we're going to create some predefined types of pizza that our users can order:

   ```
   class BuildYourOwn(init: Pizza.() -> Unit = {}) :
                        Pizza("Build Your Own Pizza") {
       init {
           init.invoke(this)
       }
   }
   class PepperoniPizza(init: Pizza.() -> Unit = {}) :
                        Pizza("Pepperoni Pizza") {
   ```

```
        init {
            toppings.add(Pepperoni)
            init.invoke(this)
        }
    }
```

Both classes take an `init` argument, which is a function with a `Pizza` receiver. This function is then called during the class initialization, giving the creators of the class a chance to configure the instance. The `PepperoniPizza` class also adds a default topping to the pizza.

If we add the `unaryPlus` operator for the `Topping` class, we can simplify how we add a topping within the context of configuring our `Pizza` instance:

```
operator fun Topping.unaryPlus() = toppings.add(this)
class PepperoniPizza(init: Pizza.() -> Unit = {}) :
                    Pizza("Pepperoni Pizza") {
    init {
        +Pepperoni
        init.invoke(this)
    }
}
```

Now, we're ready to add a `Pizza` to our order. To start, we'll create a new method on the `Order` class:

```
fun pizza(init: Pizza.() -> Unit) {
    val pizza = BuildYourOwn()
    pizza.init()
    items[pizza] = 1
}
```

This method takes a function type with the `Pizza` receiver so that the `Pizza` can be configured. It also creates a default `BuildYourOwn` instance and adds the `Pizza` to the `items` map. With that in place, we can now add a pizza to our order:

```
val order = order {
    soda(Coke)
    +Sprite
    Dr_Pepper quantity 2
    pizza {
        +Pineapple
    }
}
```

What if we want to add a predefined `Pizza` and then configure it ourselves? To do that, we can add the `unaryPlus` operator for `Pizza` within our `Order` class:

```
operator fun Pizza.unaryPlus() {
    items.put(this, items.getOrDefault(this, 0) + 1)
}
```

Now, we can use the + operator to add the pizza and then still pass in our configuration block to update the toppings:

```
val order = order {
    soda(Coke)
    +Sprite
    Dr_Pepper quantity 2

    pizza {
        +Pineapple
    }
    +HawaiianPizza {
        +Pepperoni
    }
}
```

We now have several ways of adding both `Soda` and `Pizza` instances to our order. Now, let's take a look at adding `@DslMarker` to ensure that our configuration blocks default functionality that is specific to the most local scope.

Making it easy to use

Currently, we have no `@DslMarker` annotation in place so, as we start to nest these function calls, we have access to functions for multiple different receivers. For example, in the following code snippet, we can call the `soda` function within the `init` block for `Pizza`:

```
+HawaiianPizza {
    +Pepperoni
    soda(Coke) // want to avoid this
}
```

This behavior is not ideal because it doesn't make sense to add a `Soda` to `Pizza`. So, by default, we want to limit this behavior. To do that, we can create a new `@DslMarker` annotation:

```
@DslMarker
annotation class ItemTagMarker
```

We can then add that to the base class for our `Items`:

```
@ItemTagMarker
abstract class Item(val name: String)
```

With that annotation in place, the compiler will mark it as an error if you try to access a property of the method of an implicit receiver:

```
+HawaiianPizza {
    +Pepperoni
    soda(Coke) // now an error
}
```

This also means that in cases where we do want to reference an outer receiver, then we must call it explicitly. One example of this is in our implementation of `Topping.unaryPlus()`:

```
operator fun Topping.unaryPlus() = this@Pizza.toppings.add(this)
```

Now, if we want to see how our order looks, we can add some logging functionality. To start, we'll add a print method to our `Item` base class:

```
@ItemTagMarker
abstract class Item(val name: String) {
    open fun log(indent: String = "") {
        println("$indent$name")
    }
}
```

The we'll override that behavior for `Pizza`, as follows:

```
sealed class Pizza(name: String) : Item(name) {

    val toppings: MutableList<Topping> = mutableListOf()

    operator fun Topping.unaryPlus() = this@Pizza.toppings.add(this)

    override fun log(indent: String) {
        super.log(indent)
        toppings.forEach {
            println("$indent        ${it.name}")
        }
    }
}
```

Finally, we'll add a `print()` method to the order class, which will allow us to print the entire order using a `log()` method:

```
fun log() {
    println("Order: $id")
    println("Items")
    items.forEach {
        print("${it.value} x ")
        it.key.log("   ")
    }
}
```

Now, we can print out the following order:

```
fun main() {

    val order = order {
        soda(Dr_Pepper)
        soda(Coke)

        Sprite quantity 1

        +Coke
        +Dr_Pepper

        Sprite quantity 2

        +HawaiianPizza {
            +Pepperoni
        }
        pizza {
            +Pepperoni
            +Olive
        }
    }

    order.log()
}
```

With this order, we get the following output:

```
Order:  9de6134e-23f3-44e5-88f1-2af373c399a8
Items
2 x Dr Pepper
2 x Coke
3 x Sprite
1 x Hawaiian Pizza
        Pineapple
```

```
     Pepperoni
1 x Build Your Own Pizza
     Pepperoni
     Olive
```

With that, we've built a very simple DSL for building orders for a pizza restaurant. For a production DSL, we'd likely want to build more configurability and expand the functionality, but the building blocks are the same.

Summary

Domain-specific languages, or DSLs, provide a convenient, declarative, type-safe syntax for solving a specific type of problem. DSLs written in Kotlin have been applied to problems such as declaring HTML layouts, building mobile UI frameworks, and defining HTTP routes for web servers. We've seen that, in Kotlin, DSLs are primarily composed of functions and function literals with a receiver. Through these mechanisms, we can build type-safe builders that are useful for building a human-readable, declarative syntax. We've also explored how Kotlin features such as extension functions, infix notation, and custom annotations can improve the usability and readability of our custom DSLs. Finally, we learned how to apply these features to the construction of our own domain-specific language in order to define a mobile UI.

In the next chapter, we'll dive into functional programming in Kotlin and explore specific libraries that are available for writing highly functional code.

Questions

1. What does DSL stand for?
2. Can you name two examples of domains to which DSLs can be applied?
3. What are the two primary building blocks of a DSL in Kotlin?
4. What are two mechanisms for controlling the scope of a DSL function?
5. What is the @DslMarker annotation used for?
6. What are two benefits that custom DSLs can provide?

Further reading

- *Functional Kotlin* (`https://www.packtpub.com/application-development/functional-kotlin`)
- *Hands-On Design Patterns with Kotlin* (`https://www.packtpub.com/application-development/hands-design-patterns-kotlin`)
- *Learning Kotlin by Building Android Applications* (`https://www.packtpub.com/application-development/learning-kotlin-building-android-applications`)

12
Fully Functional – Embracing Functional Programming

Functional programming can be a powerful tool for writing scalable applications as it helps developers to model data and business logic through pure mathematical operations, thereby limiting the management of state, which is one of the biggest challenges in modern object-oriented code.

This chapter will provide the reader with a better understanding of how to achieve functional programming with Kotlin. We'll review some of the benefits of functional programming, examine how Kotlin supports it through top-level and higher-order functions, and then explore how to write more functional code using the Kotlin standard library and Arrow.

This chapter will be broken down as follows:

- The characteristics and benefits of functional programming
- Writing performant higher-order functions
- Utilizing the Kotlin standard library
- Functional programming with Arrow

Technical requirements

In order to download, compile, and execute the samples found in this chapter, the following is required:

- IntelliJ IDEA 2018.3 Community or Ultimate editions, or newer
- An internet connection
- Git and GitHub (optional)

To download all of the code in this chapter, including the examples and code snippets, please refer to the following GitHub link: `https://github.com/PacktPublishing/Mastering-Kotlin/tree/master/Chapter12`.

Understanding functional programming

As we saw in `Chapter 3`, *Understanding Programming Paradigms in Kotlin*, functional programming is a declarative programming paradigm in which programs are expressed using pure mathematical functions. In this section, we'll examine what this means in practice and why you might want to embrace functional programming with Kotlin.

Pure functions

One of the core tenets of functional programming is the transformation of data through the application of pure functions. According to the strictest definitions of functional programming, these pure functions are expressed as mathematical operations. This pure, mathematical nature of functional programming gives rise to two interesting properties:

- The immutability of variables
- The lack of side effects

These properties of functional code can be of great benefit when writing code in Kotlin, or any other language, and we will explore them both in the sections that follow.

Immutability

Building any program is often an exercise in modeling and managing complex state. While object-oriented programming can make it easier to model this state, it can often give rise to problems of data synchronization and consistency. If the models representing state can be changed at any given time, then it becomes more difficult to reason about the current state of a given application. It becomes difficult to understand when and where state is being manipulated, or even how best to modify state.

This is why the immutable nature of variables and state within functional code is so appealing. If the models representing our state are immutable, then the contract with which to create or modify state becomes much more explicit. To represent a new state, we must create a new model to hold that state. This becomes easier to trace as we can now rely on the static, unchanging state of any given variable.

This becomes even more relevant when paired with the next useful property of functional programming: limited side effects.

Limited side effects

Pure mathematical functions produce no side effects. In the programming world, this means that calling a given function will produce a single output and do nothing else. A pure function will return its output without manipulating global state, making network requests, updating databases, and more.

By writing functions that produce no side effects, we are again making it easier to reason about our data flows and how the state of our applications are expressed and manipulated. When functions are hyper-focused on a single, explicit task, it becomes much easier to understand how a state is modified.

Reduced complexity

Immutability and the limitation of side effects in our programs work to reduce the complexity of those programs. Some code bases are complex out of necessity; the problem itself is complex. However, many code bases become complex because it's no longer clear how the state is expressed, managed, or manipulated. It is in cases like these where functional programming might be of great benefit.

Writing functional code in Kotlin can help us to reduce complexity in a several specific ways:

- Kotlin enables us to enforce immutability through the usage of data classes. Data classes make it extremely easy to define immutable models with which to represent state. The following is one such example in which we've defined an immutable data class to represent the current state of a UI:

```
data class ViewState(val title: String, val subtitle: String)
```

- Additionally, Kotlin provides a convenient syntax for creating a new state based on a previous one. This can be done using named arguments in conjunction with the `copy` constructor generated for any data class. Consider the following code:

```
val initialState = ViewState("Hello", "Kotlin")
val updatedState = initialState.copy(title = "Hey There!")
```

In this code, we're able to make a copy of the `initialState` variable while replacing the `title` property with the value `"Hey There!"`. This allows us to explicitly update the desired `title` property without modifying any existing state.

- Because Kotlin supports top-level functions, we can reduce the complexity of our Kotlin code bases by avoiding the creation of utility and helper classes that serve no purpose other than to contain useful methods/functions. For example, in Java, we may have a class called `DateHelpers`, which is implemented as follows:

```
class DateHelpers {
    private static final String pattern = "MM-dd-yyyy";
    public String formatDateForUI(Date date) {
        SimpleDateFormat simpleDateFormat = new
          SimpleDateFormat(pattern);
        return simpleDateFormat.format(date);
    }
}
```

In Kotlin, however, we have top-level functions, and we can implement this same functionality without the need to explicitly create a class to contain a static method. A Kotlin implementation of this same functionality might look something like this:

```
private const val pattern = "MM-dd-yyyy"
fun formatDateForUI(date: Date): String {
    val simpleDateFormat = SimpleDateFormat(pattern)
    return simpleDateFormat.format(date)
}
```

These examples of enforcing immutability, the convenient and explicit copying of data classes, and the reduction in helper classes, can help reduce complexity within our code base. One of the biggest ways in which Kotlin supports functional programming and benefits from that support is through support for higher-order functions. In the next section, we'll explore how higher-order functions improve functional programming in Kotlin.

Understanding advanced functions

In functional programming languages, functions are generally treated as first-class citizens of the language. This is true in Kotlin, which supports top-level functions as well as higher-order functions, meaning that functions can be treated as inputs and outputs of other functions.

In this section, we'll explore two important aspects of higher-order functions in Kotlin. These are as follows:

- Working with functional types
- Improving the performance of higher-order functions

Through these sections, we'll gain an improved understanding of how to efficiently use higher-order functions in our code, and how the Kotlin standard library is built.

Working with functional types

As we've seen previously in this book, Kotlin supports functions as data types. This allows us to do two things:

- Store functions as variables and properties
- Pass functions as arguments to other functions

In this section, we're going to examine each of these in more detail.

Functional variables

Let's quickly refresh how to work with function variables. We can define a variable with a functional type like this:

```
var onClickHandler: (ViewState) -> Unit = {}
```

We can then reassign that stored function as with any other variable:

```
fun main() {
    onClickHandler = { viewState ->
        println("viewState -> ${viewState.title}
                ${viewState.subtitle}")
    }
}
```

And finally, since the variable represents a function, we can invoke the function in several different ways by referencing the variable name, as follows:

```
fun main() {
    onClickHandler = { viewState ->
        println("viewState -> ${viewState.title}
                ${viewState.subtitle}")
    }
    val viewState = ViewState("Hello", "Kotlin")
    onClickHandler(viewState)
    onClickHandler.invoke(viewState)
}
```

By allowing us to store and update variables with a functional type, Kotlin enables us to start thinking in terms of functions and writing code that more heavily relies on functional operations.

Functional arguments

Now that we've reviewed working with functional types, let's take a look at how to use those functional types as arguments to other functions.

Here's a basic example of a higher-order function in which we've defined a function parameter matching the function signature of our previously defined `onClickHandler` variable:

```
class ViewModel(val viewState: ViewState, val clickHandler:(ViewState) ->
Unit)

fun createViewModel(viewState: ViewState, clickHandler: (ViewState) ->
Unit) : ViewModel {
    return ViewModel(viewState, clickHandler)
}
```

We could then pass our `onClickHandler` function variable as an argument to this newly defined `createViewModel()` function:

```
fun main() {
    ...
    createViewModel(viewState, onClickHandler)
}
```

As with any other type, we can store functions as variables and then pass them anywhere that expects that defined type. Function parameters allow us to do some interesting things. Once such example is how we can construct and configure a class using a functional constructor parameter:

```
class LoadingViewModel(config: (LoadingViewModel) -> Unit) {
    var title = ""
    var subtitle = ""
    var loadingMsg = ""
    val successMsg = ""

    init {
        config(this)
    }
}
```

This `LoadingViewModel` has several properties available that may, or may not, be needed when it's used. Rather than forcing clients to specify the value of each property when the class is instantiated, we could create and configure an instance of `LoadingViewModel` like this:

```
LoadingViewModel { loadingViewModel ->
    loadingViewModel.title = "Hello"
    loadingViewModel.loadingMsg "Loading..."
}
```

This makes use of lambda syntax and the function parameter to allow us to instantiate `LoadingViewModel` without the `()` and then configure the properties within the passed lambda. This syntax begins to feel very fluent and natural within a more functional code base as it's really just a function that is configuring the class.

As we saw in the previous chapter, we can improve on this configuration pattern by making use of a functional type with a receiver. We can refactor our function parameter, as follows, so that instead of taking a `LoadingViewModel` as its only parameter, it will have an instance of `LoadingViewModel` as its receiver:

```
class LoadingViewModel(config: LoadingViewModel.() -> Unit) {
    var title = ""
```

```
        var subtitle = ""
        var loadingMsg = ""
        val successMsg = ""

        init {
            config(this)
        }
}
```

Our `config` parameter now takes a function that requires an instance of `LoadingViewModel` as a receiver, and we can then pass the current instance to the config function within our class's `init{}` block.

By making use of a function type with a receiver, we remove the need to explicitly reference the passed `LoadingViewModel` using `this`:

```
LoadingViewModel {
    this.title = "Hello"
    this.loadingMsg = "Loading..."
}
```

We can reference the `LoadingViewModel` instance implicitly within the lambda context. With this in mind, our previous example can be simplified even further, as follows:

```
LoadingViewModel {
    title = "Hello"
    loadingMsg = "Loading..."
}
```

Notice that in this latest example, we've removed the explicit usage of `this` when referencing the `title` and `loadingMsg` properties. With this, and other, examples of higher-order functions, we've seen how they can be incredibly useful when we design and consume our classes and APIs. In the next section, we'll look at how to ensure that our higher-order functions don't negatively impact the performance of our programs.

Improving the performance of higher-order functions

Higher-order functions can be quite useful. However, their utility does not come for free. There is an overhead cost associated with using higher-order functions. This stems from how higher-order functions work at the compiler level. In this section, we'll explore how the `inline` and `noinline` modifiers can allow us to control the performance characteristics of our higher-order functions.

The inline modifier

One way in which we can control the performance of our higher-order functions is through the usage of the `inline` modifier keyword. The `inline` modifier allows us to improve the performance of our higher-order functions by indicating to the compiler that the implementation of a function can be inlined at the call site, thereby avoiding the performance overhead associated with variable capture and class instantiation of a higher-order function.

To explore how this works, let's start by defining this function, `safelyRun`:

```
fun safelyRun(action: () -> Unit) {
    try {
        action()
    } catch (error: Throwable) {
        println("Caught error: ${error.message}")
    }
}
```

This is a top-level, higher-order function that will run whatever lambda is passed to it while wrapping that call in a `try/catch` block. While this is defined as taking a function parameter, at the compiler level, it requires an instance of the `Function0` class:

```
public static final void safelyRun(@NotNull Function0 action) {
    Intrinsics.checkParameterIsNotNull(action, "action");

    try {
        action.invoke();
    } catch (Throwable var4) {
        String var2 = "Caught error: " + var4.getMessage();
        boolean var3 = false;
        System.out.println(var2);
    }

}
```

The `Function0` class will capture any variables that are referenced within the lambda in order to provide access to those values within the lambda.

So, when we use our `safelyRun()` function like this:

```
fun main() {
    val greeting = "Hello"
    safelyRun {
        println("$greeting Kotlin")
    }
}
```

The compiler will generate code, shown as follows:

```
public static final void main() {
    final String greeting = "Hello";
    safelyRun((Function0)(new Function0() {
        // $FF: synthetic method
        // $FF: bridge method
        public Object invoke() {
            this.invoke();
            return Unit.INSTANCE;
        }

        public final void invoke() {
            String var1 = greeting + " Kotlin";
            boolean var2 = false;
            System.out.println(var1);
        }
    }));
}
```

Notice that when calling `safelyRun()`, an anonymous inner class is created that then has an implicit reference to the outer class and its fields. This is how the lambda is able to capture any required state, such as properties or local variables. This anonymous inner class will be instantiated each time a lambda is evaluated.

If a higher-order function is operating on a large collection, iterating over the collection, for example, the overhead associated with capturing the lambda state will be paid for each iteration of the loop, requiring greater and greater amounts of memory and an increased number of virtual method calls.

Thankfully, we can avoid this overhead by leveraging the `inline` keyword. By adding an inline function to our higher-order function, we instruct the compiler to replace invocations of a given function with the actual implementation of that function at the call site. Let's illustrate this by updating our example.

First, we add the `inline` keyword to our `safelyRun()` function, as follows:

```
inline fun safelyRun(action: () -> Unit) {
    try {
        action()
    } catch (error: Throwable) {
        println("Caught error: ${error.message}")
    }
}
```

Now, if we look at the code generated, we'll see the impacts of adding `inline`:

```
public static final void main() {
    String greeting = "Hello";
    boolean var1 = false;

    try {
        int var7 = false;
        String var8 = greeting + " Kotlin";
        boolean var4 = false;
        System.out.println(var8);
    } catch (Throwable var6) {
        String var2 = "Caught error: " + var6.getMessage();
        boolean var3 = false;
        System.out.println(var2);
    }

}
```

The body of `safelyRun()` has been rewritten into the body of `main()`. This avoids the need to create a new instance of `Function0` to capture the `greeting` variable defined within `main()`. By avoiding the need to create a `Function0` instance on each invocation of `safelyRun()`, we've improved the performance of our code.

The noinline modifier

Adding the `inline` modifier to a higher-order function will result in all passed lambdas being inlined at the call site. However, there may be cases where this is not what you want. For these situations, we can make use of `noinline`.

We can add the `noinline` modifier to a function parameter of our higher-order function. This will indicate to the compiler to not inline that particular lambda. Let's explore this using our previous example:

1. Let's add a second function parameter to `safelyRun()`:

```
inline fun safelyRun(action: () -> Unit, action2:() -> Unit) {
    try {
        action()
        action2()
    } catch (error: Throwable) {
        println("Caught error: ${error.message}")
    }
}
```

2. Now, we will update our usage to pass a second lambda:

```
fun main() {
    val greeting = "Hello"
    safelyRun({ println("Hi Kotlin") }) {
        println("$greeting Kotlin")
    }
}
```

3. If we look at the generated code, we'll see that it looks very similar to before, with both lambdas being inlined at the call site:

```
public static final void main() {
    String greeting = "Hello";
    boolean var1 = false;

    try {
        int var7 = false;
        String var8 = "Hi Kotlin";
        boolean var4 = false;
        System.out.println(var8);
        var7 = false;
        var8 = greeting + " Kotlin";
        var4 = false;
        System.out.println(var8);
    } catch (Throwable var6) {
        String var2 = "Caught error: " + var6.getMessage();
        boolean var3 = false;
        System.out.println(var2);
    }

}
```

4. But now, let's add `noinline` to the `action2` parameter:

```
inline fun safelyRun(action: () -> Unit, noinline action2:() ->
Unit) {
    ...
}
```

5. Now, the generated code will not inline the second lambda, but will instead create a `Function0` instance to capture the required local state required for the lambda:

```
public static final void main() {
    final String greeting = "Hello";
    Function0 action2$iv = (Function0)(new Function0() {
        // $FF: synthetic method
```

```
        // $FF: bridge method
        public Object invoke() {
            this.invoke();
            return Unit.INSTANCE;
        }

        public final void invoke() {
            String var1 = greeting + " Kotlin";
            boolean var2 = false;
            System.out.println(var1);
        }
    });
    boolean var2 = false;

    String var4;
    boolean var5;
    try {
        int var3 = false;
        var4 = "Hi Kotlin";
        var5 = false;
        System.out.println(var4);
        action2$iv.invoke();
    } catch (Throwable var6) {
        var4 = "Caught error: " + var6.getMessage();
        var5 = false;
        System.out.println(var4);
    }


}
```

With `inline` and `noinline`, you have great control over how the compiler will treat any function parameters you define for your higher-order functions. IntelliJ-based IDEs will also warn you when the performance impact of inlining functions is negligible.

Leveraging the standard library

The Kotlin standard library provides a wide variety of useful functions. With these functions, we can begin writing more functional code without having to reinvent the wheel. In this section, we'll explore some common functional patterns that can be achieved by leveraging the Kotlin standard library.

Manipulating collections

Throughout this book, we've been making use of collections within our examples. The Kotlin standard library provides helper functions that make the creation of common collection types very easy:

```
fun main() {
    val list = listOf("Kotlin", "Java", "Swift")
    val mutableList = mutableListOf("Kotlin", "Java", "Swift")
    val arrayList = arrayListOf("Kotlin", "Java", "Swift")
    val array = arrayOf("Kotlin", "Java", "Swift")
    val map = mapOf("Kotlin" to 1, "Java" to 2, "Swift" to 3)
}
```

The Kotlin standard library provides numerous functions for working with these collection types once they are created. Through operations such as `filter`, `map`, `reduce`, and `find`, we can write powerful functional chains that can perform complex tasks with little code.

In this section, we will explore some of these functions and how to make use of the Kotlin standard library.

Filtering

First up, let's look at the `filter()` function. The `filter()` function allows us to provide a lambda, which returns a Boolean that is then used to filter items from a collection.

In this example, we'll use the `filter` function to print out only items that start with the letter "K":

```
fun main() {
    ...

    val list = listOf("Kotlin", "Java", "Swift")
    list.filter { it.startsWith("K") }
        .forEach { println(it) }
}
```

Notice how we are chaining functions together in this example to first filter the items and then iterate and print them out one by one. This pattern allows us to chain these operations together in more complex ways.

Mapping

Next up, let's see how we can map one value to another value. Let's map our string, `"Kotlin"`, to a corresponding data type.

First, we'll create a sealed class to represent our programming languages:

```
sealed class ProgrammingLanguage(protected val name: String) {
    object Kotlin : ProgrammingLanguage("Kotlin")
    object Java : ProgrammingLanguage("Java")
    object Swift : ProgrammingLanguage("Swift")

    override fun toString(): String {
        return "$name Programming Language"
    }
}
```

Next, we can add a call to the `map()` function to map our `String` items to a corresponding language. The `map` operator allows us to change our result type from the incoming data type to any outgoing data type we wish. In this case, we are mapping from `String` to `ProgrammingLanguage`:

```
val list = listOf("Kotlin", "Java", "Swift", "K")
list.filter { it.startsWith("K") }
    .map {
        when (it) {
            "Kotlin" -> ProgrammingLanguage.Kotlin
            else -> null
        }
    }
    .forEach { println(it) }
```

If we run this, we'll get the following output:

```
Kotlin Programming Language
null
```

Notice that we are seeing `null` printed to the console since we are unable to map the string `"K"` to `ProgrammingLanguage` and thus return `null`.

To address this, we can make use of another function, `filterNotNull()`, to filter out any values that are `null`:

```
val list = listOf("Kotlin", "Java", "Swift", "K")
list.filter { it.startsWith("K") }
    .map {
        when (it) {
```

```
                "Kotlin" -> ProgrammingLanguage.Kotlin
                else -> null
        }
    }
    .filterNotNull()
    .forEach { println(it) }
```

If we now run this code, we'll see only the non-null values:

```
Kotlin Programming Language
```

The `map()` function is quite powerful as it lets us change the nature of a data flow or map multiple values to a known set of values or types.

Associating

Sometimes, we want to associate a collection of values with some other values. One way to accomplish this is by making use of the `associate()` function. With `associate()`, we can map each value of a collection to a pair of any desired type and then save the resulting map.

In this example, we'll map each string to its length and then iterate over every pair in the map, printing them out as we go:

```
list.associate { it to it.length }
    .forEach {
        println("${it.key} has ${it.value} letters")
    }
```

Running this code will result in the following output:

```
Kotlin has 6 letters
Java has 4 letters
Swift has 5 letters
K has 1 letters
```

The `associate()` function greatly simplifies the work required to create a map of associated values based on an input collection.

Searching

The Kotlin standard library provides a variety of functions for picking items out of a collection. These include functions such as `find()`, `first()`, and `last()`. Let's take a look at a few of these functions:

- Let's look at the following example using the `first()` function:

```
val list = listOf("Kotlin", "Java", "Swift", "K")
val item = list.first()
println(item)
```

  Running this code will print out `"Kotlin"`.

- Or, we could use the `last()` function:

```
val list = listOf("Kotlin", "Java", "Swift", "K")
val item = list.last()
println(item)
```

  This time, the code will print out `"K"`.

- What if we want to take more than one item out of a collection? For this, we can use the `take()` function:

```
val list = listOf("Kotlin", "Java", "Swift", "K")
list.take(2).forEach { println(it) }
```

  In this example, we've called `take(2)` to take the first two items out of the list. When we then print those items out, we get the following output:

```
Kotlin
Java
```

- We can use the `findLast()` function to retrieve the last element in a collection that matches a given predicate:

```
val list = listOf("Kotlin", "Java", "Swift", "K")
val lastK = list.findLast { it.contains("K") }
println(lastK)
```

- Alternatively, we could use `find()` to retrieve the first element in a collection that matches the given predicate:

```
val list = listOf("Kotlin", "Java", "Swift", "K")
val firstK = list.find { it.contains("K") }
println(firstK)
```

These functions make it easy to query the items within a collection and retrieve the ones that match our current use case.

Exploring other useful functions

Beyond just functions for manipulating collections, the Kotlin standard library provides many other helpful functions. Let's explore a few examples of how these functions can make our code more concise, readable, and safe.

One such function is `isNullOrEmpty()`. This provides a convenient way to check whether a collection is either null or empty:

```
if (list.isNullOrEmpty()) {
    // handle empty case
}
```

This helps us to handle those common edge cases with a standard available function.

If we find that a collection is null, but would rather work with an empty collection than a null one, the Kotlin standard library provides functions to retrieve an empty collection of your choosing:

```
val emptyList = emptyList<String>()
val emptyMap = emptyMap<String, Int>()
val emptyArray = emptyArray<String>()
```

This can be done using a nullable collection type as well. We can use the `orEmpty()` function on a collection to return either the current non-null value or a default empty collection instead:

```
var possiblyNullList: List<String>? = null
var nonNullList = possiblyNullList.orEmpty()
```

The Kotlin standard library also provides a variety of convenience functions for working with string types. In particular, there are several functions for checking whether a string is null, blank, or empty:

```
val string: String? = null
if (string.isNullOrBlank()) {
    // handle edge cases
}
if (string.isNullOrEmpty()) {
    // handle edge cases
}
if (string?.isEmpty() == true) {
```

```
    // handle empty string
}
if (string?.isNotBlank() == true) {
    // handle non-blank string
}
```

These are quite useful when working toward eliminating `null` from your code base as much as possible.

Additionally, the `String` type has an `orEmpty()` function that can be used to return the current non-null `String` value or a default empty `String`:

```
var possiblyNullString: String? = null
var nonNullString = possiblyNullString.orEmpty()
```

The Kotlin standard library provides many helpful functions for working with strings, collections, arrays, numerical types, and more. By leveraging these functions, we can begin to write more functional code with fewer side effects, greater readability, and less code.

Functional programming with Arrow

Using higher-order functions and taking advantage of the standard library can help you begin to write more functional code with Kotlin. However, that's really only the first step toward writing pure functional code. In this section, we'll take a look at the Arrow library and see how it enables us to write more purely functional Kotlin code.

What is Arrow?

Arrow is an open source library for typed, functional programming in Kotlin. It aims to provide common syntax and functionality to achieve pure functional programming with Kotlin. This includes abstractions, interfaces, and classes including the following:

- `Functor`
- `Applicative`
- `Monad`
- `Option`
- `Try`
- `Either`
- `Eval`

For additional information about Arrow, refer to the official Arrow documentation: `https://arrow-kt.io/`.

Arrow can be used alongside your existing object-oriented, imperative code and can be used in specific places such as transforming data coming in or out of your application.

Let's explore three of the key types of abstraction that Arrow provides:

- Typeclasses
- Data types
- Effects

Typeclasses

In Arrow, typeclasses allow you to define functional logic via extension interfaces (interfaces that define extension functions). This allows us to create implementations of a typeclass for any class, even those we do not control or that are closed for extension. This also means that the behaviors are composable since they are essentially stateless functions.

Arrow provides numerous typeclasses out of the box. Examples include the following:

- `Eq`: Abstracts the comparison of two instances of any data type
- `Functor`: Abstracts the mapping from one data type to another
- `Monad`: Abstracts the sequential execution of code over some collection of data

In this snippet, we've defined a `filter` function that takes an instance of `Eq` to compare strings:

```
fun <F> List<F>.filter(other: F, EQ: Eq<F>) =
    this.filter { EQ.run { it.eqv(other) } }
```

We can then retrieve an existing `Eq` for `String` using an extension function:

```
fun main() {
    listOf("1", "2", "3").filter("2", String.eq()).forEach { println(it) }
}
```

Typeclasses in Arrow are analogous to the functions we explored previously in the Kotlin standard library.

Data types

Data types in Arrow aim to encapsulate and enforce common programming patterns. An example of this might be requesting a resource that may either succeed with a single data type, or fail. Several common data types are provided by Arrow to enforce patterns:

- Option: Represents the possible absence of data
- Either: Represents an if/else branch in a data flow
- Try: Represents an operation that may result in a success with a single result, or an exception

These data types are implemented as Kotlin data classes, or as sealed classes comprising object classes and data classes. The goal is to enforce these common patterns as well as immutability.

In this snippet, we create an instance of Some, which extends Option, and then map that to another Some instance. We can then use the getOrElse() function to access that value while providing a default value:

```
val someNumber = Some(1).flatMap { a ->
    Some(a + 1)
}.getOrElse { -1 }
```

Arrow also includes other data types for things such as collections:

- NonEmptyList: A homogeneous, non-empty list
- ListK: A wrapper around Kotlin List that is compatible with Arrow typeclasses
- MapK: A wrapper around Kotlin Map that is compatible with Arrow typeclasses

The following line of code is an example of the NonEmptyList data type:

```
val nonEmptyList = NonEmptyList.of(1, 2, 3, 4, 5)
```

Through these data types, Arrow enforces common functional programming patterns and can add/extend functionality through mechanisms such as typeclasses.

Effects

Effects are abstractions that help us to encapsulate non-deterministic operations such as network requests or disk I/O. These types of operations don't fit as nicely into the pure mathematical model of functional programming because they take time, and their result is non-deterministic.

Arrow provides several abstractions with which we can model our side effect code:

- IO: A common data type for working with external systems such as networks or databases
- Async: A typeclass that represents asynchronous code with a callback
- Promise: Represents an asynchronous operation whose result is returned as a promise

Using IO, we can define a long-running operation and then consume it using typeclasses such as attempt() or runAsync():

```
IO<Int> {
    Thread.sleep(2000)
    5
}
    .runAsync { result ->
        result.fold({ IO { println("Error") } }, { IO { println("$it") } })
    }.unsafeRunAsync { }
```

Here, we see an example of how we can define an IO operation, map both result states to desired outputs, and then evaluate the entire flow with unsafeRunAsync{ }.

Using Arrow, we can write type-safe, highly functional code with Kotlin. This code will maintain the desirable aspects of functional programming, such as immutability and pure functions, while providing standard mechanisms for side effects that are often required for modern applications. Arrow provides integrations for libraries such as Rx or Kotlin coroutines, meaning that it can be integrated with your existing code as well.

This section has just scratched the surface of using Arrow for functional Kotlin programming, but should help you to understand the key concepts and how to learn more.

Summary

In this chapter, we've taken a closer look at achieving functional programming with Kotlin. We've discussed some of the favorable characteristics of functional programs and why we might want to write functional code with Kotlin. Then, we explored how higher-order functions enable us to write standalone functions that can be used and composed to express complex data flows. We then examined how the Kotlin standard library provides a great deal of functionality for these data flows in the form of flexible, predefined functions. And finally, we reviewed Arrow, the functional programming library, and its uses in writing highly functional code with Kotlin.

In the next chapter, we'll start to explore how to write Android apps using Kotlin.

Questions

1. What is functional programming?
2. What are two beneficial characteristics of functional programming?
3. What does an `inline` modifier do to a defined function?
4. Is it true or false that higher-order functions pose a potential performance issue?
5. Can you name three functions from the Kotlin standard library?
6. What is the Arrow library used for?
7. What are the core data types when writing functional code with Arrow?

Further reading

- *Functional Kotlin* (`https://www.packtpub.com/application-development/functional-kotlin`)
- *Kotlin Standard Library Cookbook* (`https://www.packtpub.com/application-development/kotlin-standard-library-cookbook`)
- *Hands-On Reactive Programming with Kotlin* (`https://www.packtpub.com/application-development/hands-reactive-programming-kotlin`)

5
Section 5: The Wide World of Kotlin – Using Kotlin across the Entire Development Stack

This part will explore the different domains in which Kotlin can be applied. It will serve to expose the reader to how they can start using Kotlin within each domain and help them to understand why Kotlin is a viable approach.

This section comprises the following chapters:

- Chapter 13, *Kotlin on Android*
- Chapter 14, *Kotlin and Web Development*
- Chapter 15, *Introducing Multiplatform Kotlin*
- Chapter 16, *Taming the Monolith with Microservices*
- Chapter 17, *Practical Design Patterns*

13
Kotlin on Android

This chapter will explore building Android applications with Kotlin. It will detail why Kotlin is so popular for Android development and how it makes developers' lives easier.

We'll take a look at some of the tools being released by Google that make use of Kotlin, and how to create a new Android project, with Kotlin support, using Android Studio.

Finally, we'll explore the use of Android KTX and Kotlin Android Extensions in making Android development easier with Kotlin.

This chapter will be structured as follows:

- First-class Kotlin for Android
- Hello Android Kotlin
- Building with Kotlin
- First-party tooling

Technical requirements

In order to download, compile, and execute the samples found in this chapter, the following is required:

- Android Studio 3.3 or newer
- An internet connection
- Git and GitHub (optional)

To download all of the code in this chapter, including the examples and code snippets, please refer to the following GitHub link: `https://github.com/PacktPublishing/Mastering-Kotlin/tree/master/Chapter13`.

First class Kotlin for Android

Kotlin has become very popular in the Android development community. This has been an ongoing process over the past 4-5 years, and has seen Kotlin go from a small, community-driven niche to the primary development language for Android.

Adopting Kotlin for Android

This increase in popularity for Android development really started to take off in 2015, but it was two years later, in 2017, when Kotlin really came to the fore. That was when Google officially announced support for Kotlin as a development language for Android.

When Android Studio 3.0 was released in October 2017, there was no longer a major technical obstacle to the adoption of Kotlin in established projects. Organizations or teams that had been concerned about pre-release versions of plugins or IDEs could now try Kotlin with stable tools and the full, long-term support of Google. This allowed many teams to adopt the language, and thus began the surge in Kotlin's popularity that we see today.

This community support for Kotlin came about largely because of Android's dependency on Java 7 and Java 8. While newer versions of Java have much more modern functionality, Android was stuck with Java 7 and 8 for long-term compatibility. This meant that developers didn't have access to more modern features, such as lambdas, without additional plugins or updating their target language, which wasn't always feasible.

The adoption of Kotlin provided a more modern-feeling language that was still bytecode-compatible with the JVM versions that Android required. As prominent members of the Android development community began speaking out in favor of Kotlin, more and more developers started to give it a try. With official support from Google, pitching Kotlin to a team became a much easier sell, and teams could begin experimenting with Kotlin with minimal risk.

All of this has resulted in Kotlin becoming a major part of the Android ecosystem today.

Kotlin first

At Google I/O 2019, it was announced that Google would be taking a **Kotlin-first** approach to Android from now on. This means that new APIs will be built with Kotlin in mind first. And, in fact, some APIs will only be available in Kotlin.

Additionally, new courses, documentation, and samples are being created with Kotlin and generally default to Kotlin over Java when examples exist for both.

IntelliJ and Android Studio both make it incredibly easy to integrate Kotlin with existing Android projects, or to start new projects that are 100% Kotlin. Additionally, Google continues to invest in Kotlin with improved tooling and the Core-KTX Jetpack library, which makes building Android applications with Kotlin even more enjoyable.

The Android architecture components are now built with a Kotlin-first approach and include support for Kotlin features such as coroutines. To an even greater degree, the pre-alpha Jetpack Compose library from Google is an entirely new UI toolkit built with, and for, Kotlin.

As these tools mature and new ones are developed, Android will continue to become more and more Kotlin-first.

The future of Android

Google continues to invest heavily in Kotlin, and Kotlin appears to be the future of Android development. The combination of Kotlin's modern features, terrific tooling, and strong support from Google make it an incredibly appealing choice for Android developers moving forward.

Hello Android Kotlin

In this section, we're going to explore how to start building Android apps with Kotlin. We'll walk through how to create and set up a new Android Studio project with Kotlin support. Also, we'll then explore a few ways in which we can take advantage of Kotlin for Android development.

Creating an Android app with Kotlin support

Let's walk through the following steps to create an Android project with Kotlin support:

1. First, we need to open Android Studio on our development machine. If you don't already have Android Studio installed, you can find the download and installation instructions at `https://developer.android.com/studio/install`.
2. Select **Start a new Android Studio project**.

3. Select **Empty Activity**, and then click **Next**, shown as follows:

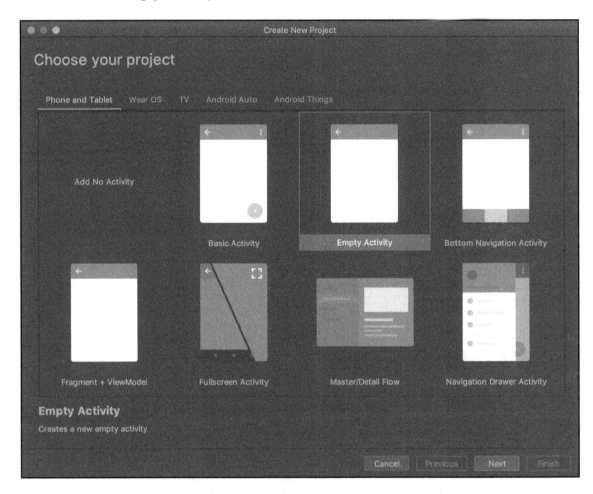

4. Update your project **Name**, **Package name**, and **Save location**, as shown in the following screenshot:

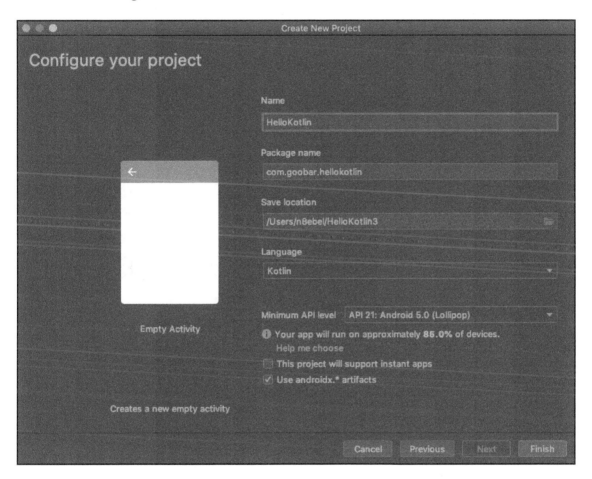

5. Ensure that **Kotlin** is selected in the **Language** drop-down menu, and then click **Finish**. This will ensure that Kotlin is the default language for the project and that the IDE generates new code using Kotlin rather than Java:

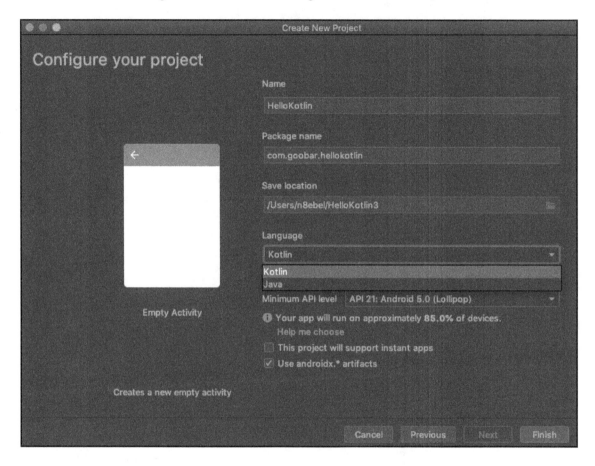

At this point, you will have a buildable Android project with Kotlin support, something similar to what is shown in the following screenshot:

To see how Kotlin is configured for the project, open the root-level `build.gradle` file. In this case, it's the `build.gradle` file labeled **Project: HelloKotlin**. See the following screenshot:

This is the project-level `build.gradle` file.

There are two key things to be aware of in this `build.gradle` file:

- The `ext.kotlin_version` variable defines the version of Kotlin used in the project, in this case, `1.3.31`.
- The Kotlin Gradle plugin has been added as a `classpath` dependency, allowing us to apply the plugin to our other Gradle modules, thereby making them Kotlin-aware.

Finally, if you open the `build.gradle` file labeled as **Module: app**, you'll notice three things:

- The `kotlin-android` plugin has been applied.
- The `kotlin-android-extensions` plugin has been applied.
- The Kotlin standard library has been added as a dependency.

The following screenshot shows these elements:

```
apply plugin: 'com.android.application'
apply plugin: 'kotlin-android'
apply plugin: 'kotlin-android-extensions'


dependencies {


    implementation"org.jetbrains.kotlin:kotlin-stdlib-jdk7:$kotlin_version"


    implementation fileTree(dir: 'libs', include: ['*.jar'])
    implementation 'androidx.appcompat:appcompat:1.0.2'
    implementation 'androidx.core:core-ktx:1.0.2'
    implementation 'androidx.constraintlayout:constraintlayout:1.1.3'
    testImplementation 'junit:junit:4.12'
    androidTestImplementation 'androidx.test.ext:junit:1.1.1'
    androidTestImplementation 'androidx.test.espresso:espresso-core:3.2.0'
}


android {
    compileSdkVersion 28
    defaultConfig {
        applicationId "com.goobar.hellokotlin"
```

At this point, you're now ready to start writing your Android app with Kotlin. In the next section, we'll explore how Kotlin can make that process easier.

Taking advantage of Kotlin on Android

Now that we have a working Android project that supports Kotlin, let's explore a few examples of common Android coding patterns that can be updated to take advantage of Kotlin.

Configuring a view reference

To get an immutable reference to a button, we could use something along the lines of the following code snippet:

```
val button = findViewById<Button>(R.id.button)
```

If we then wanted to configure multiple properties on that button, we could make use of the scoping function, `apply`:

```
val button = findViewById<Button>(R.id.button).apply {
    text = "Hello Kotlin"
    gravity = Gravity.START
    setTextColor(resources.getColor(R.color.colorAccent))
}
```

The `apply` function provides us with a receiver, in this case, `Button`, which can then be referenced implicitly within the scope of the passed lambda. This can be a useful means of grouping related method calls or property updates.

Responding to click events

When writing Android `View` code with Kotlin, we can set click listeners on our `Views` using a lambda rather than an anonymous inner class, shown as follows:

```
button.setOnClickListener {
    // handle the event
}
```

The lack of parentheses here makes this easier to read and to write. Additionally, we could combine this click listener lambda with a functional property for responding to the click:

```
var clickHandler: (() -> Unit)? = null
...
button.setOnClickListener {
    // handle the event
    clickHandler?.invoke()
}
```

By exposing a public function property for responding to the click event, we can easily defer to that property within `Button` click listener and invoke the callback function only if it's non-null.

Creating factory methods for activities and fragments

A common pattern for the creation of new activities or fragments is to create static factory methods to start an activity, or to create an intent, or to create a new instance of `Fragment`. When using Kotlin, we can accomplish this using a companion object, which is shown in the following code block with the definition of `Factory`:

```
companion object Factory {
    const val EXTRA_ID = "extra_id"

    @JvmStatic
    fun createIntent(context: Context, id: String) =
 Intent(context, DetailsActivity::class.java).apply {
 putExtra(EXTRA_ID, id)
 }
}
```

Additionally, you could use a top-level function or extension function to achieve similar behavior, as follows:

```
fun createDetailsIntent(context: Context, id: String) =
    Intent(context, DetailsActivity::class.java).apply {
        putExtra(DetailsActivity.EXTRA_ID, id)
    }
fun Context.createDetailsIntent(id: String) =
    Intent(this, DetailsActivity::class.java).apply {
        putExtra(DetailsActivity.EXTRA_ID, id)
    }
```

One possible drawback of using a top-level function is that it occupies the global namespace. If you're adding enough functions, it may become difficult for the IDE to autocomplete the function you're looking for. If this is the case for your project, using companion objects to scope your functions is likely the better choice.

Handling savedInstanceState

Kotlin allows us to perform null-safe method calls on variables that may, or may not, be null. One example of how this can reduce boilerplate in our code is in the handling of `savedInstanceState`.

A common pattern is to check whether `savedInstanceState` is non-null within `onCreate()`, and if it is, handle the restoration of that state. We can see an example of this in the following code snippet:

```
override fun onCreate(savedInstanceState: Bundle?) {
    super.onCreate(savedInstanceState)
    setContentView(R.layout.activity_details)
    savedInstanceState?.let { it }
}

fun restoreSavedState(savedInstanceState: Bundle) {
    // restore state
}
```

Using a null-safe call to the `let()` function, we can safely restore our state only if `savedInstanceState` is non-null. And because of smart casting in Kotlin, we can define the `restoreSavedState()` function to only accept a non-null `Bundle` and then rely on the compiler to smart cast `savedInstanceState` for us. This helps us to enforce type safety and reduce `NullPointerExceptions`.

These have been just a couple of examples of how Kotlin can quickly make writing Android code safer and more concise. In the next section, we'll see how Kotlin can be applied to the build configuration of our project.

Building with Kotlin

Now that we've explored how we can write Kotlin code for our Android apps, we're going to examine how we can actually configure our Gradle build scripts using Kotlin rather than Groovy. This can provide several benefits, such as static type checking and improved refactoring.

The Gradle Kotlin DSL

The Gradle Kotlin DSL is an alternative method of configuring your Gradle build. Rather than relying on Groovy, you can leverage Kotlin to define your dependencies, build variants, and so on.

Moving your Gradle configuration to make use of the Gradle Kotlin DSL has several benefits:

- Type-safe accessors allow you to reference Gradle/build entities by name.
- Improved IDE support makes it easier to find and navigate to dependencies.

Migrating to the Kotlin buildscript

To explore the Gradle Kotlin DSL, we're going to migrate our existing Android project to make use of the DSL.

The first step will be to go through both of our `build.gradle` files and ensure that all string literals are using double quotes (") instead of single quotes (') and that all Gradle function calls are using parentheses.

In the case of the top-level `build.gradle` file, this means adding parentheses to the `classpath()` function calls. This is required because Groovy allows you to omit these parentheses, whereas Kotlin requires them to be used. The following code demonstrates what this update looks like in our project-level `build.gradle` file:

```
// root-level build.gradle
buildscript {
    ext.kotlin_version = "1.3.31"
    repositories {
        google()
        jcenter()
    }

    dependencies {
        // addition of ( ) when using classpath function
        classpath("com.android.tools.build:gradle:3.5.0-beta04")
        classpath("org.jetbrains.kotlin:kotlin-gradle-plugin:$kotlin_version")
    }
}

...
```

The next step will be to rename each `build.gradle` file by adding `.kts` to the end so that the full filename is `build.gradle.kts`. This will indicate that the file is using the Kotlin Gradle DSL.

Once these filenames have been updated, we will have several errors to address. We will start by updating the root-level `build.gradle.kts` file.

First, we'll update the definition of the existing clean task as follows:

```
task(name = "clean", type = Delete::class) {
    delete(rootProject.buildDir)
}
```

Notice that we're able to make use of named parameters to define our invocation of the task function.

Next, we'll update our `kotlin_version` extension and its usage in declaring the Gradle Kotlin plugin. Consider the following code:

```
buildscript {
  extensions.add("kotlin_version", "1.3.31")
  repositories {
    google()
    jcenter()
  }

  dependencies {
    classpath("com.android.tools.build:gradle:3.5.0-beta04")
    // using extensions.get() to retrieve Kotlin version
    classpath ("org.jetbrains.kotlin:kotlin-gradle-
            plugin:${extensions.get("kotlin_version")}")
  }
}
```

We can define and retrieve extensions using `extensions.add()` or `extensions.get()`. Later on, we'll explore another means of defining our dependencies that doesn't rely on extensions.

Now, let's jump over to the app module's `build.gradle.kts` file. We'll start by updating the plugin declarations using the `plugins` block:

```
plugins {
    id("com.android.application")
    id("kotlin-android")
    id("kotlin-android-extensions")
}
```

Next, we'll update our Android configuration block as follows:

```
android {
  compileSdkVersion(28)
    defaultConfig {
      applicationId = "com.goobar.hellokotlin"
      minSdkVersion(21)
```

```
            targetSdkVersion(28)
            versionCode = 1
            versionName = "1.0"
            testInstrumentationRunner =
                "androidx.test.runner.AndroidJUnitRunner"
    }

    buildTypes {
      getByName("release") {
        isMinifyEnabled = false
        proguardFiles(getDefaultProguardFile(
            "proguard-android-optimize.txt"), "proguard-rules.pro")
      }
    }
  }
```

And lastly, we'll update our dependencies block:

```
dependencies {

    implementation("org.jetbrains.kotlin:kotlin-stdlib-jdk7:1.3.31")

    implementation("androidx.appcompat:appcompat:1.0.2")
    implementation("androidx.core:core-ktx:1.0.2")
    implementation("androidx.constraintlayout:constraintlayout:1.1.3")
    testImplementation("junit:junit:4.12")
    androidTestImplementation("androidx.test.ext:junit:1.1.1")
    androidTestImplementation("androidx.test.espresso:espresso-core:3.2.0")
}
```

At this point, our Gradle build is now using the Gradle Kotlin DSL. This gives us the familiar syntax and features of Kotlin when working with Gradle.

Simplifying dependency management with Kotlin

Now that we've migrated our build.gradle files to make use of the Kotlin Gradle DSL, let's improve the way in which we define dependencies and build constants. More specifically, we are going to use Kotlin object declarations to define our dependencies so they can be defined once and reused elsewhere. To do this, perform the following steps:

1. To start, create a new directory named buildSrc within the root project directory:

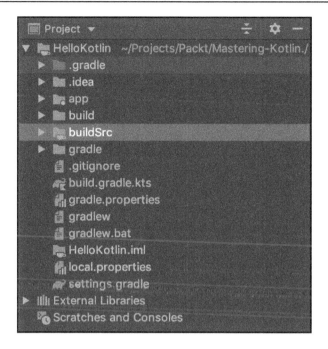

2. Next, we're going to create the following two files within the `buildSrc` directory:
   - buildSrc/build.gradle.kts
   - buildSrc/src/main/kotlin/Dependencies.kt

This `buildSrc` directory is a special directory in which we can create constants and objects that Gradle will make available to us during the configuration and building of our project. To make this work, we first need to update `buildSrc/build.gradle.kts` with the following code:

```
repositories { jcenter() }

plugins {
  'kotlin-dsl'
}
```

By applying the `'kotlin-dsl'` plugin, Gradle will use the objects and constants defined in this directory.

3. Now we can define some constants to use within our build. We'll define this within the newly created buildSrc/src/main/kotlin/Dependencies.kt file. To start, we'll define a String constant for the current version of Kotlin:

```
object Deps {
    object Kotlin {
        const val version = "1.3.31"
    }
}
```

Because we're working with a simple Kotlin file, we can define our constants as top-level properties or within an object declaration, as in the previous code snippet.

4. Once the constant is defined, we can make use of it from our other Gradle files like this:

```
// root/build.gradle.kts
buildscript {
    extensions.add("kotlin_version", Deps.Kotlin.version)
    repositories {
        google()
        jcenter()
    }
    dependencies {
        classpath("com.android.tools.build:gradle:3.5.0-beta04")
        classpath ("org.jetbrains.kotlin:kotlin-gradle-
                    plugin:${Deps.Kotlin.version}")
    }
}
```

We can access the defined constant as if it were any other type of Kotlin code that was referencing it. This approach can be used for more than just constants. We can define all of our dependencies within the buildSrc directory so they can be reused elsewhere in a consistent manner. Let's examine how this works:

1. Let's start by updating Dependencies.kt with some additional dependency constants, as follows:

```
object Deps {
    object Kotlin {
        private const val version = "1.3.31"
        const val gradlePlugin = "org.jetbrains.kotlin:kotlin-
                                  gradle-plugin:$version"
    }
    object Android {
```

```
object Tools {
    const val androidGradle = "com.android.tools.build:
                                gradle:3.5.0-beta04"
    }
}
}
```

2. Now, we can update `build.gradle.kts` to completely remove any reference to Kotlin version or plugin versions:

```
// root/build.gradle/kts
buildscript {
    repositories {
        google()
        jcenter()
    }
    dependencies {
        classpath(Deps.Android.Tools.androidGradle)
        classpath (Deps.Kotlin.gradlePlugin)
    }
}
```

This nicely encapsulates the available dependencies and their versions within the `buildSrc` directory. This makes your dependencies much easier to manage in larger, possibly multi-module, projects. This also makes it easier to navigate to dependencies from our `build.gradle.kts` files and to refactor dependencies across our project. Let's now move on to the tools used for this.

First-party tooling

As mentioned previously, Android is now Kotlin-first. With this approach comes a number of useful tools that help us take full advantage of Kotlin for Android development. In this section, we're going to explore several of these tools, including the following:

- Android KTX
- Kotlin Android Extensions
- Architecture components

For each of these, we'll examine what it is, how it takes advantage of Kotlin, and why you might consider it for your Android projects. Let's begin.

Exploring Android KTX

Android KTX is a set of different extensions for the Android framework and Jetpack. The Android KTX extensions are themselves a part of Jetpack and can be added to your project as a simple Gradle dependency. The functionality provided by Android KTX is aimed at making Android APIs more Kotlin idiomatic by taking advantage of features such as extension functions and higher-order functions.

To make the dependency more lightweight, Android KTX is broken up into several smaller dependencies, depending on the functionality they offer. Some of these are as follows:

- Core KTX
- Fragment KTX
- SQLite KTX
- ViewModel KTX
- Navigation KTX
- WorkManager KTX

The entirety of Android KTX provides a great deal of useful functionality. In the following sections, we're going to explore the functionality provided by two specific modules: Core KTX and Fragment KTX.

Adding Core KTX to your project

To start, we will update our project to make use of Core KTX. To do this, we'll first need to make sure we have the `google()` Maven repository added to our project. To add it, use the following code:

```
repositories {
    google()
}
```

Next, we'll define a constant for `core-ktx` in our `buildSrc` directory:

```
object Android {
    object Tools {
        const val androidGradle = "com.android.tools.build:gradle:3.5.0-
beta04"
    }
    object Ktx {
        const val core = "androidx.core:core-ktx:1.0.1"
    }
}
```

We'll then add the following dependency to `app/build.gradle.kts`:

```
dependencies {
    ...

    implementation(Deps.Android.Ktx.core)
}
```

Now that Core KTX is added to our project, let's explore some of the ways in which it makes developers' lives easier.

Using Core KTX

Core KTX includes packages built around a variety of core Android framework libraries and APIs, including the following:

- `androidx.core.animation`
- `androidx.core.preference`
- `androidx.core.transition`
- `androidx.core.view`

One of the best examples of using Android KTX to simplify platform APIs is in the use of `SharedPreferences`. With the functionality of Kotlin available to us, we can use a very fluent syntax for editing `SharedPreferences` that removes the need to explicitly call `commit()` or `apply()`:

```
val preferences = getPreferences(Context.MODE_PRIVATE)
preferences.edit {
    putBoolean("key", false)
    putString("key2", "value")
}
```

Another example of useful functionality provided by Android KTX is the `View.onPreDraw()` extension function:

```
button.doOnPreDraw {
    // Perform an action when view is about to be drawn
}
```

This allows us to define a lambda containing logic that will be run when `View` is about to be drawn without having to create a new listener or having to unregister that listener.

Using Fragment KTX

Let's now explore the Fragment KTX module, which contains utility functions for working with fragments. First, we'll define our new dependency constant:

```
object Android {
    ...
    object Ktx {
        const val core = "androidx.core:core-ktx:1.0.1"
        const val fragment = "androidx.fragment:fragment-ktx:1.0.0"
    }
}
```

Now, we'll update `app/build.gradle.kts`:

```
dependencies {
    ...

    implementation(Deps.Android.Ktx.core)
    implementation(Deps.Android.Ktx.fragment)
}
```

Once the dependency is added, we can define `FragmentTransactions` using the `commit()` extension function like this:

```
supportFragmentManager.commit {
    addToBackStack("fragment name")
    add(SampleFragment(), "tag")
    setCustomAnimations(R.anim.abc_fade_in, R.anim.abc_fade_out)
}
```

This makes the addition of new `FragmentTransaction` feel more Kotlin idiomatic and removes some of the boilerplate around those operations.

As we've seen with Core KTX and Fragment KTX, these libraries can really improve the Android development experience. These types of extensions and additions are available across the Android KTX dependencies and can really help you take advantage of Kotlin for Android development.

In the next section, we'll take a look at the Kotlin Android Extensions plugin and how that provides additional functionality that makes Android development easier with Kotlin.

Using Kotlin Android Extensions

The Kotlin Android Extensions plugin provides a set of additional functionality for working with Kotlin and Android. The two biggest examples of this are as follows:

- Referencing Android views without `findViewById()`
- Generating Parcelable implementations

To enable these features, we must enable the experimental features within the `androidExtensions` block of our `app/build.gradle.kts` file. The following code snippet demonstrates how to do this:

```
androidExtensions {
  isExperimental = true
}
```

Once this configuration is added to our `build.gradle.kts` file, the features included with the Android Extensions plugin will be enabled. In the next section, we'll explore one of those features to help with building our Android views.

Binding views with Kotlin Android Extensions

Once the experimental features are turned on, we can reference synthetic view bindings to access our views. This means that the Android Extensions plugin will generate view bindings for us. In `MainActivity`, we can add the following import to reference the `Button` defined in our `activity_main.xml` file:

```
import kotlinx.android.synthetic.main.activity_main.button
```

Once we've included the import, we can reference that view directly without any call to `findViewById()` or another variable declaration:

```
button.apply {
    text = "Hello Kotlin"
    gravity = Gravity.START
    setTextColor(resources.getColor(R.color.colorAccent))
}
```

By default, the view will be named after the `android:id` attribute in the XML. In this case, our button had an ID of `"@+id/button"`, so the binding generated was named button. However, if you want to use a different variable name, or have a conflict with another name, you can update the `import` statement and provide an alternative name using the following syntax:

```
import kotlinx.android.synthetic.main.activity_main.button as theButton
```

After updating the import, we can now reference our button with the name `theButton`:

```
theButton.apply {
    text = "Hello Kotlin"
    gravity = Gravity.START
    setTextColor(resources.getColor(R.color.colorAccent))
}
```

The synthetic view bindings will handle caching when used with activities and fragments and can be made to work with custom views as well. You can also control the caching strategy depending on your requirements by updating the `androidExtensions` block in your Gradle file:

```
androidExtensions {
    // HASH_MAP, SPARSE_ARRAY, NONE
    defaultCacheImplementation = "HASH_MAP"
}
```

By using the Kotlin Android Extensions for your view references, you can avoid third-party libraries such as Butterknife or multiple `findViewById()` calls. Whether you should use these synthetic bindings—`DataBinding`, `ViewBinding`, or `findViewById()`—will largely depend on your project and preferences, and you should evaluate them on a project-by-project basis.

Generating Parcelable implementations

`Parcelable` is a common interface within Android development aimed at providing a more performant serialization API. Generating implementations of the `Parcelable` interface can be a tedious and boilerplate-filled task involving the creation of a lot of simple and repetitive code. Thankfully, the Kotlin Android Extensions provide an annotation that can generate a `Parcelable` implementation for us. To make use of this functionality, we can add the `@Parcelize` annotation to any class that implements `Parcelable`:

```
@Parcelize
data class Person(val firstName: String, val lastName: String): Parcelable
```

By adding the @Parcelize annotation to our model objects, the plugin will generate the required Parcelable implementations for us. This will allow you to skip the implementation, and maintenance of that Parcelable implementation. This reduces the amount of code required for your class and means you don't have to update your Parcelable implementation each time your class is modified; the plugin will do it for you when your code is compiled. This assists in protection from errors that can commonly arise from modifying a property, but forgetting to update the Parcelable implementation.

By making use of the Kotlin Android Extensions plugin, you can reduce the amount of code you must write and maintain, and allow the plugin to generate common boilerplate code for you.

Summary

In this chapter, we've explored the relationship between Kotlin and Android development. We've walked through the history of Kotlin's adoption for Android from its early days to the recent Kotlin First announcement from Google. We detailed how to create a new Android project from scratch with support for Kotlin and how to write Kotlin-idiomatic Android code. Finally, we examined several specific Kotlin libraries and tools: Android-KTX, Kotlin Android Extensions, and the Android architecture components. We saw how these tools take advantage of Kotlin to make Android development easier and, quite possibly, more enjoyable.

In the next chapter, we'll explore how to use Kotlin outside of Android for web development.

Questions

1. When did Google first announce Kotlin support for Android?
2. When did Google decide to go Kotlin-first for Android?
3. Is it true or false that you can define your Gradle builds using Kotlin scripts?
4. How can you use the buildSrc directory when building you project with Kotlin Gradle scripts?
5. What is Android KTX?
6. What is the Kotlin Android Extensions plugin?
7. What annotation will generate Parcelable implementations for you when added to a model class?

Further reading

- *Learning Kotlin by Building Android Applications* (`https://www.packtpub.com/application-development/learning-kotlin-building-android-applications`)
- *Android Programming with Kotlin for Beginners* (`https://www.packtpub.com/application-development/android-programming-kotlin-beginners`)

Kotlin and Web Development 14

This chapter will explore the fundamentals of how Kotlin can be used for frontend web development. We will see how Kotlin can be compiled to a JavaScript target that can then be used in the development of backend services and web applications.

This chapter will help you to understand if Kotlin code can be written alongside existing JavaScript frameworks. It will also provide information of the limitations, if any, of compiling Kotlin to JavaScript and also how to build a web application that includes Kotlin.

This chapter will help us to understand these with the help of the following topics:

- Kotlin for the web
- Building a Hello Kotlin project
- Integrating with existing JavaScript

Technical requirements

In order to download, compile, and execute the samples found in this chapter, the following is required:

- IntelliJ IDEA 2018.3 Community or Ultimate editions, or newer
- Google Chrome
- npm
- An internet connection
- Git and GitHub (optional)

To download all of the code in this chapter, including the examples and code snippets, please refer to the following GitHub link: `https://github.com/PacktPublishing/Mastering-Kotlin/tree/master/Chapter14`.

Kotlin for the web

Kotlin's popularity can't be denied, and yet the vast majority of the attention given to Kotlin is within the realm of the JVM. Even more specifically, Kotlin is primarily used within the Android development community. However, one of the most interesting, ambitious, and potentially game-changing things about Kotlin is that it is becoming more and more useful beyond Android as new compilation targets become viable.

JetBrains continues to invest in support for multiple compilation targets for Kotlin. This means that it's possible to write Kotlin code that is compiled for targets other than the JVM. Currently, those targets include the following:

- JavaScript
- Native
- Multiplatform

In this section, we're going to explore the ramifications of targeting JavaScript with Kotlin. We will also see how the compilation to JavaScript works, where we can apply the compiled JavaScript, and finally, why we might want to consider building with Kotlin for the web.

Compiling Kotlin to JavaScript

Let's start at the beginning. How is it that we can write Kotlin code that is then consumed as JavaScript? Throughout this book, we've seen many examples of how Kotlin is compiled down to JVM-compatible bytecode and how Kotlin interoperates so seamlessly with Java. With this in mind, it probably sounds a bit odd at first that we can take that same Kotlin code and use it in a JavaScript environment, so let's dive a bit deeper into how this is achieved.

Transpiling to JavaScript

The magic comes from the Kotlin compiler and your project target. In a standard JVM-targeted Kotlin project, the compiler generates JVM-compatible bytecode that runs on the JVM and is intrinsically compatible with other JVM code.

When creating a Kotlin project that targets JavaScript, all of the Kotlin code within that project will be transpiled to JavaScript when you build the project. If you're unfamiliar with the term *transpile*, it refers to the compilation of a programming language by converting it from one language to another. In a sense, the code is rewritten to match the target language. In this case, the Kotlin code you write is translated into compatible JavaScript that can then be consumed as if you had written any other JavaScript code. This includes any Kotlin code within your project, including the Kotlin standard library. However, this does not include any JVM-based code or libraries that are used. So, if you're consuming a Java library in your Kotlin code, you'll need to refactor that before it will be available in the transpiled JavaScript.

As with any programming language, there are often many ways to write functionally equivalent JavaScript code. When debugging or otherwise examining the JavaScript output of transpiled Kotlin, it's desirable to make that code as readable as possible. If the code looks like something a person would write, rather than something a compiler generates, it becomes easier to understand, debug, and reason about. To this end, JetBrains continues to work to ensure that the Kotlin compiler generates human-readable JavaScript during the transpiling phase.

Now that we understand that Kotlin is transpiled to JavaScript when a project is created that targets JavaScript, how do we actually target JavaScript when creating a new project? Let's see how this is done in the next section.

Targeting JavaScript

When we create a new Kotlin project, there are several ways to go about setting up that project and defining a compilation target. Throughout this book, we've primarily been working within IntelliJ IDEA to create new Kotlin projects and modules. Those projects have all targeted the JVM and have had minimal dependencies, so the actual project creation aspect hasn't been that interesting.

Now that we're considering how to create a Kotlin project that target's JavaScript, we can consider multiple means of creating a Kotlin project. In practice, there are the following four ways we could go about creating a new Kotlin project with a JavaScript target:

- Building with Gradle
- Building with Maven
- Building within IntelliJ IDEA
- Building from the command line

In the next section of this chapter, *Building a Hello Kotlin project*, we will walk through how to set up a new Kotlin project using IntelliJ IDEA and make that project target JavaScript so that our Kotlin code can be consumed within a simple web app. Before continuing on to creating our own project, let's explore how and where we can integrate our transpiled Kotlin code.

Using the compiled JavaScript

A question that arises foremost is what we can do with our JavaScript once it's been transpiled from Kotlin. The simplest usage is to load the resulting script into an HTML page and execute whatever code we've defined in our main function.

For example, we can define a Kotlin `main()` function that prints to the console, as in the following example:

```
fun main(args: Array<String>) {
  val message = "Hello Kotlin JavaScript"
  println(message)
}
// outputs "Hello Kotlin JavaScript"
```

We can load the transpiled JavaScript equivalent of this code using a `<script>` tag with an HTML document to print out `"Hello Kotlin JavaScript"` to the console in our browser. We will see exactly how to do this in the very next section.

Beyond writing simple scripts, we could define model objects or business logic within Kotlin and then load those into our web app or server as well. Additionally, these scripts, functions, and models can be used in conjunction with other popular JavaScript frameworks, such as React. We'll discuss this in more detail in the *Integrating with existing JavaScript* section of this chapter.

Now, before diving into creating our own Kotlin project that targets JavaScript, let's explore why you might want to consider using Kotlin when targeting JavaScript.

Targeting JavaScript with Kotlin

You may be wondering *why* anyone would want to write Kotlin code that is then transpiled to Kotlin? Why go through the extra work? What are the benefits? These are perfectly reasonable questions, and ultimately, will depend a lot on your own experience and needs. However, we can explore some of the benefits to help inform your own investigation and decisions.

One benefit of using Kotlin for JavaScript is that it's statically typed. Many developers find JavaScript's lack of static typing to be disorienting and something to be desired. As such, there have been new languages that pop up, such as TypeScript, that aim to bring static typing to the JavaScript world. In this sense, Kotlin is similar to TypeScript. As a developer, you can work with static types provided by Kotlin and let the compiler work out how to translate that into proper JavaScript.

If you're an individual or team targeting multiple platforms for the same project, Kotlin could provide an avenue to achieve common code sharing. By defining common code, such as models or generic business logic, in Kotlin, that code can then be reused across multiple targets, including JavaScript, Native, and Android/JVM.

If you're a developer that is already familiar with Kotlin, targeting JavaScript can make both frontend and backend web development more approachable. Working with a familiar language can lower the barrier to entry for working in a new domain. With Kotlin for JavaScript, we can write simple JavaScript scripts, manipulate the DOM, or even write Node.js server-side code. This makes Kotlin a very powerful tool for a mobile developer, for example, who could theoretically use the same language, or even some of the same code, to write a mobile app, backend, and a web app.

With all of this in mind, let's start writing our own Kotlin project that targets JavaScript so that we can start to gain a first-hand understanding of how it works and what's possible.

Building a Hello Kotlin project

Now that we have an understanding of how the Kotlin to JavaScript compilation works, where you can make use of the compiled JavaScript, and why you might want to consider using Kotlin, let's walk through building a simple web app using Kotlin.

We're going to walk through the setup of a new Kotlin project with a JavaScript target. We'll then examine the output artifacts of the JavaScript compilation to understand what the compiler is actually producing when we build our project. And finally, we'll make use of those build artifacts to run a simple Kotlin function when our web page is loaded.

Creating a Kotlin project with a JavaScript target

To start a new Kotlin project that targets JavaScript, perform the following steps:

1. Open up IntelliJ IDEA and select **Create New Project**:

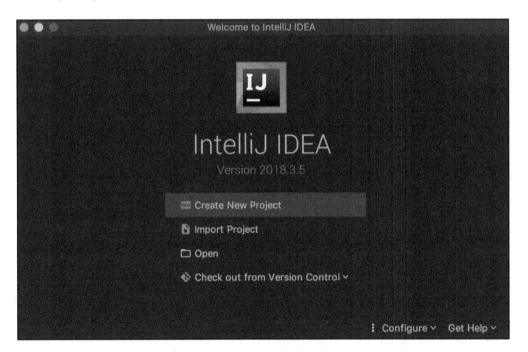

2. Navigate to the Kotlin project templates in the left-hand side of the dialog, select **JS | IDEA**, and then click **NEXT**. This will ensure that our newly created project is configured to target JavaScript using the IntelliJ IDEA build system:

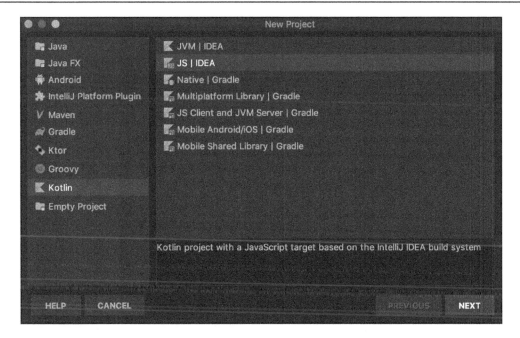

3. Next, we set our project name and project location. You can keep the **Project SDK** and **Kotlin JS library** fields as their default values unless you require a specific version of Kotlin. Once you've updated your name and project directory, click on **FINISH**:

At this point, we should now have an empty Kotlin project. Notice how the project is structured. There should be three elements in the root directory:

- The `.idea` directory for IntelliJ configuration
- An empty `src` directory
- An `.iml` file with module configuration

In the next section, we'll add a `Hello World` example in Kotlin to understand how to start building Kotlin for JavaScript.

Writing Hello World for Kotlin JavaScript

To actually start transpiling some Kotlin into JavaScript, let's add a `main.kt` file to our project. To do so, we'll walk through the following steps:

1. Right-click on the `src` directory in the project pane and select **New** | **Kotlin File/Class**.
2. In the **New Kotlin File/Class** dialog, type `main.kt` and then click **OK**.
3. Navigate to `main.kt` and add the following code. This code will log a simple string message out to the console of the target environment:

```
fun main() {
    val outputMessage = "Hello Kotlin JavaScript"
    println(outputMessage)
}
```

To this point, this should look very familiar. The Kotlin code we've written in `main.kt` is no different than what we would write if we were targeting the JVM. However, if we now build the project, we can see a difference in the resulting build artifacts, as shown in the following screenshot:

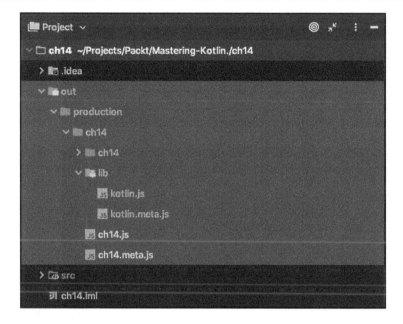

After building our project, the following four artifacts have been created:

- `lib/kotlin.js`
- `lib/kotlin.meta.js`
- `ch14.js`
- `ch14.meta/js`

In the next section, we're going to look more closely at these outputs, and what they contain.

Examining the compiled JavaScript

As discussed previously in this chapter, when we build a Kotlin project that is targeting JavaScript, the compiler will transpile our Kotlin code into human-readable JavaScript for use in whatever web application we may be building. This includes the Kotlin standard library as well. The results of this compilation process can be seen in our output directory after a project build. The following screenshot depicts this:

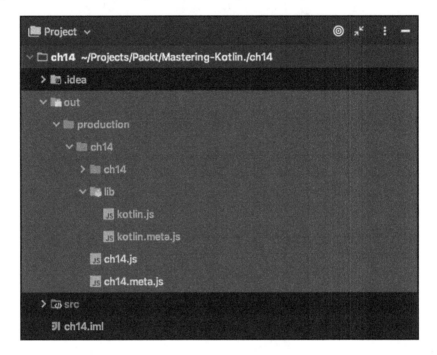

As mentioned in the last section, we have four outputs from the compilation of our current `Hello World` project:

- `lib/kotlin.js`
- `lib/kotlin.meta.js`
- `ch14.js`
- `ch14.meta/js`

Notice the pattern with these outputs? We have `ch14.js` and `lib/kotlin.js`, as well as two examples of `<file>.meta.js` that correspond to the other two output files. For each module in our project, the compiler will create a `<module>.js` file. In our example, that is `ch14.js`.

At the project level, the compiler must generate JavaScript for the Kotlin standard library, which is output as `kotlin.js`. This `kotlin.js` file should be the same for any project using the same version of Kotlin.

For each transpiled `.js` file, the compiler also then generates a corresponding `<file>.meta.js`, which is used primarily for reflection. These files are generally of less concern to us as they are not generally human-readable. However, the `.js` files generated for the Kotlin standard library and each of our modules is designed to be human-readable, so we can understand what the transpiled JavaScript is doing.

If we open up `ch14.js`, we can see the JavaScript code equivalent of our `Hello World` Kotlin example, as shown here:

```
if (typeof kotlin === 'undefined') {
  throw new Error("Error loading module 'ch14'. The dependency 'kotlin'
                   was not found. Please, check whether 'kotlin' is
                   loaded prior to 'ch14'.");
}
var ch14 = function (_, Kotlin) {
  'use strict';
  var println = Kotlin.kotlin.io.println_s8jyv4$;
  function main() {
    var outputMessage = 'Hello Kotlin JavaScript';
    println(outputMessage);
  }
  _.main = main;
  main();
  Kotlin.defineModule('ch14', _);
  return _;
}(typeof ch14 === 'undefined' ? {} : ch14, kotlin);
```

This JavaScript is the result of the compiler transpiling the Kotlin standard library, our own code, and then ensuring that all of the dependencies are still met. The result of this JavaScript is a variable assigned the result of a self-executing, anonymous function call. When that function is declared, it is executed, which, in turn, executes the transpiled version of our `main()` function from `main.kt`. In this case, this results in our "Hello Kotlin JavaScript" message being printed out to the console.

Now that we've seen how our Kotlin has been transpiled into usable JavaScript, let's look at how we can actually start consuming this code.

Consuming Kotlin through compiled JavaScript

Possibly the easiest way to start consuming our transpiled JavaScript is to load that JavaScript with a `<script>` tag within an HTML document. In doing this, we can run our `main()` function when the script is loaded and examine the output in the developer console.

To demonstrate this, let's walk through the following steps:

1. Add a new `index.html` file under the root directory, as in the following code snippet:

```
<!DOCTYPE html>
<html lang="en">
    <head>
        <meta charset="UTF-8">
        <title>HelloKotlinJS</title>
    </head>
    <body bgcolor="#E6E6FA">
        <!-- will load our JavaScript here -->
    </body>
</html>
```

By adding this file, we give ourselves an entry point from which to load and run our JavaScript. If you then open this `index.html` file in your browser, you should see an empty page with a colored background. We will be updating this shortly.

2. Within the `<body>` tag, add two `<script>` tags, one for `kotlin.js` and one for `ch13.js`:

```
<!DOCTYPE html>
<html lang="en">
    <head>
        <meta charset="UTF-8">
        <title>HelloKotlinJS</title>
    </head>
    <body bgcolor="#E6E6FA">
        <script type="text/javascript"
          src="out/production/ch14/lib/kotlin.js"></script>
        <script type="text/javascript"
          src="out/production/ch14/ch14.js"></script>
    </body>
</html>
```

By adding these `<script>` tags, we will load the Kotlin standard library and our module's JavaScript code. Note the order of these scripts. It's important that `kotlin.js` is loaded first because `ch14.js` relies on the Kotlin standard library. If `ch14.js` is loaded first, you'll receive an *uncaught error* when loading your script.

3. Next, we'll save our `index.html` file, and then use IntelliJ to open `index.html` in Google Chrome. With `index.html` open, you should see several icons representing available web browsers that can be used to view the HTML page, as shown in the following screenshot:

```
<!DOCTYPE html>
<html lang="en">
    <head>
        <meta charset="UTF-8">
        <title>HelloKotlinJS</title>
    </head>
    <body bgcolor="#E6E6FA">
        <script type="text/javascript" src="out/production/ch14/lib/kotlin.js"></script>
        <script type="text/javascript" src="out/production/ch14/ch14.js"></script>
    </body>
</html>
```

Opening this into our browser will enable us to examine the results of running our JavaScript. Once `index.html` is open, you should see an empty web page.

4. To view the results of our JavaScript within Google Chrome, navigate to **View** | **Developer** | **Developer Tools** | **Console**:

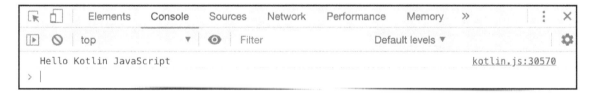

This will allow us to view any console output from our web page. Once the **Developer Tools** pane has opened, reload your web page and you should then see `"Hello Kotlin JavaScript"` printed out to the console. This is the result of running our `main()` function that has been transpiled into `ch14.js`.

With that, we've completed the journey of creating a new Kotlin project, writing a simple `Hello World` function in Kotlin, and then consuming that code as JavaScript within a simple web page. While this is a very basic example, it covers the primary workflow of targeting JavaScript with Kotlin.

In the next section, we'll explore more about how to integrate Kotlin code with other JavaScript, and we'll build on our example to use Kotlin to actually manipulate the content of our web page.

Integrating with existing JavaScript

We've now seen how to set up a basic Kotlin project that targets JavaScript and can then be run in a simple web app. But how can we start to build something more interesting using Kotlin? These days, web development is largely dominated by different libraries and frameworks aimed at making the development process easier and more efficient.

How does Kotlin fit in with these frameworks? How can you build a scalable web application with Kotlin? In this section, we're going to start answering these questions. We'll start with an overview of popular frameworks that are compatible with Kotlin, and then we'll dive a bit deeper and explore manipulating the DOM from our Kotlin code.

Working with other JavaScript frameworks

As was mentioned previously, the landscape of JavaScript development today is filled with third-party frameworks such as React, Node.js, and Vue.js. They enable JavaScript developers to be more efficient and to build better applications and services. This begs the question: Can we use Kotlin in conjunction with popular third-party JavaScript libraries?

Thankfully, the answer is yes. We can leverage our Kotlin code alongside these frameworks in a few different ways:

- Without direct interaction
- By converting TypeScript definitions to work with strongly typed APIs
- Interacting with non-strongly typed APIs directly using dynamic types

The most basic example of mixing Kotlin and JavaScript is writing Kotlin that doesn't rely on any direct interaction with other JavaScript frameworks. This is the approach we've seen so far in this chapter. Our `Hello World` code didn't know it was going to be run in a JavaScript environment. It didn't work with any framework, manipulate the DOM, or do other domain-specific tasks. This would be the same if we were simply writing our model objects in Kotlin so that they could be reused across multiple Kotlin projects. If we're working with simple data classes, there's a high likelihood they wouldn't need to be dependent on any specific JavaScript APIs.

What happens if we want to use a library that the Kotlin standard library doesn't provide JavaScript bindings for? Examples of this may include jQuery or React. In these cases, we have two options:

- Our first option is to search for any available TypeScript headers for the library and convert them to Kotlin bindings using the conversion tool available at `https://github.com/kotlin/ts2kt`. The `DefinitelyTyped` project is a repository of static TypeScript bindings for JavaScript libraries and frameworks. The repository contains definitions for thousands of libraries. If you find definitions for a library you wish to use, you can convert those definitions to Kotlin using the freely available `ts2kt` tool. When using `ts2kt`, we can generate a Kotlin file containing strongly typed bindings for whichever library we want to use. We can then reference those definitions from our Kotlin code.

> You can learn more about the `DefinitelyTyped` project for TypeScript definitions by visiting the GitHub repository: `https://github.com/DefinitelyTyped/DefinitelyTyped`.

- The second option is to use Kotlin's dynamic types to gain access to JavaScript functions that are available at runtime, but for which we don't have access to static bindings. By defining a variable as `dynamic`, we can call anything we would like on it, and it will not result in a compiler error. Take the following code snippet, for example:

```
// results in runtime error if invokeAnything() doesn't exist
val someObject: dynamic = null
someObject.invokeAnything()
```

This code compiles, but unless the `invokeAnything()` function is defined somewhere at runtime, this code will result in an exception, as demonstrated in the following screenshot:

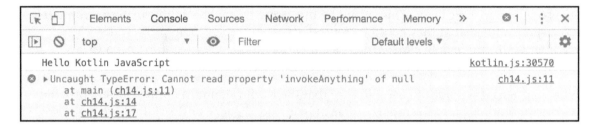

By using `dynamic` types, we have the flexibility to work with any JavaScript we need to, even if we don't have access to static bindings. As mentioned previously, we can find bindings for many popular libraries in the `DefinitelyTyped` repository that we can then make use of by converting them to Kotlin using `ts2kt`.

Additionally, JetBrains has provided its own repositories for several popular frameworks. Some of these are listed here:

- Wrappers for popular libraries such as React and Redux—https://github.com/JetBrains/kotlin-wrappers.
- A starter project for building a React app with Kotlin—https://github.com/JetBrains/create-react-kotlin-app.

Between available TypeScript definitions, the JetBrains-provided `kotlin-wrappers` repository, and dynamic types, Kotlin can potentially harness the full power and functionality of the JavaScript ecosystem.

To illustrate this, in the next section, we're going to generate jQuery bindings for Kotlin and use jQuery to manipulate our web page using Kotlin.

Manipulating the DOM via Kotlin

Let's walk through this concept of generating bindings to a third-party library to modify our web page using jQuery through our Kotlin code. To do this we're going to need to find TypeScript bindings for jQuery, convert those to Kotlin with `ts2kt`, and then use those bindings to manipulate our page from Kotlin.

By following these steps, we'll be able to add HTML elements to our web page programmatically from our Kotlin code:

1. First, install the `ts2kt` tool using the following `npm` command: `npm -g install ts2kt`.
2. Then, from the root directory of our project, install jQuery on your machine using `npm install jquery`. We'll need to test our project in our local development environment. This should result in a `node_modules` directory being added to the root level of the project. Within that folder, you should see a `jquery` directory.
3. Next, download the `jquery.d.ts` TypeScript definition file and save it to your root project directory. You can find the definitions here: `https://github.com/DefinitelyTyped/DefinitelyTyped/blob/types/jquery/jquery.d.ts`.
4. We can then convert those headers into Kotlin with the following command: `ts2kt -d src jquery.d.ts`. This will generate a `src/jquery.kt` file under the root directory. This file will contain all the required Kotlin bindings for jQuery. If you open the file, you'll notice most of the bindings are implemented as `external interface`.

At this point, we're ready to start using jQuery within our Kotlin code. Let's start off by adding a basic header to our page. To do so, we can use the following code:

```
fun main() {
    val outputMessage = "Hello Kotlin JavaScript"
    println(outputMessage)

    jQuery("body").append("<h1>We Added A Heading!!</h1>")

    ...
}
```

Running the code will append an `<h1>` tag to our `<body>` element when our script is loaded. Before we can see the results of this change, we need to include `jquery.js` as a script within `index.html`. This is what will allow our jQuery bindings to bind to the actual jQuery implementations. To include our local jQuery installation, add the following `<script>` tag to `index.html`:

```
<!DOCTYPE html>
<html lang="en">
    <head>
        <meta charset="UTF-8">
        <title>HelloKotlinJS</title>
    </head>
    <body bgcolor="#E6E6FA">
        <script src="node_modules/jquery/dist/jquery.js"></script>
```

```
        <script type="text/javascript"
         src="out/production/ch14/lib/kotlin.js"></script>
        <script type="text/javascript"
         src="out/production/ch14/ch14.js"></script>
    </body>
</html>
```

Now, we can rebuild our project and then reload `index.html` in our browser. Once you do, your page should now look like this:

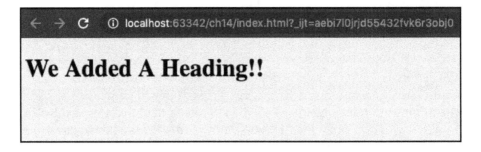

You can see that our `<h1>` element has been successfully added to our page. This is a small visual change, but a pretty large conceptual step. We were able to generate bindings for a popular JavaScript library, leverage those bindings from Kotlin, and use them to manipulate the content of our web page using a statically typed API.

Now, let's expand on this a bit by leveraging more Kotlin features to generate a more interesting web page. Here's how this is done:

1. Let's start by creating a `ViewState` data class that will contain the information to display on the page:

   ```
   data class ViewState(val title: String, val topics: List<String>)
   ```

2. Next, we'll create a `PagePresenter` class that will omit `ViewState` instances through a callback:

   ```
   class PagePresenter(private val viewStateListener: (ViewState) ->
   Unit) {

       init {
           viewStateListener(ViewState("Hello KotlinJS", headings))
       }
   }
   ```

3. We'll also define a list of topics that can be passed to our `ViewState`:

```
private val headings = listOf("Kotlin", "Programming",
"JavaScript")
```

4. Now, within `main.kt`, we can create a new instance of `PagePresenter`. Within the callback lambda, we can use jQuery to bind our `ViewState` properties to our web page:

```
val presenter = PagePresenter() {
    jQuery("body").append("<h1>${it.title}</h1>")
    it.topics.forEach {
        jQuery("body").append("<h2>${it}</h2>")
    }
}
```

Notice that within this callback, we're able to take advantage of Kotlin features such as String templates, and our Kotlin standard library functions such as `forEach()`. This makes it very easy to bind our `ViewState` to the UI by calling the appropriate jQuery functions.

If we rebuild this project and reload our web page, you should see that it now has a title and three subheadings:

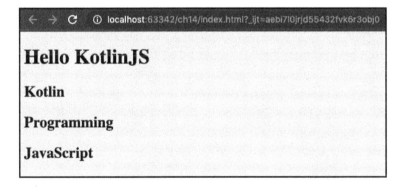

This example has shown how to start building for the web using JavaScript that is transpiled from type-safe Kotlin code. When writing in Kotlin, we can take advantage of familiar Kotlin features such as data classes and the Kotlin standard library and rely on the compiler to generate appropriate JavaScript for us. The ability to use existing, or generate new, JavaScript bindings for popular libraries means we aren't limited in how we can write JavaScript. Whether we want to use jQuery, React, Redux, Node.js, or other frameworks, the possibility of using Kotlin is available to us. In `Chapter 15`, *Introducing Multiplatform Kotlin*, we'll build on another, more interactive, example of using Kotlin for web development as we work within a multiplatform project.

Summary

In this chapter, we've explored how Kotlin can be used for frontend web development. We saw how Kotlin can target JavaScript, and be transpiled into human-readable JavaScript code that can then be consumed like any other JavaScript. We also discussed how Kotlin can work alongside existing popular JavaScript libraries by using dynamic types, or by generating Kotlin bindings using TypeScript definitions and the `ts2kt` tool. Finally, we put these concepts together to create a simple Kotlin project that targets JavaScript. This project's resulting JavaScript was loaded into a simple HTML document, and then manipulated programmatically from Kotlin using generated jQuery bindings. This sample project demonstrated several of the potential benefits of using Kotlin for web development: strong typing, the Kotlin standard library, and a familiar programming language for those who don't use JavaScript.

In the next chapter, we'll continue to explore additional compilation targets for Kotlin.

Questions

1. Does Kotlin run natively in a JavaScript environment?
2. How is your Kotlin project made usable within a JavaScript project?
3. What does it mean to transpile code?
4. What are two potential benefits of using Kotlin for JavaScript development?
5. What are two ways of building a Kotlin project with a JavaScript target?
6. Which common JavaScript modules is Kotlin compatible with?
7. Is it true or false that Kotlin is compatible with third-party JavaScript frameworks?

Further reading

- *Hands-On Cross-Platform Development with Kotlin* (https://www.packtpub.com/application-development/hands-cross-platform-development-kotlin)
- *Professional JavaScript* (https://www.packtpub.com/application-development/professional-javascript-0)

Introducing Multiplatform Kotlin

15

Kotlin multiplatform is an exciting new option for achieving code sharing across multiple build targets. With a Kotlin multiplatform project, we can write Kotlin code that is then used across the web, Android, iOS, and a variety of native targets. By writing common implementations of model objects, key business logic, and so on, we can reduce the amount of overall code we have to write and can write, test, and reuse common components. In this chapter, we'll explore Kotlin's take on multiplatform programming, including how to create a new multiplatform project, how to target multiple platforms with shared code, and some of the pros and cons of using Kotlin multiplatform in its current state.

The following topics will be covered in this chapter:

- Introducing Kotlin multiplatform
- Creating your first Kotlin multiplatform project
- Building a Kotlin multiplatform project
- Understanding the limitations of Kotlin multiplatform

Technical requirements

In order to download, compile, and execute the samples found in this chapter, the following is required:

- IntelliJ IDEA 2018.3 Community or Ultimate editions or newer
- Xcode 10.2 or newer
- CocoaPods installed
- Android SDK installed (refer to the README.md file of this chapter)
- An internet connection
- Git and GitHub (optional)

To download all of the code in this chapter, including the examples and code snippets, please refer to the following GitHub link: `https://github.com/ PacktPublishing/Mastering-Kotlin/tree/master/Chapter15`.

Introducing Kotlin multiplatform

For many years, new and different solutions have been developed for sharing code across multiple build targets. They all have their own unique take on the idea of multiplatform support, and often achieve that goal in very different ways. With Kotlin, developers have yet another possible solution for writing code once and reusing it for varying build targets.

In this section, we're going to take a look at how Kotlin approaches multiplatform support and how the Kotlin multiplatform approach differs from other cross-platform solutions. Primarily, we'll illustrate the fact that Kotlin multiplatform enables developers to share code across multiple projects in a relatively low-risk fashion not present in other cross-platform solutions.

Understanding how Kotlin approaches multiplatform

What is Kotlin multiplatform? What does it mean to build a Kotlin multiplatform project, and what are the benefits? We're going to answer those questions in this section.

Understanding the value of Kotlin multiplatform

Kotlin multiplatform is Kotlin's approach to the sharing of data models, logic, and domain expertise across multiple target platforms. The goal is to remove the need to write code multiple times for each of the various platforms you target. By leveraging shared expertise, shared code, and shared validation, developers can potentially reduce bugs, reduce the amount of code written, limit maintenance costs, and ship projects more quickly.

Because Kotlin can be compiled to many different build targets, developers can write code that can be deployed to these various targets while also still leveraging native components when needed.

Targeting multiple platforms

The key characteristic of Kotlin that makes Kotlin multiplatform possible is that it can be compiled to a wide variety of build targets. Currently, these build targets include the following:

- JVM
- Android
- JavaScript
- Native:
    - iOS (`arm32`, `arm64`, simulator `x86_64`)
    - Windows (`mingw32` and `x86_64`)
    - Linux (`x86_64`, `arm32`, MIPS, MIPS little endian, Raspberry Pi)
    - macOS (`x86_64`)
    - WebAssembly (`wasm32`)

While Kotlin compiles to each of these platforms, these platforms don't share the exact same functionality. Instead of trying to provide a common set of functionality that works across all possible platforms, Kotlin enables developers to define platform-specific implementations of types, interfaces, classes, and so on. This is founded on the `expect` and `actual` keywords, which operate very similarly to an interface.

By defining a type with `expect`, we can inform the compiler that within our shared code, we can rely on some expected API to be available. For each individual platform, we can then use `actual` to define what that platform-specific implementation looks like. This allows developers to rely on native APIs whenever possible while still writing shared, platform-agnostic Kotlin code.

When a Kotlin multiplatform project is then compiled, only the actual implementations for that platform are included in the build artifact. That artifact might be JavaScript, which is to be included within a web page, a shared library for use within an iOS application, or it could be native Kotlin itself within an Android application. In any case, Kotlin multiplatform projects aim to provide mechanisms with which to share code without taking a heavy-handed approach and limiting how that code must be shared or consumed.

This less heavy-handed approach is a bit different from other cross-platform solutions and, in the next section, we'll dive deeper into what makes Kotlin multiplatform different to these existing solutions.

Differentiating Kotlin multiplatform

The potential to target multiple platforms with a single code base isn't a new concept. In the world of mobile development alone, there have been several popular cross-platform solutions, including Cordova, Xamarin, React Native, and, quite recently, Flutter. All of these, in theory, enable developers to write a single application and then deploy that application to multiple targets, typically, Android and iOS. So, what makes Kotlin multiplatform different from these solutions?

Sharing logic, not UI

Possibly the greatest differentiating factor between Kotlin multiplatform and other existing cross-platform approaches is the fact that Kotlin multiplatform aims to share logic, not UI elements. With Kotlin multiplatform, you can share things such as model objects, important business logic, and tests. However, it is likely that you wouldn't be sharing any UI elements across your build targets. This is in stark contrast to solutions such as React Native or Flutter, which tightly integrate the logic and UI for an application.

In a typical Kotlin multiplatform project, models, business logic, high-level architecture, tests, and more would be defined in common Kotlin code. That code would then be consumed by each individual platform and bound to the UI using native components. This means that any Kotlin multiplatform application is likely to have a native look and feel, whereas some cross-platform solutions struggle to feel truly native.

By limiting the scope of what is shared in Kotlin code, Kotlin multiplatform projects also come with a desirable trait of more limited risk.

Limiting risk

Because Kotlin multiplatform projects don't share both logic and UI across build targets, it becomes easier to integrate Kotlin multiplatform modules within an existing project. The shared code can simply be consumed as if it were any other dependency. It also means that a new Kotlin multiplatform application is still going to rely on familiar native tools and tech stacks in at least the UI layer.

All of these things together lead to lower the risk of adopting Kotlin multiplatform when compared to a more heavy-handed cross-platform approach such as React Native or Flutter. In a Kotlin multiplatform code base, if a shared component is not performant enough, it can't wrap a native API properly, or if it has any other issue, it can easily be swapped out for a native implementation with minimal impact. This is not always the case with other cross-platform approaches.

Because of an emphasis on shared logic and a low barrier to entry, Kotlin multiplatform is well positioned for existing applications that want to start sharing code but can't afford to migrate large portions of their code to a new tech stack, or want to minimize the number of new tools/languages required to share code.

In the next section, we'll walk through the setup of a new Kotlin multiplatform project to better understand how to share Kotlin code across multiple build targets.

Creating your first Kotlin multiplatform project

In this section, we're going to walk through what is required to create a simple Kotlin multiplatform project that targets Android, iOS, and the web. We'll break the process down, module by module, to highlight the differences in project setup for each build target.

By the end of the chapter, we'll have a simple `Hello World` project running on all three target platforms using code from a shared Kotlin module.

Creating a shared module

At the core of Kotlin multiplatform is shared code. To start building our project, we'll begin by creating a new Gradle module that will contain our shared Kotlin code:

1. First, we'll create a new, empty Gradle project within IntelliJ. When we're finished, we should have a project structure that looks similar to the following:

```
root
  .gradle/
  .idea/
  gradle/
  build.gradle
  gradlew
  gradlew.bat
  settings.gradle
```

2. We now want to update `build.gradle` so that we can define `classpath` dependencies, which will be needed by other modules. The resulting `build.gradle` file should look something like this:

```
buildscript {
    ext {
        kotlin_version = '1.3.31'
    }

    repositories {
        google()
        jcenter()
        mavenCentral()
    }
    dependencies {
        classpath 'com.android.tools.build:gradle:3.2.0'
        classpath "org.jetbrains.kotlin:kotlin-gradle-
                    plugin:$kotlin_version"
    }
}

allprojects {
    repositories {
        google()
        jcenter()
        maven { url 'https://dl.bintray.com/kotlin/kotlin' }
    }
}
```

With this in place, our Android project will have the Gradle plugins it needs once that project is added.

3. Next, within this new project directory, we're going to create another Gradle module named `:core` to store our shared Kotlin code. This module should have the following structure:

```
root/core
    build.gradle
    src/commonMain/kotlin
    src/androidMain/kotlin
    src/iosMain/kotlin
    src/jsMain/kotlin
```

This `:core` module is where we will configure which platforms our multiplatform project will target, and it's where we will define common Kotlin types, interfaces, and models. Within the `src/` directory, we've defined source sets that will correspond to each of our target platforms, and a common source set to define the common types.

To ensure that our root-level project recognizes the new `:core` module, we will update `settings.gradle` to include the new module:

```
// settings/gradle
include 'core'
```

As we continue adding new modules to our project, we'll be updating `settings.gradle` accordingly.

4. Now that our `:core` module is in place, we will update `core/build.gradle` to define our multiplatform build targets using the `kotlin-multiplatform` Gradle plugin, as follows:

```
plugins {id "org.jetbrains.kotlin.multiplatform" }

kotlin {
    js()
    jvm("android")
// Change to iosArm64 (or iosArm32) to
// build library for iPhone device
    iosX64("ios") {
        binaries { framework("core") }
    }

    sourceSets {
        commonMain {
            dependencies {
                implementation kotlin('stdlib-common')
            }
        }
        androidMain {
            dependencies {
                implementation kotlin('stdlib')
            }
        }
        iosMain { }
        jsMain {
            dependencies {
                implementation kotlin('stdlib-js')
            }
```

```
            }
        }
    }
```

Notice at the top of `core/build.gradle` that we've added `plugins {id "org.jetbrains.kotlin.multiplatform" }`. This plugin gives us access to Kotlin multiplatform configuration functions that control how our multiplatform project should be built. Within the `kotlin {}` block, we define each of our build targets using the various platform-specific functions:

- `js()`
- `jvm("android")`
- `iosX64("ios")`

These indicate to the compiler what build targets we are expecting. Finally, within the `sourceSets {}` block, we can define further configuration and dependencies for specific platforms. Notice that we've added Kotlin standard library dependencies for each build target. By providing platform-specific dependencies, we can ensure that we have common Kotlin functionality in the source files for each platform.

5. With our build configuration in place, it's time to start adding some shared Kotlin code. To begin, we'll create a new Kotlin file, `core/src/commonMain/kotlin/Sample.kt`, and this file will define a `Platform` class to be available across all source sets:

```
expect object Platform {
    val name: String
}
```

The `Platform` object contains a single property, `name`, which we will use to provide platform-specific names from our shared `:core` module. This is possible because of the `expect` modifier we've added to the declaration of `Platform`. By using `expect`, we indicate to the compiler that each of our target source sets should contain a platform-specific implementation of the `Platform` type.

6. Now that we've added an `expect Platform` object, we will create the platform-specific implementations within our other source sets, starting with Android. We'll create a new file, `core/src/androidMain/kotlin/AndroidSample.kt`, and define `Platform` for our Android source set. The following code shows this:

```
// core/src/androidMain/kotlin/AndroidSample.kt
actual object Platform {
    actual val name: String = "Android"
}
```

Notice that our declaration of `Platform` looks very similar to the original, but with two key differences:

- We've added the `actual` modifier to the declaration of `Platform`.
- We've added the `actual` modifier to the declaration of the `name` property.

The `actual` modifier is how the compiler knows which `actual` types to match to any `expect` types that have been defined in our common source sets.

Now, we'll repeat this process for our iOS and JavaScript targets:

1. First, we'll add the `actual` modifier for our iOS sources:

```
// core/src/iosMain/kotlin/iosSample.kt
actual object Platform {
    actual val name: String = "iOS"
}
```

2. Now, we'll add the `actual` modifier for our JavaScript sources:

```
// core/src/jsMain/kotlin/JsSample.kt
actual object Platform {
    actual val name: String = "Javascript"
}
```

With those added files in place, we now have a `Platform` object that can be used generically from any shared code, but will be swapped out with platform-specific implementations at compile time for each target. The `expect` and `actual` modifiers allow us to define types similarly to how we might define an interface, and then provide actual implementations for each platform based on the needs of that platform.

Now that our `:core` module is in place, we'll start adding platform-specific projects that will consume our common code. We'll start by adding the Android project.

Adding an Android app

We now want to create a new Gradle module in our project that will contain the Android project. You can do this by right-clicking the root package in the IDE and navigating to **New** | **Module**. We'll name this module `:androidapp` and, after its initial creation, it should have the following structure:

```
root/androidapp
    build.gradle
    src/main/java/com/packt/kotlinmultiplatform/MainActivity.kt
    src/main/res/*
    AndroidManifest.xml
```

The `src/main/res/` directory will simply contain the default resources created by Android Studio or IntelliJ and these aren't a factor in how we will consume our shared Kotlin code.

`androidapp/build.gradle` is a standard Android `build.gradle` file as we saw previously in Chapter 13, *Kotlin on Android*, with one key difference. We've added a dependency to the `:core` module. The following code snippet demonstrates this:

```
apply plugin: 'com.android.application'
apply plugin: 'kotlin-android'
apply plugin: 'kotlin-android-extensions'

android {
    compileSdkVersion 28
    defaultConfig {
        applicationId "com.packt.androidmultiplatform"
        minSdkVersion 21
        targetSdkVersion 28
        ...
    }
    ...
}
```

```
dependencies {
    implementation project(":core")
    implementation fileTree(dir: 'libs', include: ['*.jar'])
    implementation"org.jetbrains.kotlin:kotlin-stdlib-jdk7:1.3.31"
    ...
}
```

The dependency on :core allows us to access the common Kotlin types, functions, and more that have been defined. We can consume those types within our Android app's code.

Then, within our MainActivity.kt file, we can access Platform.name and use that String value to update our UI. Consider the following code for it:

```
// MainActivity.kt
class MainActivity : AppCompatActivity() {

  override fun onCreate(savedInstanceState: Bundle?) {
    super.onCreate(savedInstanceState)
    setContentView(R.layout.activity_main)

    val textView = findViewById<TextView>(R.id.textView)
    textView.text = Platform.name
  }
}
```

Once our :androidapp module is updated to consume the Platform class, we just need to update settings.gradle to recognize our new :androidapp module, as follows:

```
// settings.gradle
include ':core', ':androidapp'
```

Our Android app is now able to consume any shared code we add to the :core module. We'll look at consuming more interesting shared code later on in this chapter. For now, let's move over to iOS and see how to add and configure the iOS project.

Adding an iOS app

Now we're ready to add the iOS project to our Kotlin multiplatform project. To try this, perform the following steps:

1. To get started, we'll create a new root-level directory in our project named `iosapp`. Within this directory, we will then need to create a new iOS Xcode project using the **Single View App** template:

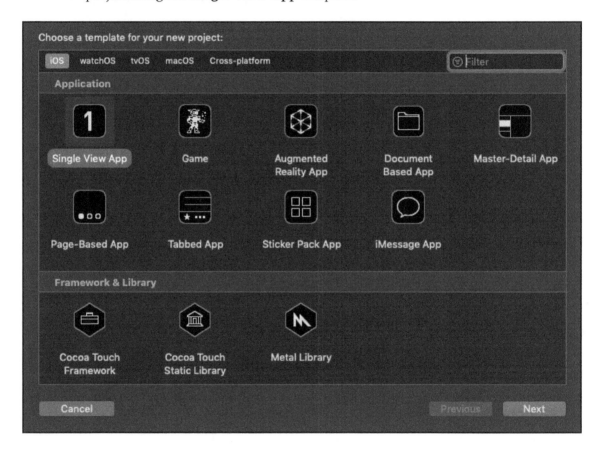

2. After clicking **Next**, you'll be prompted to fill in your project details:

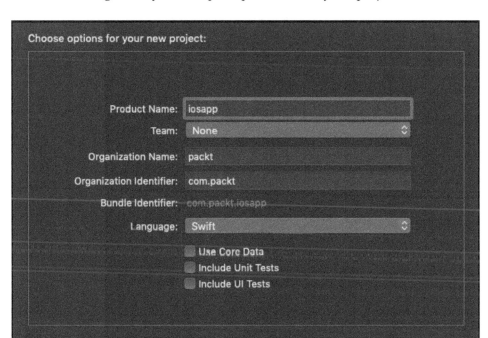

In this case, we'll name this project `iosapp` and then click **Next** to choose the project directory. Here, we'll specify our `root/iosapp` directory and click **Create**.

When that default project is created, we should have a project structure similar to the following:

```
root/iosapp
    iosapp/
    iosapp.xcodeproject/
    iosapp.xcworspace/
```

3. Now, we'll work on integrating our shared Kotlin code with our newly created iOS project. To do this, we will use the `native-cocoapods` plugin within our `:core` module. We can add this plugin by updating `core/build.gradle`:

```
plugins {
    id "org.jetbrains.kotlin.multiplatform"
    id 'org.jetbrains.kotlin.native.cocoapods'
```

```
    }

    // CocoaPods requires a podspec version be defined
    version = "1.0"

kotlin {

    cocoapods {
        // Configure fields required by CocoaPods.
        summary = "https://packt.com"
        homepage = "Example of Kotlin multiplatform project"
    }
    ...
}
```

Adding this plugin will generate a new Gradle task called `podspec`. Before we run this new Gradle task, we need to add the following line to `gradle.properties`:

```
// gradle.properties
-Pkotlin.native.cocoapods.generate.wrapper=true
```

This line will help to prevent Xcode compatibility issues, and will ensure that the output of the task is correct. Running the `podspec` task will create a `core.podspec` file within our `:core` module. Using `core.podspec`, we can add our `iosMain` source set as a framework dependency of our iOS project using Cocoapods.

4. Now that we have our `core/core.podspec` file, we need to create a Podfile within our `iosapp` directory. This Podfile will allow us to include our shared Kotlin code as a native framework. For this basic example, our Podfile should look something like this:

```
target 'iosapp' do
# Comment the next line if you don't want to use dynamic frameworks
  use_frameworks!

  # Pods for iosmultiplatform
  pod 'core', :path => '../core'
end
```

There are three key things to note within this Podfile:

- The `target 'iosapp' do` should refer to whatever the name of our Xcode project is. In this case, it refers to a project called `iosapp`.
- The `use_frameworks!` declaration is required to allow us to build our Kotlin framework when the Xcode project is built.
- When defining the pod, the name and path of the pod should match what is defined within `core/core.podspec`.

Once the Podfile is defined, navigate to the `iosapp` directory and run `pod install` from the command line. Once this is complete, you should be able to build your Xcode project and consume the shared Kotlin framework.

To demonstrate the consumption of the shared framework, we can update the default `ViewController.swift` file to display `Platform.name` on the screen. The following code snippet demonstrates this:

```
// ViewController.swift
import UIKit
import core

class ViewController: UIViewController {

    override func viewDidLoad() {
        super.viewDidLoad()
        let label = UILabel(frame: CGRect(x: 0, y: 0,
                             width: 300, height: 21))
        label.center = CGPoint(x: 160, y: 285)
        label.textAlignment = .center
        label.font = label.font.withSize(25)
        label.text = Platform.init().name
        view.addSubview(label)
    }

}
```

All that is required to use the shared Kotlin code is a build of the Xcode project to generate the framework. Then, we simply import the framework using `import core`, and we are free to use our `Platform` type.

Now that our iOS project is set up, let's examine how to set up a simple HTML page that uses the shared Kotlin code.

Adding a web page

To consume the JavaScript target of our shared Kotlin code, we will create a new Gradle module called `:webapp` and then create a simple HTML page that will consume the compiled JavaScript code. Perform the following steps for this:

1. To start, create a new Gradle module, `:webapp`, with the following structure:

   ```
   root/webapp
       build.gradle
       src/main/kotlin
       src/index.html
   ```

2. Within `webapp/build.gradle`, we will use the `kotlin2js` plugin to configure how our `:webapp` module should be built:

   ```
   apply plugin: 'kotlin2js'

   dependencies {
       compile "org.jetbrains.kotlin:kotlin-stdlib-js"
       implementation project(':core')
   }

   compileKotlin2Js.kotlinOptions.sourceMap = true
   compileKotlin2Js.kotlinOptions.outputFile =
   "${projectDir}/output/js/app.js"
   compileKotlin2Js.kotlinOptions.suppressWarnings = true
   compileKotlin2Js.kotlinOptions.verbose = true
   ```

   Notice that we've added a dependency to `:core` that will allow us to reference our shared Kotlin types with this module. We've configured several properties of the `kotlin2js` plugin, the most important one being `outputFile`. This `outputFile` path is where the JavaScript output for our `:webapp` directory will be saved.

3. Before we can start writing new Kotlin code and build our web page, we need to add a new Gradle task to our `:webapp` module. This task will be responsible for expanding the build artifacts of our JavaScript built target from `:core`. This is required because we need to be able to include the JavaScript implementations of the Kotlin standard library along with whatever Kotlin code we write/deploy within our `:webapp` module. To add this task, we can make the following updates to `webapp/build.gradle`:

   ```
   // webapp/build.gradle
   ...
   ```

```
task assembleWeb(type: Sync) {
    configurations.compile.each { File file ->
        from(zipTree(file.absolutePath), {
            includeEmptyDirs = false
include { fileTreeElement ->
def path = fileTreeElement.path
path.endsWith(".js") && (path.startsWith("META-INF/resources/") ||
!path.startsWith("META-INF/"))
}
})
}
from compileKotlin2Js.destinationDir
into "${projectDir}/output"

    dependsOn classes
}

assemble.dependsOn assembleWeb
```

 This code is part of the official documentation for setting up the `kotlin.js` portion of a Kotlin multiplatform project.

4. Now, we're ready to start building our web page. First, we'll define a new file, `webapp/src/main/kotlin/main.kt`, and define the following Kotlin function:

```
fun main() {
    val outputMessage = "Hello Kotlin ${Platform.name}"
    println(outputMessage)
}
```

This function will access `Platform.name` and print that out to the console.

5. Next, to compile the required build artifacts for `:webapp`, run the `assemble` and `assembleWeb` Gradle tasks. This should generate two important build artifacts:
   - `webapp/output/kotlin.js`
   - `webapp/output/js/app.js`

6. Now, we can consume those build artifacts from `index.html`. We will load them as scripts so that when the web page is loaded, `Platform.name` is printed out to the console, as follows:

```html
<!DOCTYPE html>
<html lang="en">
<head>
    <meta charset="UTF-8">
    <title>JS Multiplatform</title>
</head>
<body bgcolor="#E6E6FA">
<script type="text/javascript" src="../output/kotlin.js"></script>
<script type="text/javascript" src="../output/js/app.js"></script>
</body>
</html>
```

7. Once `index.html` is updated, you should be able to open the page in your browser from IntelliJ, as we did previously in this book, and see the console output using the developer tools.

With our HTML page consuming our compiled JavaScript, we now have three different projects in place that are making using of our shared Kotlin code.

In the next section, we'll further explore how to go about writing shared Kotlin code that can be consumed by various build targets.

Building a Kotlin multiplatform project

We've now seen how we can set up a Kotlin multiplatform project that shares Kotlin code across multiple build targets. In this section, we'll discuss more about how you can write and architect your multiplatform code, and also explore the current state of available multiplatform libraries that can be leveraged to build a multiplatform project.

Writing multiplatform Kotlin

In this previous section, we shared a single, simple class that exposed a platform-specific string. This demonstrated how we can leverage the `expect` and `actual` modifiers, but the overall example was quite simple. In this section, let's look at a slightly more interesting example of how we can architect common code and consume it across the different projects we've created.

For this, we perform the following steps:

1. First, we're going to create a data class called `ViewState` to represent the data
    we want displayed to the screen. We'll define that class in a new
    file, `core/src/commonMain/kotlin/ViewState.kt`:

    ```
    data class ViewState(val title: String, val subtitle: String)
    ```

    `ViewState` will simply hold two strings: a title and a subtitle. We'll be using
    those shortly to update our UI.

2. Next, we're going to create a `Presenter` class within our `:core` module. This
    `Presenter` class will expose a listener that will provide instances of `ViewState`,
    and it will have a method for handling clicks:

    ```
    class Presenter {

        private var count = 0
        private var viewState = ViewState(Platform.name,
                                    "Clicked ${++count} times")
            set(value) {
                field = value
                viewStateListener?.invoke(value)
            }

        var viewStateListener: ((ViewState) -> Unit)? = null
            set(value) {
                field = value
                value?.invoke(viewState)
            }

        fun onClick() {
            viewState = viewState.copy(subtitle =
                            "Clicked ${++count} times")
        }
    }
    ```

    With this `Presenter` class, we can define how state and interactions are managed
    in a platform-independent way, and then reuse this class across our different
    build targets.

3. Now, we're going to make use of our new `Presenter` class within our
   `:androidapp` module. We'll update `MainActivity.kt` to use the presenter to
   respond to click events and to update our UI:

```kotlin
class MainActivity : AppCompatActivity() {

    lateinit var title: TextView
    lateinit var subtitle: TextView
    lateinit var button: Button

    override fun onCreate(savedInstanceState: Bundle?) {
        super.onCreate(savedInstanceState)
        setContentView(R.layout.activity_main)

        title = findViewById(R.id.titleText)
        subtitle = findViewById(R.id.subtitleText)
        button = findViewById(R.id.button)

        val presenter = Presenter().apply {
            viewStateListener = {
                title.text = it.title
                subtitle.text = it.subtitle
            }
        }

        button.setOnClickListener { presenter.onClick() }
    }
}
```

We've updated `MainActivity.kt` to work with three views: two `TextViews`
and a `Button`. We create an instance of `Presenter`, and then assign
`viewStateListener` so that we can respond to changes in the `ViewState` by
updating our UI. We then set a click listener on the button that calls
`Presenter.onClick()`.

The result is that when the button is clicked, UI should be updated to display the
number of times the button has been clicked.

4. To demonstrate the fact that `Presenter` can be used across various targets, we'll
   now update our iOS app to use `Presenter` in the same way as the Android app.
   To do this, we'll update `iosapp/iosapp/ViewController.swift`:

```swift
class ViewController: UIViewController {
    let presenter = Presenter()

    override func viewDidLoad() {
```

```
        super.viewDidLoad()
        let title = UILabel(frame: CGRect(x: 0, y: 0,
                            width: 300, height: 21))
        title.center = CGPoint(x: 160, y: 285)
        title.textAlignment = .center
        title.font = title.font.withSize(25)
        view.addSubview(title)
        let subtitle = UILabel(frame: CGRect(x: 0, y: 0,
                            width: 300, height: 21))
        subtitle.center = CGPoint(x: 160, y: 385)
        subtitle.textAlignment = .center
        subtitle.font = subtitle.font.withSize(25)
        view.addSubview(subtitle)
        let button = UIButton(frame: CGRect(x: 0, y: 0,
                            width: 300, height: 21))
        button.center = CGPoint(x: 160, y: 485)
        button.setTitle("Click Me", for: .normal)
        button.backgroundColor = UIColor(red: 0, green: 50/255,
                                    blue: 51/255, alpha: 0.5)
        view.addSubview(button)
        presenter.viewStateListener = {
            title.text = $0.title
            subtitle.text = $0.subtitle
            return KotlinUnit()
        }
        button.addTarget(self, action: #selector(buttonClicked),
                        for: .touchUpInside)
    }
    @objc func buttonClicked() {
        presenter.onClick()
    }
}
```

Once again, we are using `Presenter` to listen to changes in `ViewState`, and to respond to click events. Notice that the changes to the iOS project look very similar to that of the Android project. With a Kotlin multiplatform project, if you can define common abstractions in the shared code, then the work remaining for every specific platform is mostly to perform simple binding of the data to the UI. Because the general pattern becomes unified across platforms, the ultimate implementation of the UI layer across all platforms will likely be quite similar.

In the next section, we'll see how we can use available multiplatform libraries to simplify the development process and to help make our common architecture unique across all platforms.

Leveraging multiplatform libraries

We've now seen several examples of how to write and share common Kotlin code. However, if you're building a real application today, you likely don't want to build everything from scratch. You're probably going to need things such as networking, serialization, settings, and dependency injection. You might want to leverage reactive programming paradigms, or use common tools such as Firebase. For these situations, it's of great benefit to have third-party libraries available that you can rely on for multiplatform implementations.

As of today, the third-party library ecosystem for Kotlin multiplatform is pretty limited. Because the technology is relatively new, there aren't many options out there yet. However, there are a few libraries available that may be quite helpful:

- `ktor`—a Kotlin-based framework for asynchronous servers and clients that can be leveraged for multiplatform networking.
- `kodein`—a dependency injection framework.
- `sqldelight`—provides APIs for working with SQLite across JVM, Android, and iOS.
- `multiplatform-settings`—a multiplatform implementation of simple key/value pairs.
- `kotlinx.coroutines`—coroutines are supported in multiplatform projects and can be used in your common code to solve structured concurrency problems.
- `kotlinx.coroutines.flow`—provides, cold, asynchronous data streams similar to what you might be familiar with from RxJava. When combined with coroutine-based channels, you can achieve highly reactive code within Kotlin.
- `Reaktive`—a Kotlin multiplatform implementation of reactive extensions.

While this is a small set of well established libraries, many more libraries are in active development, including implementations for Firebase, logging, and I/O. As more and more developers begin to work with Kotlin multiplatform, the developer ecosystem should continue to expand, making it easier to find existing tools and libraries.

While quite exciting in its current state, like everything, Kotlin multiplatform has some drawbacks. In the next section, we will study a few limitations of the Kotlin multiplatform approach to cross-platform code.

Understanding the limitations of Kotlin multiplatform

Kotlin multiplatform presents an interesting new opportunity for sharing mission-critical business logic and operational expertise. However, as with any technical solution, there are limitations and trade-offs.

In this section, we're going to examine some of these limitations to help you better understand the requirements of Kotlin multiplatform and when you may want to consider it for your project.

Understanding operational requirements

Perhaps the largest consideration when evaluating Kotlin multiplatform for your projects, teams, and organizations is whether or not you want a fully cross-platform solution, or want to share models and logic but stick to native UI. As was discussed previously in the *Sharing logic, not UI* section of this chapter, Kotlin multiplatform doesn't generally touch the UI layer of your application. As such, building applications with Kotlin multiplatform still requires knowledge of native platforms and the building of native UI for each of those platforms. This is in stark contrast to solutions such as React Native or Flutter, in which the business logic and UI are both defined in common code and shared across the various platform targets.

The difference in shared UI versus shared business logic impacts the team structure as well. With any cross-platform solution, knowledge of the native platforms is useful. However, with Kotlin multiplatform, it's truly critical. Without native code for the UI layer and integration of shared Kotlin code, there will be no application. React Native, Flutter, Xamarin, and so on present the possibility of the entire application being written in shared code. For example, you could build a mobile development team consisting of primarily JavaScript developers that leverage React Native to build your apps, and it's likely that the majority of these developers would rarely need to interact with native platform tools or code. When considering Kotlin multiplatform, React Native, Flutter, or any other cross-platform solution, it's important to think about your current team structure, skills, and long-term hiring strategy.

As you consider how to build a team that is leveraging some form of code-sharing or cross-platform solution, it's important to consider the skills and technologies required in relation to your current team, along with potential future hiring needs.

With Kotlin multiplatform, each application will still require native code and tools. For example, your web team can still use familiar frameworks such as React and Redux while consuming shared Kotlin code. Your Android and iOS developers will still likely be working within Android Studio and Xcode as they integrate the shared Kotlin code and build out native UI components. If you have several existing platform development teams, Kotlin multiplatform might represent a low barrier-to-entry solution with which to start sharing code among those existing teams. This is quite different to a solution such as Flutter, which is a much more all-or-nothing approach to cross platform.

Because of the reliance on existing native tools, code, and expertise, Kotlin multiplatform is a relatively low-risk option for experimenting with code sharing. Integrating Kotlin multiplatform code with an existing project is quite simple, especially for Android and JavaScript, and can be done in very small increments with little to no impact on existing code. This makes it very easy to try out within a team, as well as easy to replace if it doesn't meet your needs. These two traits significantly lower the operational risk involved when compared to solutions such as React Native and Flutter.

Beyond the conceptual differences between Kotlin multiplatform and other cross-platform solutions, there are more tangible differences and limitations in the development ecosystems of the various approaches. In the next section, we're going to discuss the current state of the Kotlin multiplatform ecosystem and what limitations this may entail.

Understanding Kotlin multiplatform ecosystem limitations

The developer ecosystem around a technology can be an important consideration when evaluating said technology. That evaluation may include things such as first- and third-party documentation, third-party libraries, samples, and tools. These can all make it much easier to develop with a technology, and act as a rough metric for the support behind that technology; both of which are desirable when investing in a solution.

Currently, the Kotlin multiplatform ecosystem is quite new and limited. There are not a lot of third-party Kotlin multiplatform libraries available at the moment. Examples and documentation are also very limited when compared to native development, or even other cross-platform solutions such as React Native and Flutter.

Because Kotlin multiplatform is so new, and supporting tools, libraries, and examples are limited, if you start building a Kotlin multiplatform project today, you may find yourself having to solve problems on your own. If you find a need for a particular API, you may have to write it yourself rather than defaulting to a commonly used library specific to a platform.

As Kotlin multiplatform tooling improves, and more developers begin to adopt the Kotlin multiplatform approach, it's likely that the developer ecosystem around Kotlin multiplatform will mature as well. In the next section, we'll explore some of the areas in which tooling will be improving.

Understanding framework and tooling limitations

Kotlin's support for multiplatform projects continues to evolve as JetBrains invests more energy into making it work smoothly across all Kotlin compilation targets. Currently, the developer experience for Kotlin multiplatform projects varies quite a bit depending on which platform you're targeting.

For JVM and Android projects, shared Kotlin code can be consumed very easily. In fact, it can sit right alongside the rest of your project. This isn't much of a surprise considering the popularity of Kotlin for Android. For iOS and other native targets, the experience is not as smooth. Generating a shared framework for a native target, or incorporating it into an iOS project as a Cocoapod is fairly straightforward. However, debugging this shared Kotlin code is currently quite difficult. It's possible to attach a command-line debugger, but debugging directly from Xcode or other IDEs is currently under development. Targeting JavaScript is a straightforward process, as we've seen in Chapter 14, *Kotlin and Web Development*, though there are fundamental platform differences that must be considered when writing Kotlin code for a JavaScript target.

One area of Kotlin multiplatform projects that will require careful attention is that of threading and concurrency. For example, the JVM is multithreaded, while JavaScript is single-threaded. If you're used to writing JVM or Android applications, you will have to rethink how you write and manage currency abstractions when targeting JavaScript. If you're leveraging coroutines across these shared targets, you may also have to consider that coroutines are not currently multithreaded, so you can't simply rely on them to solve your concurrency needs. It's entirely conceivable that you would need to write your own abstraction layer that can default to platform-specific concurrency paradigms when necessary.

All of these limitations are things that can be fixed, and are being worked on. As JetBrains, Google, and other developers continue to invest in Kotlin, and specifically Kotlin multiplatform, the overall developer experience should continue to improve.

Summary

This chapter has hopefully illustrated the interesting potential of Kotlin multiplatform to achieve code sharing between multiple targets. Kotlin multiplatform differs from other cross-platform solutions. In this, it aims to share logic and models, not UI. Because of this distinction, Kotlin multiplatform offers a lower-risk proposition when compared to frameworks such as React Native or Flutter. It is quite simple to write a small function or model in Kotlin and then share that across multiple platforms, where it can be consumed as a simple dependency.

Kotlin multiplatform projects can be configured and built via Gradle, making it easy to define various build targets and then generate any required build artifacts. Within a Kotlin multiplatform project, implementations can be shared across all platforms, or they can be customized based on each platform using the `expect` and `actual` keywords. By leveraging these keywords, and clean software engineering practices, it's possible to create common APIs that leverage platform-specific tools and implementations where needed.

While Kotlin multiplatform is a promising proposition for achieving code sharing, it does have its limitations. The Kotlin multiplatform ecosystem is still in its infancy, and may not have third-party libraries available for tools/services you're accustomed to using such as Firebase, or simple logging. Additionally, there are complexities associated with how threading works across various platforms that may require a strong understanding of concurrency to ensure your applications are performant and error free. As the Kotlin multiplatform ecosystem and support continue to advance, it will likely become easier and easier to build applications using shared Kotlin code.

In the next chapter, we'll explore how Kotlin can be used to build backend services.

Questions

1. What is Kotlin multiplatform?
2. How does Kotlin multiplatform differ from other cross-platform solutions such as React Native or Flutter?
3. What are four compilation targets supported in Kotlin multiplatform projects?
4. What is the significance of the `expect` keyword?
5. What is the significance of the `actual` keyword?
6. What are two potential benefits of Kotlin multiplatform?
7. What are two limitations of Kotlin multiplatform?

Further reading

- *Mastering Android Development with Kotlin* (`https://www.packtpub.com/application-development/mastering-android-development-kotlin`)
- *Building Applications with Spring 5 and Kotlin* (`https://www.packtpub.com/application-development/building-applications-spring-5-and-kotlin`)
- *Hands-On Microservices with Kotlin* (`https://www.packtpub.com/web-development/microservices-kotlin`)

16
Taming the Monolith with Microservices

Kotlin isn't limited to client-side applications and, in this chapter, we will examine the use of Kotlin on the backend. We'll explore the concept of a microservices architecture and how it can help build scalable and maintainable applications. We'll see how Kotlin fits in to that microservices architecture and ecosystem, illustrating where you will be able to apply existing Kotlin knowledge to the development of backend services. And finally, we'll learn how to start using Kotlin to write our own microservices by building our own simple microservice using Ktor, a Kotlin-based framework for building both server- and client-side code.

The following topics will be covered in this chapter:

- Understanding microservices
- Writing microservices with Kotlin
- Deploying your first Kotlin microservice

Technical requirements

In order to download, compile, and execute the samples found in this chapter, the following is required:

- IntelliJ IDEA 2018.3 Community or Ultimate editions, or newer
- An internet connection
- Git and GitHub (optional)

To download all of the code in this chapter, including the examples and code snippets, please refer to the following GitHub link: `https://github.com/PacktPublishing/Mastering-Kotlin/tree/master/Chapter16`.

Understanding microservices

Modern software applications arc required to be performant, scalable, and maintainable if they are to effectively contribute to the long-term success of any project, team, or company. To achieve these objectives, the architecture used to build these services is of paramount importance. To date, many large-scale applications have been built as monolithic services that grow and grow over time. However, many organizations are turning away from the monolith because of a tendency toward mixed responsibilities, poor performance, and costly maintenance. Instead, these organizations are embracing a microservices architecture.

In this section, we're going to provide some context to the discussion around monoliths versus microservices so we can better understand how Kotlin may fit into a modern services architecture.

Exploring the limits of the monolith

Let's first discuss what a monolith is. In software development, a monolith is thought of as a single application, service, or class that has many responsibilities. In reference to backend services, it generally refers to a single large service that manages all the domain responsibilities needed for the team or organization. This type of service may often be the result of an early prototype or implementation that has grown over time, responding to an ever-expanding list of business requirements. This often leads to functionality being bolted on, small hacks being applied here and there, and a general increase in complexity for the entire system.

This accumulation of complexity, patchwork features, and technical debt may weigh heavily on the system over time, and can start to have a genuine business impact for a team or organization. Monolithic services tend to be very interconnected as they handle many different responsibilities. It may be difficult to understand where to make a change when adding a new feature, and it may be unclear how that change may impact the system as a whole. This leads to increased maintenance costs. If it's more difficult and time-consuming to improve the system, two things may happen:

- Any critical bug fixes or improvements will inherently require more time, energy, and money.
- As these costs increase, the fixes may be deemed less and less critical and, therefore, the quality of the system may begin to decrease even further.

The interdependencies in a monolithic system make it difficult to monitor, trace, and debug issues within the application. How can you isolate a single data flow? How do you measure performance of a single aspect of the system? These types of questions may become impossible to answer.

Because monolithic applications are more challenging to monitor and debug, it becomes equally as difficult to truly understand the performance characteristics of the system. This opens the door for inefficiency both in the code, and in the deployment hardware used to host the system. If we can't become more performant through code improvement, the next best option is to throw more hardware and money at the system in the hope of masking performance issues with faster machines. While this may work for a time, it likely isn't the best way to scale your services in the long run.

Over the years, these are the challenges in maintaining and scaling applications that have lead organizations to explore and adopt microservices architectures.

In the next section, we'll discuss what microservices are and how they aim to improve on monolithic systems.

Embracing microservices

Microservices. This is likely one of the most popular buzzwords in software development today; but what does it actually mean? Microservices are, in many ways, a direct response to the challenges of monolithic applications. Instead of a single, large service that grows and grows over time, a microservices architecture comprises smaller, focused services that perform a single task. This is similar to how we might think of a class in object-oriented programming as doing one thing, or modeling a single piece of domain knowledge.

In any large system, it is likely that there are multiple different areas of the domain that can be broken down and separated out. This could be things such as authentication, user registration, video encoding, or content delivery. In a monolithic application, these would likely be managed by the same large service, but with a microservices approach, each of these domain tasks could be managed by their own small service.

How does this increase in services improve the overall effectiveness and efficiency of the system? To begin with, smaller and more focused services are easier to understand, maintain, and therefore more easily owned by a specific individual or team. Because microservices are specialized and have clear responsibilities, it makes it easier to understand how a change in one microservice will affect others in the system. Fixing a bug, adding functionality, or increasing performance therefore becomes a much more manageable task, thereby increasing the likelihood that the service scales well over time.

By focusing an individual service on a specific task, it becomes very clear where to look when that task is experiencing performance degradation or other problems. Individual services can be more easily monitored, debugged, and improved because they are largely isolated from the rest of the system. What's more, because they are isolated from the system, they aren't necessarily tied to the same types of monitoring tools as the rest of the system. If a particular service requires a specialized tool, it can be applied locally to that single service.

This notion of specialized tooling doesn't just apply to performance monitoring. In reality, because each service is self-contained and ideally exposes a common set of APIs for other services to interact with, it doesn't matter how the service is built.

In a microservices architecture, it's possible for individuals and teams to build their services with whichever tools, languages, and frameworks they see fit. This enables developers to adopt new tools, experiment with new languages, and generally work toward finding the ideal tech stack for their organization.

The freedom provided by focused individual services can lead to a more scalable system. As individual services are fixed more quickly and more often, and performance bottlenecks are monitored and fixed, the overall system improves. When a service needs to be replaced, the rest of the system may not even know about it. Teams are more free to focus on their own services without as much concern for how it may impact unrelated services. All of this can lead to faster teams, more performant services, and ultimately a better application.

While this microservices architecture has many benefits, it has its drawbacks as well. One of these is that, in enabling services to be developed with whatever languages and frameworks a developer sees fit, it opens us up to endless possibilities for how to build our microservices. This potentially increases the complexity of the overall system by increasing the number of languages and frameworks required to maintain that system. However, it's also very powerful because it enables developers to use whatever tools they are most comfortable with when building their services.

In the next section, we're going to use this freedom by focusing on how we may begin using Kotlin to build services within our microservices architecture.

Writing microservices with Kotlin

With Kotlin, we have another modern language available with which we can build our microservices architecture. Whether it's an entire system or a single service, Kotlin is a viable option for writing scalable, performant applications.

In this section, we'll look at some specific examples of how to leverage Kotlin to write microservices.

Understanding Kotlin's relation to microservices

How, and where, can we use Kotlin to develop backend services? To answer this, we could examine where can we use Java to write backend services. Java has long since been a popular choice for building backend applications, and because Kotlin targets the same JVM, we can deploy Kotlin services using similar frameworks and deployment methods.

Perhaps most popular is Spring, which has long been a go-to choice for Java developers when building enterprise applications. Today, this also includes Spring Boot and Spring Cloud, which aim to make it even easier to build individual services, or even an entire microservices architecture. When building with Spring, we can take advantage of Kotlin's popular language features while leveraging the tooling and architecture principles Spring provides. Starting with Spring 5.0, it's possible to generate a Spring project with Kotlin support by default.

Another framework that can enable us to build backend services with Java, Kotlin, and several other languages is Vert.x. Vert.x helps developers build scalable, reactive services around non-blocking, event-driven programming. Using Vert.x with Kotlin feels very natural as it provides idiomatic APIs for all supported languages.

To host our Kotlin services, we can generally turn to any service that hosts JVM applications. This includes popular options such as Amazon Web Services, Google Cloud Platform, and Heroku. The actual deployment process will vary based on which frameworks you're using to build your service and the platform to which you're deploying.

With existing frameworks such as Spring and Vert.x that support multiple languages, why would we want to choose Kotlin to develop our backend services? We're going to explore this question in the following section.

Choosing Kotlin for your microservices

With so many languages available to develop our backend services, why would we choose Kotlin? As we've seen throughout this book, Kotlin is a powerful modern language. It's expressive, it's concise, it has a terrific standard library, and it's fully compatible with any existing Java framework you may want to leverage in your service. Kotlin is also well suited to highly asynchronous programming through its support for coroutines. Finally, Kotlin has excellent tooling with which to build and debug your services. All of these factors add up to a very productive development experience for Kotlin on the backend.

Adding to the potential benefits of using Kotlin to build a microservices architecture is the Ktor framework. Ktor is a Kotlin-based framework for building asynchronous client and server code. Ktor takes advantage of Kotlin's features, including higher-order functions and custom DSLs, to provide a framework that is very Kotlin idiomatic and easy to use as a Kotlin developer. Ktor also supports Kotlin multiplatform, enabling developers to share Kotlin code between their backend services and client code.

In the next section, we're going to build our own service using Kotlin and Ktor. We'll walk through the setup process, write the simple service, and then deploy our service locally so that we may start developing against it.

Deploying your first Kotlin microservice

Now that we've explored what microservices are, and how we can use Kotlin to develop these services using several different frameworks, we're going to build our own simple service with Kotlin. We'll use Ktor to develop a simple service using Kotlin, and see how easy it can be to deploy and use that service locally.

Creating a Ktor project

To create a Ktor project, perform the following steps:

1. First, open IntelliJ and select **New Project**, as follows:

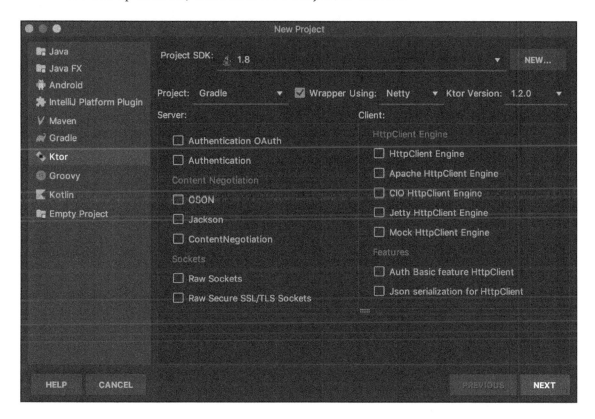

2. Next, in the **Client** section, select **Jetty HttpClient Engine** and then click **Next**:

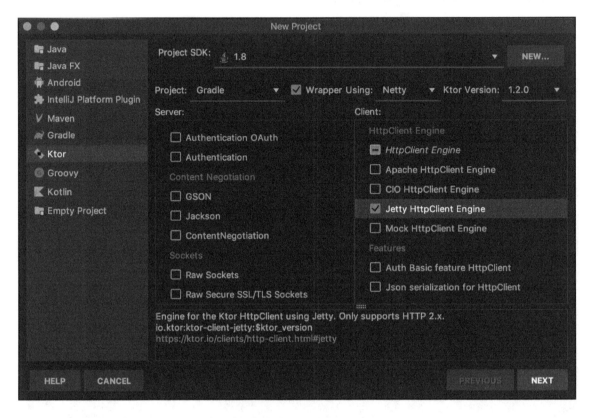

3. Now, go ahead and set your `groupId`, `artifactId`, and `versionId` to be whatever you want and select **Next**.

4. Choose where you would like your project to be saved, and then click **Finish**.

At this point, you should have a new Gradle module created based on whatever name you assigned to your project. Within that module, you should have a file, `Application.kt`. This file will be the entry point for our new service and should look similar to the following code snippet:

```
// Application.kt
fun main(args: Array<String>): Unit =
io.ktor.server.netty.EngineMain.main(args)
@Suppress("unused") // Referenced in application.conf
@kotlin.jvm.JvmOverloads
fun Application.module(testing: Boolean = false) {
    HttpClient(Jetty) { }
}
```

Before adding functionality to our service, we want to ensure we're on Ktor version 1.2.1. This version enables us to use a simplified syntax when building our service. To verify the version, open up the `gradle.properties` file, and update the `ktor_version` to 1.2.1 as follows:

```
// gradle.properties
ktor_version=1.2.1
```

Now that our project is set up, we'll start adding functionality to our service by defining several endpoints that will return data when accessed.

Writing a simple microservice

To start adding to our new service, let's update `Application.kt`. When we look at `Application.kt`, we currently see two things. First, we have a top-level `main()` function that acts as the entry point for the service:

```
fun main(args: Array<String>): Unit =
io.ktor.server.netty.EngineMain.main(args)
```

That function calls into the Netty deployment engine, which performs the work required to actually deploy our service. Netty is a network application framework that simplifies the deployment of our service. We'll look more closely at this in the next section.

The next item of interest is the `Application.module()` extension function. This function will be used within the deployment configuration of our service, shown as follows:

```
@kotlin.jvm.JvmOverloads
fun Application.module(testing: Boolean = false) {
    HttpClient(Jetty) {
        routing {
            event()
        }
    }
}
```

It's within this function that we will actually be building our service.

Adding a route

To begin adding endpoints to our service, we will install a routing feature into our application.

1. We can do this using an available `Application.routing()` function. The following code shows this:

```
@kotlin.jvm.JvmOverloads
fun Application.module(testing: Boolean = false) {
    HttpClient(Jetty) {
        routing {
            // add routes here
        }
    }
}
```

Because `Application.routing()` takes in a configuration function, we can call `routing {}` with a lambda, which will enable us to configure the available endpoints for our service.

2. Now, we'll add a route that will return `"Hello World"` when the base endpoint of our service is accessed. We'll do this by adding a `get()` call within our `routing {}` block. By passing `"/"` to `get()`, we define what happens at the root URL path:

```
@kotlin.jvm.JvmOverloads
fun Application.module(testing: Boolean = false) {
    HttpClient(Jetty) {
        routing {
            get("/") {
                call.respondText("Hello World",
                                    ContentType.Text.Plain)
            }
        }
    }
}
```

When the `"/"` path is accessed, our route will respond with `"Hello World"`. We will see this in action by deploying our service locally, which we'll take a look at in the next section.

Deploying our microservice

When building your services, at some point, you're going to want to deploy them. It's likely you'll want to deploy the service publicly if the service is intended for production use, but you'll also likely want to be able to test your service in some type of local or testing environment. In this section, we'll discuss options available for deploying a Ktor-based service in production and then we'll walk through how to deploy our service locally so that we can test it.

Deploying Kotlin services in production

When building a web service using Ktor, there are a variety of different methods available for deploying your service for production use. The specifics of these options are beyond the scope of this book, but to help point you in the right direction, several of these deployment options are listed here:

- Google App Engine
- Heroku
- Docker containers
- Fat JARs

For more details on the production deployment of Ktor services, you can visit the Ktor deployment site: `https://ktor.io/servers/deploy.html`.

Deploying local Ktor services

To test our new service, we can easily deploy that service locally and validate its function. The local deployment of the service is configured through the `application.conf` configuration file that was generated when we created our project. That file should look something like the following code snippet:

```
// application.conf
ktor {
    deployment {
        port = 8080
        port = ${?PORT}
    }
    application {
        modules = [ com.packt.ApplicationKt.module ]
    }
}
```

In this file, there are two key things:

1. We define the local port to which our service will be deployed and be available.
2. We define `module` as our static entry point with which to begin running our service.

The reference to `ApplicationKt.module` corresponds to the `Application.module` extension function we've defined in `Application.kt`:

```
@kotlin.jvm.JvmOverloads
fun Application.module(testing: Boolean = false) {
    ...
}
```

With this configuration, when we call our `main()` function, the `Application.module()` function will be run and available locally at `http://0.0.0.0:8080`.

To actually deploy the service, open `Application.kt` within IntelliJ, and then click the green arrow in the left gutter of the IDE window:

```
▶   fun main(args: Array<String>): Unit = io.ktor.server.netty.EngineMain.main(args)

    @Suppress( ...names: "unused") // Referenced in application.conf
    @kotlin.jvm.JvmOverloads
    fun Application.module(testing: Boolean = false) {
        HttpClient(Jetty) { this: HttpClientConfig<JettyEngineConfig>
            routing { this: Routing
                get( path: "/") { this: PipelineContext<Unit, ApplicationCall>
                    call.respondText( text: "Hello World", ContentType.Text.Plain)
                }
            }
        }
    }
```

Once this has been clicked, the service will be deployed using Jetty, which will log the deployment status to the run window in IntelliJ. If everything is successful, you should see output similar to the following:

```
[main] INFO Application - Responding at http://0.0.0.0:8080
```

Now that our service is deployed, if we open `http://0.0.0.0:8080` in our browser, we should see `Hello World` printed out to the screen as our endpoint response:

And with that, we've now completed the process of creating a simple service in Kotlin, and then deploying that service locally to test and potentially build upon. In the next section, we'll expand on this service by adding additional routes and taking advantage of Kotlin language features to make our service easier to build and maintain.

Scaling our routes

When embracing a microservices architecture, or really any scalable software, we want our code to be easy to read, modify, and debug. Currently, our service has its sole route defined directly within the `routing {}` block of `Application.kt`. This is fine for a trivial example, but it's not scalable. In this section, we're going to see how we can leverage extension functions to make our routing easier to understand, and we are then going to walk through the process of installing an additional route to our service.

Defining routes with extension functions

Using Kotlin extension functions, we can make the definition and installation of our service's routes easier to read and maintain. To do this, perform the following steps:

1. Start by creating a new package under the `/src` directory, and name that package `routes`:

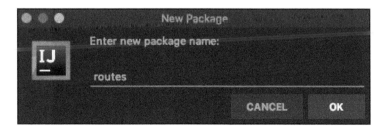

2. Now, we'll create a new file within this package named
`/src/routes/route_root.kt`.

3. Without `route_root.kt`, we will define an extension function on the `Route` type to define how our root endpoint route should be handled:

```
// route_root.kt
fun Route.root() {
    get("/") {
        call.respondText("Hello World", ContentType.Text.Plain)
    }
}
```

You'll notice that we've simply moved our existing route definition out from `Application.kt` to the function body, `Route.root()`. Now, we can use this extension function to simplify the `routing {}` block within `Application.module()` as follows:

```
@kotlin.jvm.JvmOverloads
fun Application.module(testing: Boolean = false) {
    HttpClient(Jetty) {
        routing {
            root()
        }
    }
}
```

Because the `routing {}` block has a receiver of the `Route` type, we can call our `Route.root()` extension function without explicitly referencing the receiver using `this`. Now, let's see how we can leverage this pattern to simplify the installation of additional routes.

Installing additional routes

Any real service is likely going to support multiple routes, so let's add an additional route to our service.

1. To begin, we'll create a new file, `/src/routes/route_agenda.kt`.

2. Next, we'll define an extension function, `Route.agenda()`, as we did previously.

3. Within `route_agenda.kt`, we will create `const` sample JSON `val`, which will be served from our endpoint, as follows:

```
// route_agenda.kt
const val AGENDA_JSON_SAMPLE = """
{
  "days":[
```

```
{
  "title":"Day 1",
  "date":"6\/4\/20",
  "sessions":[
    {
      "id":0,
      "title":"Kotlin 101",
      "speaker":"John Smith"
    },
    {
      "id":1,
      "title":"Kotlin 201",
      "speaker":"Jane Smith"
    }
  ]
},
...
]
}
"""
```

4. Now, we'll use that JSON to build our new route for the /agenda endpoint:

```
fun Route.agenda() = get("/agenda") {
    call.respondText(AGENDA_JSON_SAMPLE.trimIndent(),
ContentType.Text.Plain)
}
```

5. Now, once we install route, we can serve that JSON from
   http://0.0.0.0:8080/agenda.

6. To install our route, once again, we will simply add to the routing {} block of
   Application.module as follows:

```
@kotlin.jvm.JvmOverloads
fun Application.module(testing: Boolean = false) {
    HttpClient(Jetty) {
        routing {
            root()
            agenda()
        }
    }
}
```

7. And if we redeploy the service and navigate to `http://0.0.0.0:8080/agenda`, we should see the following output:

```
{
  "days":[
    {
      "title":"Day 1",
      "date":"6\/4\/20",
      "sessions":[
        {
          "id":0,
          "title":"Kotlin 101",
          "speaker":"John Smith"
        },
        {
          "id":1,
          "title":"Kotlin 201",
          "speaker":"Jane Smith"
        }
      ]
    },
    {
      "title":"Day 2",
      "date":"6\/5\/20",
      "sessions":[
        {
          "id":4,
          "title":"Kotlin 301",
          "speaker":"John Smith"
        },
        {
          "id":5,
          "title":"Advanced Kotlin",
          "speaker":"Jane Smith"
        }
      ]
    }
  ]
}
```

Now, once this is deployed, we can continue to build our service, adding additional routes as needed and serving static text, JSON, or any other response types that we need in order to scale our application, be they a single service or a collection of microservices.

Summary

In this chapter, we've taken a close look at how Kotlin can be used within a microservices architecture to build server-side code. We discussed some of the benefits of a microservices architecture and dived into how Kotlin fits into that architecture. We learned how Kotlin can be used to write microservices with existing JVM frameworks, and we explored Ktor, a Kotlin-based framework for writing asynchronous server code. Finally, we brought these concepts together by writing a simple microservice with Kotlin using Ktor. By building on the lessons learned in this chapter, we can begin leveraging Kotlin outside of our client-side applications.

In the next chapter, we'll explore common design patterns and how they can be achieved using Kotlin.

Questions

1. Why are "monoliths" difficult to manage at scale?
2. What is a "microservice architecture"?
3. What is a microservice?
4. Can you name a server-side framework that is compatible with Kotlin?
5. What is Ktor?
6. Why might Kotlin be a good choice for writing backend code?
7. How would you deploy a Kotlin-based microservice?

Further reading

- *Hands-On Microservices with Kotlin* (`https://www.packtpub.com/web-development/microservices-kotlin`)
- *Microservices Development Cookbook* (`https://www.packtpub.com/application-development/microservices-development-cookbook`)
- *Microservices Deployment Cookbook* (`https://www.packtpub.com/virtualization-and-cloud/microservices-deployment-cookbook`)

17
Practical Design Patterns

Design patterns are a powerful tool for a software developer. They help to solve common problems, such as ensuring the uniqueness of a class instance or how to encapsulate and swap behaviors at runtime. Design patters also give us a common vocabulary with which to discuss architectural challenges and decisions.

In this chapter, we will revisit some familiar Java design patterns and see how those patterns can be reimagined while harnessing the power of the Kotlin programming language.

The following topics will be covered in this chapter:

- Understanding design patterns
- Revisiting the Singleton pattern in Kotlin
- Revisiting the Factory pattern in Kotlin
- Revisiting the Builder pattern in Kotlin
- Revisiting the Strategy pattern in Kotlin

Technical requirements

In order to download, compile, and execute the samples found in this chapter, the following is required:

- IntelliJ IDEA 2018.3 Community or Ultimate editions, or newer
- An internet connection
- Git and GitHub (optional)

To download all of the code in this chapter, including the examples and code snippets, please refer to the following GitHub link: `https://github.com/PacktPublishing/Mastering-Kotlin/tree/master/Chapter17`.

Understanding design patterns

When building software, we often find ourselves coming across similar challenges on a regular basis. How can we avoid creating unnecessary instances of a particular class? How can we control how a class is instantiated? How might we separate the way a specific decision is made from the rest of an algorithm? These are just a few examples of the types of problems software developers regularly face and that are potentially solved through the application of common design patterns.

So, let's begin by understanding what design patterns are. Design patterns collect common vocabulary, patterns, and best practices for solving some of the common software development challenges. Common design patterns will typically include descriptions of the problem they aim to solve, the motivations behind how they solve the problem, and some guidance for when you may want to use that pattern.

As the problem area of software development is quite broad, so is the number of common design patterns. The full list of established design patterns would be very large, and beyond the scope of this chapter. However, the following list provides a subset of design patterns that you may be familiar with, either directly or indirectly:

- Singleton
- Factory
- Builder
- Strategy
- Delegate
- Command
- Façade
- Iterator

Design patterns manifest themselves at many different levels of the software development stack. You might apply the Iterator pattern when traversing an individual set of elements, you might leverage the Command pattern to implement undo/redo functionality for a user, or you might perhaps use the abstract Factory pattern to control how entire families of elements are created within your application.

Setting out to master all common design patterns could be quite the undertaking, something best cultivated over a career. However, learning when and how to apply any pattern can help make you a more efficient developer.

In this chapter, we're going to explore several design patterns that are common to object-oriented programming languages such as Java, and see how we can apply those patterns with Kotlin.

So, let's begin to study them in the following sections.

Revisiting the Singleton pattern in Kotlin

One of the most common software design patterns is the Singleton pattern. With this pattern, developers can ensure that only a single instance of any class exists within an application. In this section, we'll revisit this pattern, understanding why this pattern may be useful, and how to implement this pattern in Kotlin.

Understanding the Singleton pattern

As previously mentioned, the Singleton pattern helps developers ensure that only a single instance of a class exists at any time for an application. This is generally achieved through limiting how a class may be instantiated by making the class constructor private, and providing a public static method that can configure, instantiate, and provide a single instance of that class for the entire application.

In Java, a simple implementation of the Singleton pattern might look something like this:

```java
public class SimpleSingleton {
    // initialize instance when loading class
    private static final SimpleSingleton instance = new
        SimpleSingleton();

    // private constructor prevents outside instantiation
    private SimpleSingleton() { }
    // public method to access instance
    public static SimpleSingleton getInstance() {
        return instance;
    }
}
```

There are problems associated with this simple approach, however; namely, that the static instance of `SimpleSingleton` will be created and take up system resources even if it's never used. A more efficient, and safer, Singleton implementation might look something like this:

```
public class ThreadSafeSingleton {
    private static ThreadSafeSingleton instance;

    // private constructor prevents outside instantiation
    private ThreadSafeSingleton() { }

    public static ThreadSafeSingleton getInstance() {
        if (instance == null) {
            // synchronized to prevent simultaneous access from
            // multiple threads
            synchronized (ThreadSafeSingleton.class) {
                if (instance == null) {
                    // initialize if not already created
                    instance = new ThreadSafeSingleton();
                }
            }
        }
        return instance;
    }
}
```

This more complex version ensures that our Singleton pattern works as expected across multiple threads and ensures that we are only allocating the memory for the static instance if and when it's actually needed. We can help illustrate whey this is important in the following example:

```
public static void main(String[] args) throws InterruptedException {
    String language = args[0];
    Thread thread1 = new Thread() {
        @Override
        public void run() {
            super.run();
            if (language.equals("Kotlin")) {
                SimpleSingleton singleton =
                    SimpleSingleton.getInstance();
            }
        }
    };
    Thread thread2 = new Thread() {
        @Override
        public void run() {
            super.run();
```

```
            if (language.equals("Kotlin")) {
                SimpleSingleton singleton =
                    SimpleSingleton.getInstance();
            }
        }
    };

    thread1.start();
    thread2.start();
}
```

In this code snippet, we're only ever accessing our `SimpleSingleton` instance if our first program argument is equal to `"Kotlin"`. This means, in all other cases, that we are saving memory by not initializing `SimpleSingleton`. Additionally, because we are initializing our instance in a thread-safe manner, we can be sure that we're always getting a single instance even when accessing `SimpleSingleton` from multiple different threads. These guarantees are very useful, but do add complexity to the implementation.

So why might you want to use the Singleton pattern in your application? That is a question to consider carefully. While Singleton is a well-known design pattern, it's often referred to as an anti-pattern as it can lead to undesirable traits such as the following:

- A shared, global state
- Mixed dependency graphs

You may still want to rely on Singleton in some cases, however. Perhaps you have some configuration type that stores data that is always the same. You may determine that the best way to share a global state is through a Singleton rather than global variables, or you may want to leverage a Singleton when implementing another pattern such as the Prototype pattern, which creates new instances based on a common instance.

Whatever your reasons for using the Singleton pattern, Kotlin makes it extremely easy to implement. We're going to see how to implement a Singleton in Kotlin in the following section.

Implementing the Singleton pattern in Kotlin

To create thread-safe Singletons in Kotlin, we can rely on object declarations, as we discovered in `Chapter 5`, *Modeling Real-World Data*. To create a Kotlin equivalent implementation of our `ThreadSafeSingleton` example from the previous section, we can write the following Kotlin code:

```
object ThreadSafeSingleton
```

With this single line, we can now access `ThreadSafeSingleton` from anywhere in our code base in a thread-safe manner. Adding the `object` keyword rather than `class` ensures that the compiler will generate bytecode that enforces the Singleton pattern for us.

We can now add a property to our `ThreadSafeSingleton` object to demonstrate how to access properties of an object declaration. Consider the following code snippet:

```
object ThreadSafeSingleton {
    const val platform = "JVM"
}
```

To reference the newly added `platform` property, we simply reference the property name preceded by the object declaration name, shown as follows:

```
fun main() {
    ThreadSafeSingleton.platform
}
```

By leveraging object declarations, we can quite easily implement the Singleton pattern using Kotlin. This is a common pattern when defining sealed class hierarchies and defining types that only need to exist in memory a single time.

Using object expressions to enforce single instances of classes that don't require configuration is convenient, but what about classes that do require a constructor? We'll explore this use case in the next section.

Revisiting the Factory pattern in Kotlin

When we want to create common class types, and need to configure those types without exposing that configuration logic to our client code, we can turn to the Factory design pattern. So let's see how this helps by learning more about this pattern.

Understanding the Factory pattern

The factory design pattern is an object creation design pattern for creating objects with a shared type without exposing implementation details about how individual instances are configured. We've already seen an example of this pattern in Chapter 13, *Kotlin on Android*, when we wrote a Factory method for creating new `Intent` instances. Consider the following code snippet:

```
fun createIntent(context: Context, id: String) =
        Intent(context, DetailsActivity::class.java).apply {
            putExtra(EXTRA_ID, id)
        }
```

In this example, details about *how* the `Intent` is actually created are hidden from the caller of `createIntent()`. Callers of that API only need to understand what arguments to pass in and that they will receive a properly configured `Intent` in return.

The Factory pattern can be useful in many situations. It can shield client code from changes as to how a class is configured by providing a consistent API through the Factory. It can encapsulate the configuration and instantiation of a class into a single location, or it could provide a convenient way to retrieve test implementations of a type to assist in unit testing.

In the next section, we'll walk through a simple example of leveraging the Factory pattern in Kotlin.

Implementing the Factory pattern in Kotlin

Let's walk through an example of implementing the Factory pattern to retrieve difficulty settings for a particular game. What we want to achieve is something like this:

```
val settings = DifficultySettings.getSettings(GameDifficulty.HARD)
println("Difficulty Settings = ${settings.label}")
```

Our goal is to use our Factory method, in this case `getSettings()`, to retrieve an instance of some settings type and be able to work with that type without needing to understand how that type is actually instantiated. To implement this, perform the following steps:

1. First, we will create an `enum` class to represent the available difficulties we want our client code to be aware of:

    ```
    enum class GameDifficulty {
        EASY, NORMAL, HARD
    }
    ```

2. Next, we will create a `DifficultySettings` class, which is what our client code will access to represent the individual settings for the game:

```
class DifficultySettings private constructor(
    val label: String,
    val lives: Int,
    val enemySpeed: Float,
    val enemyHealth: Float
)
```

Notice that we've made the constructor for this class `private`. This is because we don't want our client code to be able to instantiate instances of this class. We want to hide that work behind our Factory method.

3. Now, we will add our Factory method to the `DifficultySettings` class using a companion object:

```
class DifficultySettings private constructor(
    val label: String,
    val lives: Int,
    val enemySpeed: Float,
    val enemyHealth: Float
) {

    companion object Factory {
        @JvmStatic
        fun getSettings(difficulty: GameDifficulty):
            DifficultySettings {
            return when (difficulty) {
                GameDifficulty.EASY -> DifficultySettings(
                                        "EASY", 5, .5f, .5f)
                GameDifficulty.NORMAL -> DifficultySettings(
                                        "NORMAL", 3, .75f, .75f)
                GameDifficulty.HARD -> DifficultySettings(
                                        "HARD", 1, 1f, 1f)
            }
        }
    }
}
```

We've named our companion object `Factory` to provide some additional semantic meaning to this companion object, and the use of `@JvmStatic` ensures that our new method will be readily available from both Kotlin and Java with the same syntax.

With this companion object in place, we can now retrieve instances of
`DifficultySettings` through our Factory method, `getSettings()`:

```
fun main() {
    val settings = DifficultySettings.getSettings(GameDifficulty.HARD)
    println("Difficulty Settings = ${settings.label}")
}
// outputs: Difficulty Settings = HARD
```

By leveraging a factory to retrieve our instance of `DifficultySettings`, we've hidden the
initialization details from our calling code and insulated it from future changes in how
`DifficultySettings` must be constructed. The Factory pattern is a great tool for
encapsulating this type of instantiation and retrieval, and it is easy to implement in Kotlin.

In the next section, we'll see how Kotlin enables us to rethink the Builder pattern.

Revisiting the Builder pattern in Kotlin

The Builder pattern is an object creation pattern for creating instances of classes that have a
large number of potential optional parameters. For classes like these, with many optional
parameters, we could rely on a Builder class to provide an improved API for constructing
instances of the class. This API enables us to build different representations of our class
using a common API.

In this section, we'll explore both what a traditional Builder might look like and how Kotlin
enables us to simplify our concept of a Builder in many cases by leveraging default
parameter values and named arguments.

Understanding the Builder pattern

The Builder pattern helps us to configure different representations of a class, typically, for
classes that have many optional parameters. In the world of Java, this is often done by
creating an inner class called Builder for whichever type we are looking to configure. Client
code then sets fields on the Builder, and eventually calls a `build()` method. Within
`build()`, the Builder can create an instance of the desired class using any fields set on the
builder, and using sensible defaults for any of the optional fields. This enables client code to
ignore any fields that aren't relevant.

Let's take an example of what this looks like in Java so that we can compare it effectively to our Kotlin implementation in the next section. We'll create a Builder for configuring a `SearchRequest` class for an API.

1. We'll start by creating our `SearchRequest` class:

```
public class SearchRequest {

    private String queryTerm;
    private String[] categories;
    private int resultCount;

    private SearchRequest() { }

    private SearchRequest(String queryTerm, String[] categories,
                          int resultCount) {
        this.queryTerm = queryTerm;
        this.categories = categories;
        this.resultCount = resultCount;
    }

    public String getQueryTerm() {
        return queryTerm;
    }

    public String[] getCategories() {
        return categories;
    }

    public int getResultCount() {
        return resultCount;
    }

}
```

This class exposes three getters: `getQueryTerm()`, `getCategories()`, and `getResultCount()`. These correspond to each of the relevant fields for making an API search request. Notice, however, that the constructor of this class is private. This is to ensure that a client can only instantiate `SearchRequest` through our `Builder` class.

2. Now, let's add that `Builder` class to `SearchRequest`:

```
public class SearchRequest {

    . . .
```

```
public static class Builder {
    private String queryTerm;
    private String[] categories;
    private int resultCount;

    public Builder queryTerm(String queryTerm) {
        this.queryTerm = queryTerm;
        return this;
    }

    public Builder categories(String[] categories) {
        this.categories = categories;
        return this;
    }

    public Builder resultCount(int resultCount) {
        this.resultCount = resultCount;
        return this;
    }

    public SearchRequest build() {
        return new SearchRequest(queryTerm, categories,
                                 resultCount);
    }
}
}
```

Within our `Builder` class, we mirror the fields available on `SearchRequest` so that we may store the values when they are set on the `Builder`, and then use them to construct an instance of `SearchRequest` in `build()`.

3. To then create an instance of `SearchRequest` from our client code, we could work with `SearchRequest.Builder` like so:

```
public static void main(String[] args) {
    SearchRequest.Builder builder = new SearchRequest.Builder();
    SearchRequest request = builder
            .queryTerm("Kotlin")
            .resultCount(5)
            .build();
}
```

We first create an instance of `SearchRequest.Builder`, and we then set field values on the builder using a fluent API that allows us to chain those setters together. Finally, we call `build()` to create our configured instance of `SearchRequest()`.

This example of the Builder pattern in Java illustrates how useful the pattern can be, but also how verbose it is in many languages.

In the next section, we'll revisit this pattern in Kotlin and see how Kotlin language features enable us to greatly simplify this implementation.

Implementing the Builder pattern in Kotlin

To solve the same problems as the Builder pattern in Kotlin, we can turn to default parameter values and named arguments. Remember that the key problem the Builder pattern solves is allowing client code to easily configure different representations of some class without having to know about or understand any optional parameters that are not relevant to current usage. This is something that functions in Kotlin provide out of the box through default parameter values and named arguments. Let's take a look at how we could rewrite our `SearchRequest` class in Kotlin to make it easier to configure without the use of a Builder.

To achieve the same results in Kotlin, we can reimplement `SearchRequest` using a simple data class along the lines of the following:

```
data class SearchRequest(
    val queryTerm: String = "",
    val categories: List<String> = listOf(),
    val resultCount: Int = 10
)
```

In this data class, we've added each property to our primary constructor and provided a default value for each of these properties. This enables us to instantiate an instance of this class by passing 0, 1, or all of the parameters. Any parameter that is not specified will rely on the default value. The following code snippet demonstrates how we can instantiate instances of `SearchRequest` by passing 0, 1, or multiple parameters to the constructor:

```
fun main() {
    val request1 = SearchRequest()
    val request2 = SearchRequest(
        categories = listOf("Kotlin", "Android"),
        queryTerm = "Kotlin"
    )
    val request = SearchRequest(resultCount = 20)
}
```

We see in this example that we can configure different representations of `SearchRequest` quite simply without the use of a Builder. Default parameter values allow us to only specify which parameters we care about, and named arguments let us pass those parameters in any order we wish. This frees us from having to understand the exact order of the parameters and what sensible defaults might be.

While the Builder concepts are still applicable in Kotlin, the actual requirement of a Builder class is not. This is one of the best examples of Kotlin incorporating common Java patterns and best practices into the language feature set itself.

In the next section, we'll explore how higher-order functions simplify how we can realize the Strategy pattern in Kotlin.

Revisiting the Strategy pattern in Kotlin

The Strategy pattern is a useful pattern for encapsulating algorithms, or pieces of algorithms, in self-contained units of computation, and which then enable your code to delegate to those encapsulated *strategies* when needed. In this section, we'll take a look at how higher-order functions in Kotlin can make the Strategy pattern easier to implement.

Understanding the Strategy pattern

How should two objects be compared when sorting? What action should be performed when a game controller's button is pressed? How should a computer-controlled player choose which chess piece to move? All of these questions are examples of problems where the Strategy pattern could be applied to make our algorithms and programs more flexible and easier to maintain.

Let's take the example of writing a bot to play chess. We may want to create several different levels of difficulty. Let's see how to do this:

1. We could do this by defining a common interface such as the following:

```
interface BotBehavior {
    fun generateBoardState(currentState: Array<Array<Int>>)
}
```

2. We could then define different types of specific behavior by implementing that interface in concrete behavior classes such as the following:

```
object EasyBot : BotBehavior {
    override fun generateBoardState(currentState:
Array<Array<Int>>) {
        // pick first available action
    }
}

object DifficultBot : BotBehavior {
    override fun generateBoardState(currentState:
Array<Array<Int>>) {
        // perform look ahead search
    }
}
```

3. With these different behaviors in mind, we might then create a Chess class that takes BotBehavior and delegates to that behavior in its implementation of the game:

```
class Chess(var behavior: BotBehavior) {
    fun play() {
        // game loop
        // relies on behavior
    }

    fun pause() { }
}
```

4. Finally, we can create an instance of Chess with a specific encapsulated behavior, pause the game, and update the behavior. Once the behavior is swapped out, the behavior of the Chess instance as a whole may be very different. The following code shows this:

```
fun main() {
    val game = Chess(EasyBot)
    game.play()
    game.pause()
    game.behavior = DifficultBot
    game.play()
}
```

By using the Strategy pattern to encapsulate these behaviors, we can change the overall behavior of the game without modifying its code, and this can be updated at runtime, making it more flexible still.

In the next section, we'll look at using higher-order functions to define our strategies with Kotlin.

Implementing the Strategy pattern in Kotlin

In our previous example of Chess, we defined concrete strategies by implementing the BotBehavior interface. This interface was quite simple and defined only a single method. In situations like these, we could simplify our Strategy pattern implementation by relying on higher-order functions instead of concrete types. Let's see how this is done:

1. Let's create a new chess class called FunctionalChess:

```
class FunctionalChess(val behavior: (Array<Array<Int>>) -> Unit) {
    fun play() {
        // game loop
        // relies on behavior
    }

    fun pause() { }
}
```

This new FunctionalChess class takes a function parameter instead of an instance of BotBehavior. This will enable us to define our behavior strategies as functions and pass them to FunctionalChess.

2. We can now define an easy behavior and a difficult behavior as top-level function variables:

```
val easyBehavior:(Array<Array<Int>>) -> Unit = { gameState ->
    // pick first available action
}

val difficultBehavior:(Array<Array<Int>>) -> Unit = { gameState ->
    // perform look ahead search
}
```

3. Now, we are able to use those defined function variables to configure how our `FunctionalGame` class should operate:

```
fun main() {
    val functionalGame = FunctionalChess(easyBehavior)
    functionalGame.play()
    functionalGame.pause()
    functionalGame.behavior = difficultBehavior
}
```

As in the previous example, we can swap out behaviors as needed to control how the game plays, but we don't need to create several new classes in order to do so. We are able to rely on simple functions.

This pattern of relying on higher-order functions to control the behavior of an algorithm is how the Kotlin standard library works. If we look at the `sortedBy()` function from the Kotlin standard library, we can see that it takes a function parameter that helps determine how elements should be sorted. Consider the following code snippet:

```
/**
 * Returns a list of all elements sorted according to natural sort order of
the value returned by specified [selector] function.
 *
 * The sort is _stable_. It means that equal elements preserve their order
relative to each other after sorting.
 */
public inline fun <T, R : Comparable<R>> Iterable<T>.sortedBy(crossinline
selector: (T) -> R?): List<T> {
    return sortedWith(compareBy(selector))
}
```

From the preceding code, we can see that the function allows us to change how elements are sorted by changing the lambda passed to our call to `sortedBy()`. If we look at the following example, we'll see we are choosing to sort based on the length of the string:

```
listOf("programming languages", "foo", "Kotlin")
    .sortedBy { it.length }
    .forEach { println(it) }
// prints "foo", "Kotlin", "programming languages"
```

However, if we sort based on the value of the first character in the string, we get a different output:

```
listOf("programming languages", "foo", "Kotlin")
    .sortedBy { it[0] }
    .forEach { println(it) }
// prints "Kotlin", "foo", "programming languages"
```

By changing the strategy defined by our function parameter, we were able to change the output of the operation. This flexibility is really powerful. By writing code that defers key decisions to swappable components such as an interface or higher-order function, we can make our code more flexible and easier to reuse.

Summary

In this chapter, we've revisited a handful of common software design patterns and seen first hand how Kotlin makes the implementation and utilization of these patterns very easy. We saw how Kotlin provides first-party support for the Singleton pattern through the use of `object` classes. We explored how to implement the Factory pattern using companion objects. We examined how the use of named arguments and default parameter values enables us to forgo the traditional Builder pattern implementation in favor of simple functions. And finally, we explored how Kotlin's support of higher-order functions simplifies the implementation of the Strategy pattern.

Whether it's the patterns shown in this chapter, or your own favorite design patterns, Kotlin enables developers to reimagine existing patterns or conventions from popular languages such as Java in order to write clean, concise, and expressive code.

Whether it's reimagining existing design patterns, or revolutionizing how Android apps and backend services are written, Kotlin is a powerful tool for developers. Throughout this book, we've explored how Kotlin works, the features that enable developers to write more concise and expressive code, and how to use that code to build applications across mobile, browsers, and the backend. Hopefully, this has empowered and inspired you to take a closer look at Kotlin so that you may add it to your developer toolbox, thereby helping you to become a more efficient developer.

Questions

1. What are design patterns?
2. Why are design patterns helpful?
3. What is the benefit of the Singleton pattern?
4. What is the purpose of the Factory pattern?
5. What two Kotlin language features simplify the implementation of the Builder pattern?
6. What is the Strategy pattern?

Further reading

- *Design Patterns and Best Practices in Java* (https://www.packtpub.com/application-development/design-patterns-and-best-practices-java)
- *Hands-On Design Patterns with Kotlin* (https://www.packtpub.com/application-development/hands-design-patterns-kotlin)

Assessments

Chapter 1: A New Challenger Approaches

1. **Which company started development of the Kotlin programming language?**

   - JetBrains

2. **When was Kotlin announced to the world?**

   - 2011, at the JVM Language Summit

3. **Who is the lead designer of Kotlin?**

   - Andrey Breslav

4. **Which platforms did Kotlin initially target?**

   - JVM platforms

5. **Which platforms are currently supported by Kotlin?**

   - JVM, Android, JavaScript, Native

6. **For which platform has Kotlin gained the most popularity?**

   - Android

7. **List two factors that have contributed to the rapid growth of Kotlin?**

   - Compatibility with Java and existing tools
   - Adoption within the Android community
   - Google's support for Kotlin as a first-class language for Android
   - The ability to target multiple platforms

Chapter 2: Programmer's Multi-Tool

1. **Can you name two programming paradigms that Kotlin supports?**

   - Function, reactive, object-oriented

2. **Is it true or false that Kotlin requires everything to be contained within classes?**

   - False

3. **What is a top-level function?**

   - A function that exists independently of any containing class. Top-level functions are typically defined at the top of a .kt file, but can be placed anywhere within a .kt file as long as it's not within a class or object declaration.

4. **What are higher-order functions?**

   - Functions that return other functions, or functions that take other functions as parameters.

5. **How do you declare a nullable type in Kotlin?**

   - By adding a ? operator to the end of the type declaration, for example, String?.

6. **What are the three ways to handle null?**

   - Using an it/else check
   - Using the Elvis operator
   - Using the let() function

7. **Is it true or false that Kotlin code can't be used from Java code?**

   - False—Kotlin and Java are highly interoperable.

Chapter 3: Understanding Programming Paradigms in Kotlin

1. **What is a programming paradigm?**

   - A programming paradigm is a way of classifying a programming language based on common features or patterns of that language.

2. **Can you name three programming paradigms supported by Kotlin?**

   - Imperative
   - Functional
   - Object-oriented
   - Reactive
   - Generic

3. **What is the difference between imperative and declarative code?**

   - Imperative describes "how" to do something. Declarative describes "what" to do.

4. **Can you name one declarative programming language?**

   - SQL

5. **What are the three core principles of object-oriented programming?**

   - Encapsulation
   - Polymorphism
   - Inheritance

6. **What are two core principles of functional programming languages?**

   - First-class functions
   - Pure functions

7. **What is reactive programming?**

   - A style of programming in which computation is done in response to streams of events

8. **What is the difference between RxJava and RxKotlin?**

   - RxKotlin is a set of helper functions meant to extend RxJava to make it more Kotlin idiomatic.

Chapter 4: First-Class Functions

1. **What is the significance of the fun keyword?**

   - The `fun` keyword is used to denote the start of a function definition.

2. **How do you add a parameter to a function?**

   - You must add parentheses after the function name. Within the parentheses you must use the `name:Type` syntax.

3. **What are named arguments?**

   - When passing arguments, you can specify which parameter to assign an argument value by including the parameter name followed by = and then the value.

4. **What are default parameter values?**

   - You can specify a default value for a parameter that will be used if the parameter is omitted when passing arguments to a function call.

5. **How do you define a local function?**

   - You define it like a regular function but within another function.

6. **What is a top-level function?**

   - A function not associated with any class that is defined within any Kotlin file

7. **How do you define an infix function?**

   - You must add the `infix` keyword and ensure that the function takes only a single non-`vararg` parameter.

8. **What are higher-order functions?**

   - Functions that either return another function or take another function as a parameter.

9. **How do you define an extension function?**

   - You specify a receiver type to be associated with the function by using the `Type.functionName` syntax.

Chapter 5: Modeling Real-World Data

1. **How do you define a class in Kotlin?**

   - Use the `class` keyword followed by a name. You can then optionally add properties and methods.

2. **How do you define an interface in Kotlin?**

   - Use the `interface` keyword followed by a name. You can then optionally add properties and functions.

3. **What are data classes?**

   - Special classes that generate the `equals()`, `hashCode()`, and `toString()` implementations, and are ideal for immutable data classes

4. **What are sealed classes?**

   - A special type of class useful for creating restricted class hierarchies. They are similar to enums, but allow each type in the hierarchy to have unique properties and methods.

5. **How is a sealed class different from an enum?**

   - Sealed classes can include multiple different classes within the hierarchy and can include different data and methods.

6. **What is an object expression?**

   - Kotlin's way of implementing anonymous classes

7. **What is an object declaration?**

   - A native way of supporting the Singleton pattern

8. **What is a companion object?**

   - An object declaration that is scoped to a specific class instance

9. **What are the four visibility modifiers in Kotlin?**

   - Public
   - Private
   - Internal
   - Protected

10. **What are the differences between a primary and secondary constructor?**

    - There can only be one primary constructor.
    - Primary constructors can define properties.
    - There can be multiple secondary constructors.
    - Primary constructor initialization happens before anything else.

Chapter 6: Interoperability by Design

1. **Can you name two reasons why interoperability with Java and Kotlin was important to JetBrains?**

   - To work with existing JetBrains tools and code.
   - To enable developers to adopt the language slowly.
   - Making Java and Kotlin work together makes IntelliJ more useful.

2. **Is it true or false that Kotlin files cannot be in the same source directory as Java files?**

   - False

3. **Is it true or false that Java can be quickly converted to Kotlin using IntelliJ?**

   - True

Chapter 7: Crossing Over – Working across Java and Kotlin

1. **Is it true or false that it's possible to call Kotlin code from Java?**

    - True

2. **Is it true or false that it's possible to call Java code from Kotlin?**

    - True

3. **Is it true or false that Kotlin's strict null typing is persisted when calling into Java?**

    - False

4. **What are the two ways of managing the lack of static methods in Kotlin?**

    - Companion objects
    - Top-level functions
    - Extension functions

5. **How are top-level functions accessed from Java?**

    - Using a generated static class that takes the form of
      `<filename>Kt.<nameOfFunction>()`

6. **How are extension functions accessed from Java?**

    - Using a generated static method that takes the receiver class as the first parameter of the method

7. **Is it true or false that default parameter values can be used from Java?**

    - False

Chapter 8: Controlling the Story

1. **What is the @JvmName annotation used for?**

    - It can be used to change the name of the Java class generated by the Kotlin compiler to contain top-level functions and properties.

2. **What is the @JvmStatic annotation used for?**

   - It indicates that the compiler should generate JVM static elements such as methods, getters, and setters for the annotated element.

3. **What does the @JvmOverloads annotation do when applied to a Kotlin function?**

   - It denotes that the compiler should generate overloaded methods for a function that provide the Kotlin-defined default parameter values, making them available from Java through the overloaded methods.

4. **What are use-site targets used for?**

   - They are used to specify which compiler-generated element an annotation should be applied to. For example, an annotation applied to a `var` property could use a use-site target to define whether the annotation should be applied to the generated field, getter, or setter for the annotated property.

5. **Is it true or false that companion objects can be given more meaningful names?**

   - True. A name can be given to a companion object by adding the name after the `object` keyword in the companion object declaration.

6. **What are two uses for companion objects?**

   - Factory methods
   - Scoping of properties and methods to avoid polluting the namespace

Chapter 9: Baby Steps – Integration through Testing

1. **What are two common approaches for integrating Kotlin into an existing project?**

   - Feature first
   - Tests first

2. **What are two advantages to incorporating Kotlin via a test-first approach?**

   - It can test the interop experience between Java and Kotlin code.
   - It doesn't ship the new code to production.

3. **What is one drawback to incorporating Kotlin via a test-first approach?**

   - You don't typically get to take full advantage of all Kotlin features.

4. **How does writing tests with multiple languages improve interop between Java and Kotlin?**

   - It forces you to exercise your classes and APIs in whichever language they aren't written. This helps highlight pain points in the interop experience.

5. **What is one way to handle the testing of Kotlin classes that are final by default?**

   - Using Mockito-Inline
   - Using the all-open compiler plugin

6. **What is the purpose of the kotlin.test package?**

   - It provides testing utilities and annotations that are platform independent, which can then be used for specific platforms or in multi-platform projects.

7. **Can you name one Kotlin-focused testing library?**

   - Mockito-Kotlin

Chapter 10: Practical Concurrency

1. **Can you name two mechanisms for executing code in the background for JVM applications?**

   - Thread
   - Executors
   - CompleteableFuture
   - RxJava

2. **When was CompleteableFuture introduced to Java?**

   - Java 8

3. **What is RxJava?**

   - It is the JVM implementation of Reactive Streams, which can be used for simple asynchronous operations or for fully reactive programming.

4. **What are coroutines?**

   - They are a solution for structured concurrency that enable us to write asynchronous code in an imperative, non-blocking way.

5. **What is structural concurrency?**

   - It is the concept of scoping coroutines and their execution to different scopes that can be controlled and canceled throughout the lifetime of an application.

6. **Why are different coroutine builders useful?**

   - They enable us to control how our coroutines are configured, run, and responded to. They could be used to bridge non-blocking and blocking portions of our code base, or to control the scopes in which our coroutines are associated.

7. **What are suspending functions?**

   - They are functions with the suspend function added to their declaration, which indicates that the function can suspend the operation of a coroutine. They can be used to write functions that perform long-running tasks that can then be called from within a coroutine.

Chapter 11: Building Your Own Tools – Domain-Specific Languages (DSLs)

1. **What does DSL stand for?**

   - Domain-Specific Language

2. **Can you name two examples of domains to which DSLs can be applied?**

   - Building web pages
   - Defining static layouts
   - Testing

3. **What are the two primary building blocks of a DSL in Kotlin?**

   - Extension functions
   - Higher-order functions

4. **What are two mechanisms for controlling the scope of a DSL function?**

   - Functions with a receiver
   - `@DslMarker` annotations

5. **What is the @DslMarker annotation used for?**

   - It controls which receivers a lambda has access to by default so that a lambda only has access to the current receiver if annotated.

6. **What are two benefits that custom DSLs can provide?**

   - They provide a very human-readable API for common tasks.
   - They can simplify the construction or representation of an artifact (such as a web page) using the declarative syntax of a DSL

Chapter 12: Fully Functional – Embracing Functional Programming

1. **What is functional programming?**

   - A style of programming in which state and business logic are expressed through pure mathematical operations without the use of shared state or side effects.

2. **What are two beneficial characteristics of functional programming?**

   - Reduction in state management
   - Limiting of side effects

3. **What does an inline modifier do to a defined function?**

   - It indicates that the compiler should include the function's implementation at the functional call site to improve the performance characteristics of the code.

4. **Is it true or false that higher-order functions pose a potential performance issue?**

   - True

5. **Can you name three functions from the Kotlin standard library?**

   - `map()`
   - `filter()`
   - `orEmpty()`
   - `first()`
   - `last()`

6. **What is the Arrow library used for?**

   - It's used as a framework for writing purely functional code in Kotlin.

7. **What are the core data types when writing functional code with Arrow?**

   - Typeclasses
   - Data types
   - Effects

Chapter 13: Kotlin on Android

1. **When did Google first announce Kotlin support for Android?**

   - 2017 at Google IO

2. **When did Google decide to go Kotlin-first for Android?**

   - At Google IO 2019

3. **Is it true or false that you can define your Gradle builds using Kotlin scripts?**

   - True

4. **How can you use the buildSrc directory when building your project with Kotlin Gradle scripts?**

   - You can statically define dependency definitions so they can be reused across multiple Gradle or Kotlin buildscripts.

5. **What is Android KTX?**

   - KTX is a set of Kotlin extensions for the Android framework and supports library classes aimed at making working with certain APIs easier and more Kotlin-idiomatic.

6. **What does the Kotlin Android Extensions plugin do?**

   - It provides additional functionality for using Kotlin on Android, such as using Kotlin synthetic view accessors.

7. **Which annotation will generate Parcelable implementations for you when added to a model class?**

   - `@Parcelize`

Chapter 14: Kotlin and Web Development

1. **Does Kotlin run natively in a JavaScript environment?**

   - Kotlin can be transpiled to JavaScript code and then run natively in a JavaScript environment.

2. **How is your Kotlin project made usable within a JavaScript project?**

   - A `.js` file is generated for each Kotlin source file in your project, and a `.js` file is created for JavaScript implementations of the Kotlin standard library. Those `.js` files can then be imported and run in your JavaScript project.

3. **What does it mean to transpile code?**

   - It is a translation from one language or standard to another. For example, the Kotlin JS compiler transpiles Kotlin to JavaScript.

4. **What are two potential benefits of using Kotlin for JavaScript development?**

   - Static typing
   - Excellent standard library functionality
   - The application of existing Kotlin skills and understanding to a web project

5. **What are two ways of building a Kotlin project with a JavaScript target?**

   - Starting a new KotlinJS project from scratch using IntelliJ
   - Compiling your Kotlin code to JavaScript and then integrating it with your existing project

6. **Which common JavaScript modules is Kotlin compatible with?**

   - AMD
   - UMD
   - CommonJS

7. **Is it true or false that Kotlin is compatible with third-party JavaScript frameworks?**

   - True

Chapter 15: Introducing Multiplatform Kotlin

1. **What is Kotlin multiplatform?**

   - It is an approach to sharing data models and business logics across multiple application targets using a common Kotlin code base.

2. **How does Kotlin multiplatform differ from other cross-platform solutions, such as React Native of Flutter?**

   - Kotlin multiplatform aims to share models and business logic, but not UIs.

3. **What are the four compilation targets supported in Kotlin multiplatform projects?**

   - JVM
   - Android
   - iOS
   - JavaScript

4. **What is the significance of the expect keyword?**

   - Indicates to the compiler that there will be a function/class/interface/and suchlike available in a target platform's source code that matches the signature defined in common Kotlin code. It can be thought of as similar to how a concrete class is an implementation of an interface or abstract class.

5. **What is the significance of the actual keyword?**

   - It indicates to the compiler that a function/class/interface/and so on is the platform-specific implementation of some element defined in the common code base.

6. **What are two potential benefits of Kotlin multiplatform?**

   - Sharing of data models
   - Sharing of business logic
   - Greater thought into application architecture

7. **What are two limitations of Kotlin multiplatform?**

   - Tooling is not great on all platforms, native in particular.
   - It requires all developers to know some Kotlin to be able to work on the entire code base.
   - It doesn't include UI development, which may be seen as a good or bad thing depending on your teams' needs.

Chapter 16: Taming the Monolith with Microservices

1. **Why are "monoliths" difficult to manage at scale?**

   - Services and responsibilities become tightly coupled. It can become difficult to understand the entirety of the system and how a single change may impact other parts of the code. It therefore may become challenging to maintain, modify, and optimize the system.

2. **What is a microservice architecture?**

   - An application architecture in which individual functionality is broken down into individual services that work together.

3. **What is a microservice?**

   - A small, specialized service that works as a part of a larger system of services.

4. **Can you name a server-side framework that is compatible with Kotlin?**

   - Ktor
   - Spring
   - Spring Boot

5. **What is Ktor?**

   - A Kotlin-based framework for asynchronous client/server code

6. **Why might Kotlin be a good choice for writing backend code?**

   - It's JVM and JavaScript compatible, and is compatible with a variety of frameworks such as Spring and Ktor, as well as having modern language features with an active developer community behind it.

7. **How would you deploy a Kotlin-based microservice?**

   - You can deploy locally from your IDE with Jetty, or you could deploy to a variety of production services such as AWS or Google Cloud. These production deployments would likely involve generating an executable JAR file and any associated resources, which would then be run in the service container.

Chapter 17: Practical Design Patterns

1. **What are design patterns?**

   - They are common patterns, implementations, and rationales for solving software challenges.

2. **Why are design patterns helpful?**

   - They can help us discuss solutions to software challenges using common language and context, and they help implement solutions to those same challenges.

3. **What is the benefit of the Singleton pattern?**

   - It ensures that only a single instance of some object exists within an application.

4. **What is the purpose of the Factory pattern?**

   - To control how instances of classes are instantiated

5. **What two Kotlin language features simplify the implementation of the Builder pattern?**

   - Named arguments
   - Default parameter values

6. **What is the Strategy pattern?**

   - It encapsulates the key logic and decisions of a larger algorithm so the algorithm can be made more flexible by allowing different behaviors to be substituted via different strategies.

Other Books You May Enjoy

If you enjoyed this book, you may be interested in these other books by Packt:

Learn Kotlin Programming - Second Edition
Stephen Samuel, Stefan Bocutiu

ISBN: 978-1-78980-235-1

- Explore the latest Kotlin features in order to write structured and readable object-oriented code
- Get to grips with using lambdas and higher-order functions
- Write unit tests and integrate Kotlin with Java code
- Create real-world apps in Kotlin in the microservices style
- Use Kotlin extensions with the Java collections library
- Uncover destructuring expressions and find out how to write your own
- Understand how Java-nullable code can be integrated with Kotlin features

Hands-On Data Structures and Algorithms with Kotlin
Rivu Chakraborty, Chandra Sekhar Nayak

ISBN: 978-1-78899-401-9

- Understand the basic principles of algorithms and data structures
- Explore general-purpose data structures with arrays and linked lists
- Get to grips with the basics of stacks, queues, and double-ended queues
- Understand functional programming and related data structures
- Use performant searching and efficient sorting
- Uncover how Kotlin's collection framework functions
- Become adept at implementing different types of maps

Leave a review - let other readers know what you think

Please share your thoughts on this book with others by leaving a review on the site that you bought it from. If you purchased the book from Amazon, please leave us an honest review on this book's Amazon page. This is vital so that other potential readers can see and use your unbiased opinion to make purchasing decisions, we can understand what our customers think about our products, and our authors can see your feedback on the title that they have worked with Packt to create. It will only take a few minutes of your time, but is valuable to other potential customers, our authors, and Packt. Thank you!

Index

G

H

I

CPSIA information can be obtained
at www.ICGtesting.com
Printed in the USA
FSHW010143040220
66783FS

This cookbook is not just for the person ambitious to get healthy and rebuild their beneficial, healthy and can rebuild anyon

If you have not read my book about my amazing transformation: Alopecia & Wellness: HOW I GOT MY HAIR BACK TREATMENT FREE, I highly encourage you to do so. You will learn how health equals hair.

My books and videos can be found conveniently on my website: alopeciaandwellness.com

---

INTRODUCTION

"When diet is wrong, medicine is of no use.

When Diet is correct, medicine is of no need"

-Ancient Ayurvedic Proverb

During Alopecia, the mirror was my worst enemy.

I was to focused on the unappealing image of myself and lack of hair to even begin to recover from the disease.

Every effect in the body is a sign that something is wrong by the foods that do not digest well. What happens when the food doesn't come out? It stays in, rots, putrefies and ferments. In one simple word: the undigested food gets <u>old</u>. Would you leave smelly garbage in your house?

Of course not. The same goes for your body. Get rid of the old and begin to maintain a healthy clean body full of <u>new</u> organic digestible foods. Unless you get rid of the old, you will never accept the new and neither will your body be able to transform into a radiantly healthy being.

Bad breath, body odor, pimples etc. all seem small but are huge signs that something is wrong in the body.

Instead of shifting our mental energy to health and reverse the disease to rebuild the body, we smell our bad odor or knit pick the little symptoms in remorse and patch it. We settle to the masking our deficiencies: applying creams, deodorant, medication or even under-going treatments and surgery!

"Every effect has its cause" – David Wolfe

Change and see change.

Sometimes with challenge comes change. Focus your effort in the right places, and you can only succeed.

The food you choose to put into your body can be your best friend or your worst enemy. Food can feed a disease or reverse it.

If the food you are putting into your body is not real, organic and clean than your only hurting yourself by not giving your body the nutrients it needs to regenerate and rebuild itself.

The body constantly cleans itself out, which speeds up the healing process to heal itself on an on going basis, but it can't if the foods aren't the proper building blocks. Non-organic, poison, pesticide filled foods will not do the job. You become what you eat and the effects will eventually show.

Alopecia is a disease. Your body is out of balance, confused (hints the name: dis-ease) and is attacking itself because of the lack of nutrients in order to thrive and regenerate itself.

Get your body on track with these recipes I've given to you. Do yourself a favor and be sure to buy organic foods. Not only will you be promoting clean food for your own body, but generations to come for a cleaner future.

"If we were to use the knowledge regarding foods that is now available to us, sickness could be wiped out in one generation"

– Dr. Jonathan Forman, M.D an English Physician

The Goal is to consume foods with live nutrients and enzymes that kick up old toxic waste lingering in the colon/intestines (the core of all disease). Fresh fruits and green leafy vegetables and all other Vegetables in the forms of juices, smoothies, salads and soups or just eaten as is. They all promote powerful healing that pharmaceutical medicine cannot.

"If the body fails to be healthy, it is obvious that the lack of deficiency of regenerative elements in the food is the cause of, and the responsibility for, whatever ailment, sickness or disease overtakes it."

- *Dr. Norman W. Walker*

Whether this is all understood fully right now or you are overwhelmed should not be an excuse to overlook the simple answer of our human design when it comes to health.

No matter the dis-ease: being over weight, acne, body odor, Bloated stomach, gas, greasy or dry skin or signs of any other effect other than radiant glowing health are all signs and effects of a body out of balance. Most people in todays society that aren't eating for health have there own kind of eating disorder, not caring about anything that goes in or even comes out!

Fresh Organic Food, Fresh Air, Exercise that you actually Enjoy, and a Positive Mindset to keep your whole life in the correct order are the key elements to Eliminate, enhance and evolve your health back to normal function.

"Food is not just a factor that affects us, it is the primary thing that affects us. If what we put inside our bodies does not affect us, what could?" – David Wolfe, *Eating for Beauty*

ALOPECIA & WELLNESS COOKBOOK:

RECIPES TO RECREATE YOURSELF

STARTS OUT WITH SMOOTHIES & JUICES, SALADS, SOUPS, VEGETABLE DISHES, GRAINS AND LASTLY DESSERTS THAT WILL BLOW YOUR MIND AND YOUR TASTEBUDS.

SMOOTHIES & JUICES

A High-powered Commercial Blender is recommended

(**For** the sake of your kitchen blender!)

Vita-mix is the brand I use

THE GREEN SMOOTHIE

Serves 1

1 Cup H20

1 Banana

1 Apple

A handful of Strawberries, or berry of your choice

1 Celery stalk (or cucumber)

2c of greens, spinach, kale or lettuce

Blend until smooth

BANANA HEMP GREEN SMOOTHIE

Serves 1

1 Cup H20

 2 Banana's

1-2 Tsp Hemp seeds

1 Cup Spinach

Blend until smooth

TINTED GREEN "COOKIES & CREAM"

Serves 1

20 oz Cup

1 Cup Hemp milk (vanilla, unsweetened)

1/4 Cup Coconut milk (unsweetened)

2 Tbs Raw protein powder (vanilla) sun warrior or raw meal

1-2 Handfuls of spinach

½ Frozen banana (non-frozen is fine just add 2 -3 ice cubes)

2 Tsp Almond butter

1 Tbs Cacao nibs (raw crushed chocolate bean*)

1 Tbs Coconut oil

Add the liquid ingredients in a blender first with the banana. Blend in high speed until smooth. Add the rest of the ingredients and blend until smooth.

- *You can find this in a health food store 'Whole Foods Market' now carry cacao nibs*

JOLLY GREEN SMOOTHIE

SERVES 1

4 Kale leaves

2 Bananas

1c Fresh Strawberries

½ c Cold Water

3 Ice cubes (optional to make colder)

Blend in a blender

FIG PLUM SMOOTHIE

Serves 1

1c Figs (dried or fresh)

3 Plums

1c Cold water

3 Ice cubes

Blend until smooth

AUTUMNS APPLE SMOOTHIE

Serves 1

1c Figs (fresh or dried)

2 Fuji Apples

dash of Cinnamon (optional)

3 Ice cubes

Blend all of the ingredients together until smooth

PEAR- MINT SMOOTHIE

Serves 1

1 Celery stalk

2 Pears

4-6 Mint Leaves

4 Kale leaves

½-1c Cold water

3 Ice cubes

Dash of cinnamon (optional)

Blend until smooth

BANANA CANDY SMOOTHIE

Serves 1

2 Bananas (ripe bananas have dark spots)

1/2c Fresh Parsley (flat leaf)

1 large Green Apple

Blend until smooth

SWEET JUNGLE DREAM

Serves 1

1 Apple

1c Fresh Strawberries

3 Kale leaves

1c Water

3 Ice cubes

DAD'S FAVORITE

Serves 1

1 Cup water

2 Frozen banana's (non-frozen is fine)

3-4 Handfuls spinach

TROPIC SMOOTHIE

Serves 1

1 Cup water

2 Tbs Coconut oil

2 Kale leaves

2 Handfuls of spinach

½ Orange, peeled

¼ Cup Fresh pineapple

BLUEBERRY BLUES

Serves 1

1 Cup water

2 Handfuls frozen Blueberries (fresh is fine)

2 Kale leaves

1-2 Handfuls of spinach

Blend each recipe's ingredients in a blender until smooth and enjoy.

MOLLY'S FAV. FRUITLESS GREEN SMOOTHIE

Serves 1

1 Cup Coconut (water)

2 Large handfuls spinach

2 Kale leaves

1 Carrot

½ Head of lettuce

½ Tbs Spirulina

½ Cucumber

1 Celery stalk

Blend until smooth.

'Great for digestion'

BEET BEET, SO UNIQUE SMOOTHIE

Serves 1

1 Cup cold water

2 Handfuls of spinach

½ Beet, chopped

1 Carrot, chopped

½ Cucumber, chopped

Lemon wedge

¼ Cup Goji Berries

½ Cup Blueberries

1 Tbs Flaxseeds

1 Tbs Chia seeds

A handful of macadamia nuts

Blend water, cucumber and spinach until you have a good liquid consistency. Next add the remaining ingredients and blend until smooth.

RICHIE RICH SMOOTHIE

Serves 1

1 Cup Rice milk, nut milk or hemp seed milk

2 Bananas, 1 frozen 1 fresh

1-2 Kale leaves

1 Tbs Almond butter

2 Dates, pitted

Blend until smooth

ALLISONS SMOOTHIE

1 Frozen banana

1 Fresh banana

½ Cup Blackberries, frozen

½ Cup Fresh rasberries

½ Cup H2o, cold

Mix in a blender and enjoy

GREEN JOLLY RANCHER SMOOTHIE

1 Frozen banana

1 Fresh banana

6 Fresh strawberries

3-4 Kale leaves

½ Cup H2o, cold

Mix in a blender and ejoy

This smoothie literally tastes like a green jolly rancher, to kick up the sweetness just add more strawberries

BANANA ICECREAM SMOOTHIE

Serves 1

3-4 Frozen Bananas

1/2c Water

3 Ice cubes

Blend In a high speed blender until smooth.

Eat with a spoon or sip with a straw....top with anything you like!

STRAWBERRY DAIQUIRI JUICE

Serves 1

3 Kale leaves

1 Cup Strawberries

½ Cucumber

1 Head of Lettuce

½ Lemon with rind

½ Juice of a lime

Blend all ingredients until smooth

This smoothie puts me in vacation mode all year round

SUPER FAST SUPER FOOD DRINK

Serves 1

8 oz Raw organic coconut water

Pinch vanilla powder

1 Tbsp. cocoa powder

Dash cinnamon powder

1 Tsp. Greens powder, I use 'Amazing grass, green super food'

Spirulina* (to taste)

Blend all ingredients in a blender and enjoy.

- *Spirulina is an acclaimed type of super food, it is a blue-green algae rich in proteins, vitamins, minerals and antioxidants. It helps protect cells from damage and has a similar makeup to sea vegetables. You can find it in a health food store or online. Be mindful that this is a very unique super food for acquired taste.*

FAMOUS GREEN SODA /JUICE

Serves 1

2 Inches of fresh ginger

1 Apple

1 Collard Leaves with stem

2 Kale Leaves

1 Head of lettuce

Feed ingredients through a juicer and enjoy

PINEAPPLE EXPRESS/JUICE

½ Pineapple juice

½ Green pear

4 Bok Choy leaves and stem, chopped (or lettuce)

½ Cucumber

Feed ingredients through a juicer and serve

RASPBERRY LEMONADE

Serves 1

½ Lemon

1-2 Handfuls fresh raspberries

1 Apple

1 Cup Fresh parsley

1 Cucumber, chopped

1 Celery

Feed all the ingredients through a juicer, then just transfer the juice into a blender with 2-3 ice cubes and enjoy your delicious frozen drink.

PURPLE RAIN JUICE

Serves 1-2

1 Large Cucumber

2 Cups Black seeded grapes, or Red grapes

2 Cups Broccoli stems, large

½ of 1 Lemon, chopped

Feed ingredients through a juicer and enjoy

LIGHT BREAKFAST

I have a juice, smoothie or both in the morning for my breakfast. Sometimes I need more to fill me…

EGG WHITE SCRAMBLE

Serves 1

1 Tbsp. Coconut oil or olive oil

4 Egg whites

¼ Cup Coconut milk, rice milk or nut milk

Handful spinach

½ Tomato, diced

Adobo to taste

In a bowl whisk the egg whites and milk together. Heat a frying pan with the oil and pour in the egg mix. Scramble the eggs in the pan by "sweeping" the eggs with your spatula, when half cooked add the remaining ingredients.

EGGWHITE FRITTATA

3 Egg whites

1 Cherry tomatoes, cut in half

Handful spinach

3 Tbsp. Coconut milk

1 Tbsp. Coconut oil or Olive oil

Sea salt

Garlic powder

Black pepper

Hot sauce optional

Whisk together the egg whites with coconut milk, Toss in the veggies.

Heat a pan with the oil on the stove on medium heat.

When oil is warm, pour in the egg mixture.

When the bottom side is cooked, flip on the other side or fold in half for an omelet.

Once both sides are cooked sprinkle with spices to taste and serve. Drizzle on some hot sauce if you want some heat in your bite!

VANILLA NUT CRUNCH CEREAL

Serves 1

¼ Cup Whole almonds and pistachios

¼ Cup Sunflower seeds, pumpkin seeds and flax seeds

1 ½ Tbsp. Coconut oil, melted

2Tbs Vanilla (powder or extract)

1 Tsp. Almond extract

1 Tsp. Coconut extract

2 Tbsp. Agave or pure maple syrup

1 Tsp. Cinnamon

1 Hand full of shredded coconut

¾ Cup slivered almonds

½ Tsp. Maca powder

Place all ingredients in a food processor, blend until nuts are bite size pieces. Spread onto baking sheet and bake until nuts are golden brown.

Eat as a trail mix or serve with rice or nut milk as a great alternative to regular cereal

MAMA'S BREAKFAST BOWL

Serves 2

4 Poached organic eggs

¼ Head of cauliflower (to make cauliflower rice)

½ Avocado diced

1 Small diced tomato

Fresh lime to taste

Pinch of chili powder

Pinch of curry powder

Pinch of coriander (optional)

Pinch of cumin (optional)

CAULIFOWER RICE

Steam the cauliflower. Then place in a food processor and blend with:

1 Garlic clove

1 Tsp. Tahini

1Tbs Coconut oil

1 Tbsp. Fresh lime juice

In a bowl make a bed of the cauliflower rice then place the poached eggs on top. Garnish with the remaining ingredients.

I usually add Basil and cilantro to my bowl, these ingredients add a great fresh flavor and added nutrients

APPLE CINNAMON SPICE CEREAL

Serves 1

1 Cup Store bought, gluten free granola

½ Tsp. Vanilla extract

Dash cinnamon

¼ Apple, diced

Mix together in a bowl and serve over nut or rice milk

Chia seed 'oatmeal'

1/4c chia seeds

1/4c water

In a small saucepan on low heat: add in chia seeds and water. Stir occasionally and remember that it cooks really quick so don't leave the area. Once the chia mix starts to gel up than its done. Transfer immediately to a bowl. Option is up to you to pour coconut, rice or almond milk over. Top with seeds, fruit and/or cinnamon.

Chia seeds can absorb up to 12x its weight in water which is incredible for hydration. They are tiny seeds but are high in fiber and omega 3s essential fatty acids which makes them incredibly nutritious and great for digestion.

Other Suggestions for breakfast options are:

-Fruit!

- Avocado with sea salt

-Steel Cut Oats with honey and topping of choice (fruit, nuts, seeds or dried fruit)

-Gluten free, Sprouted grain bread with almond butter ,or avocado

-Boiled Egg with sea salt and black pepper or even some mustard and dill

SALADS

Always have a fresh organic salad before main meals. The live enzymes will ease digestion and help move the bulk through from your more dense meal.

GARLICKY DILL BEAN SALAD

Serves 5

1 lb. Small dried fava beans

½ Cup olive oil

1 ½ Tbsp. Parsley, minced

3 Tbsp. Dill, minced

1 Tsp. Ground cumin

4 Garlic cloves, minced

Juice of a lemon

Sea salt and freshly ground pepper to taste

Drain beans and place in a 4qt saucepan, cover with water by 2 inches, and bring to a boil over a high heat. Then reduce heat to a medium low, simmer, stirring occasionally until tender, about an hour. Drain the beans and transfer to a bowl, add the oil, parsley, dill, cumin, garlic, juice, salt and pepper. Let stand for 30 minutes to let the flavors marry before serving.

CRANBERRY, CABBAGE & ALMOND CHOPPED SALAD

Serves 1

¼ Green cabbage, chopped

½ Red bell pepper

1 Large carrot, chopped

¼ Cup Almonds

1/3 Cup Dried cranberries

Juice of lime

2 Tbsp. Flax seed oil

2 Tbsp. Agave nectar

1/3 Cup red onion, minced

1 Large Avocado, chopped

Place all the ingredient's into a large food processor and pulse until chopped and enjoy.

THE BEST KALE SALAD

Serves 1-2

1 Head of Kale

2 Handfuls of sprouts

3 Tomatoes, chopped

1-2 Avocados, chopped

1 Handful fresh dill

Take the kale leaves of the stems (you can juice the stems later), add a dash of sea salt to the kale leaves, tear them into pieces and place them into a bowl along with all the other ingredients.

Dressing :

Juice of 2 lemons

4 Tbsp. Nutritional yeast*

1 Tsp. Paprika (I use smoked paprika or chipotle spice for a spicy and smoky taste)

1 Tsp. Mustard powder

4 Tbsp. Dulse flakes

Pinch of sea salt

2 Tbsp. olive oil

Wisk all the ingredients together and toss into salad.

*Nutritional yeast is deactivated yeast that is dried and flakey. I use it as a spice or to add a cheese like flavor to simple salads and salad dressing. It is fortified with vitamin B12

SUPER EASY MEXICAN SALAD

Serves 2

15 oz. Black beans

15 oz. pinto beans

2 Tomatoes, diced

1 Bell pepper, diced

½ Cup cilantro, chopped

3 Scallions, diced

2 Tbsp. Avocado oil

2 Tbsp. Lemon juice

1 Tbsp. Apple cider vinegar

Mix all the ingredients together and let the flavors marinate in the fridge for 1-2 hours, then serve !!

LIGHT ITALIAN DRESSING

Makes 1 cup

3 Tbsp. Apple cider vinegar

2 Tsp. Mustard

1 Tsp. Sea salt

2 ½ Tsp. Italian seasoning

1 Cup water

Wisk together and pour over any salad of you choice !!!

CAJUN SALAD

Serves 1

1 ½ Cup Greens of your choice

1 Handful chopped basil

½ Cup Sundried tomatoes

½-1 Ripe avocado, diced

1 Handful sprouts

3-4 Radishes

1 Tbsp. Ground flax seeds

Mix all ingredients in a large bowl.

DRESSING:

2-3 Tbsp. Nutritional yeast

2-3 Tbsp. Dulse flakes

¾-1 Tbsp. Cajun spice mix

Juice of a lemon

Olive oil

Wisk ingredients and drizzle over salad.

Inspired by Author and Nutritionist: Kimberly Snyder. This salad is bursting with flavor.Eevery mouthful is just amazing.

MY FAVORITE SALAD

Serves 1

1 Head greens of choice

1-2 Avocado, sliced

1 Lrg. Hot house tomato, sliced (or 3 small, your choice)

2 Handfuls Alfalfa sprouts (or sprouts of your choice)

Place all ingredients in a large salad bowl and drizzle with the dressing.

DRESSING:

1 Tbsp. Olive oil

2 Lemons, juice

4 Tbsp. Nutritional yeast

1 Tsp. Mustard

2 Tbsp. Dulse flakes

Wisk together all the ingredients

This salad is very similar to the 'Best kale salad' except it's quicker and lighter

MEXICAN SPINACH SALAD

Serves 1

5 Cup Spinach

½ Red bell pepper, diced

½ Red onion, diced

½ Cucumber, diced

¼ Green onions, diced

½ Cup Cilantro, chopped

½ Lemon, juice

½ Lime, juice

1 Avocado, diced

½ Cup Corn

Mix all ingredients in a large salad bowl and enjoy!!!

This salad is great Mexican night meal for the whole family, I usually eat it in lettuce wraps

SESAME CREAM

Serves 1

1/3 Cup Whole sesame seeds

4 Plum tomatoes

Grind the sesame seeds in a coffee grinder. Blend the tomatoes in a blender until smooth, then add the ground sesame seeds and blend together. If you have a vita-mix, you can actually blend everything all at once with no problems. This recipe creates a delish cream that you can enjoy as a dressing or a snack on gluten free toasted bread.

CUCUMBER MINT SALAD

Serves 4

3 Medium cucumbers, diced into ½ inch cubes

¼ Cup Red onion, chopped

¼ Cup Fresh dill, finely chopped

1 Tsp. Fresh dill, chopped

¼ Fresh mint leaves, chopped

2 Tbsp. Olive oil

½ Tsp. Agave

1 Tsp. Lime juice

Place the cuke pieces in a bowl. Add in the onion, dill and mint. In a separate bowl whisk together the wet ingredients to make the dressing. Drizzle over the cukes and enjoy.

HEMP SEED DRESSING

½ Cup Hemp seed, shelled

1/3 Cup Soaked raisin

1/3 Cup Fresh lemon juice

2 Tsp. Lemon zest

1 Tsp. Ginger, minced

1 Tbsp. Coconut aminos*

1 Clove raw garlic

1 Tsp. Cayenne

½ -1 Cup Fresh water

Sea salt to taste

Blend all of the ingredients together, and chill in a glass container in the refrigerator. Serve over you favorite salad.

*Coconut Aminos is an a soy sauce alternative. It's raw, vegan and gluten free plus has less sodium. It is made from the sap of a coconut tree and soooo delish.

SALAD WITH CARROT GINGER DRESSING

Makes 1 cup

1 inch Fresh Ginger, chipped

2 Carrots, grated

2 Tbsp. Coconut Secret aminos or gluten free Tamari

2 Tbsp. Fresh Lemon or Lime juice

1t Sesame oil (completely optional, I leave it out)

Blend ingredients together in a blender until smooth. Serve over a large salad. My favorite greens for this salad is Spinach anf I top it with Saurkraut

GRAND GREEN SALAD

Serves 4

4 Scallions

½ Cucumber, chopped

1 Handful Fresh basil leaves, chopped

2 Ripe avocados, peeled and sliced

1 Butter head lettuce, chopped

1 Handful Alfalfa, chopped

2 Oz Vegan cheese, or raw Goat cheese grated

6 Tbsp. Extra virgin olive oil

2 Tbsp. Red wine vinegar

1 Tsp. Mustard powder

Sea salt and black pepper to season

Place all your dry ingredients on a large chopping board. Mix together by further chopping. Place in a large salad bowl to serve and sprinkle the cheese over the top of your salad. Next whisk the olive oil, vinegar and mustard powder together in a small bowl and drizzle over the salad and enjoy.

RICE SALAD

Serves 4

1 ¼ Cups Long grain and wild rice

1 Tbsp. Fresh basil, chopped

1 Tbsp. Fresh mint, chopped

1 Tbsp. Fresh parsley, chopped

8 Oz Roasted red bell peppers, chopped

½ Fresh red Chile, chopped

½ Cup Lemon juice

2 Tbsp. Olive oil

Cook the rice in a large pan, drain and let cool. Whisk together the olive oil and the lemon juice and drizzle over the cooled down rice and mix well. Add in all your chopped herbs and peppers and toss your rice salad. Season to taste and enjoy.

MOLLYS HOMEMADE CEASER DRESSING

¼ Cup Fresh lemon juice

2 Tsp. Coconut vinegar, or apple juice cider

2 Tsp. Yellow mustard

2 Garlic cloves, minced

½ Tsp. Sea salt

½ Tsp. Black pepper

¾ Cup Olive oil

1 Tsp. Honey

½ Cup Coconut milk, unsweetened

1 Tabs Tahini

1 Tbsp. Onion, chopped

Toss all the ingredients in a blender and blend until smooth, pour over you favorite salad or enjoy as a dipping sauce.

CAESAR SALAD

Serves 6

2 Heads Romaine lettuce, chopped

½ Cup Kalamata olives, pitted

1 Cup sourdough croutons

DRESSING OR MOLLYS HOMEMADE CEASER DRESSING

8 Oz Soft silken tofu

3 Tbsp. Lemon juice

1 Tbsp. Chickpea miso

3 Tbsp. Apple cider vinegar

3 Garlic cloves, minced

1 Tsp. Ginger, grated

2 Tsp. Brown rice syrup

1 Cup Extra virgin olive oil

1 Tbsp. Fresh chopped coriander

Place the lettuce in a bowl and top with the olive oil and the croutons. In a food processor whip the tofu until smooth. Add in the remaining ingredients and process until combined. Pour the dressing over the salad, toss and serve.

PESTO DRESSING

Serves 2

½ Cup Pesto

2 Tbsp. Fresh lemon juice

¼ Cup Fresh Lime juice

Place ingredients in a bowl and combine well.

TAHINI LEMON DESSING

Serves 4

½ Cup Raw tahini

½ Cup H20

¼ Cup Fresh Lemon juice

½ Tsp. Garlic, minced

¼ Tsp. Sea salt

Dash cayenne

1 Tbsp. Fresh parsley, minced

Place tahini, H20, Lemon juice, cumin, garlic, salt and cayenne in a blender and puree until smooth. Add parsley and puree further.

SPINACH STRAWBERRY SALAD

Serves 4

1 Tbsp. Coconut oil, melted

3 Cups Baby spinach

1 Cup Arugula

10 Fresh Strawberries, hulled and sliced

¼ Cup Frozen raspberries

Juice of one navel orange

Toss the spinach and arugula with the sliced strawberries in a bowl. Combine raspberries, orange and coconut oil in a blender and puree until smooth. Toss the dressing with the spinach and strawberries and mix until evenly coated.

TUNA CEVICHE SALAD

Serves 6

2 Tbsp. Coconut oil, melted

1 Cup Fresh lemon juice

1 Cup Fresh lime juice

1 Garlic clove, minced

1 Jalapeno pepper, diced

½ Tsp. Sea salt

1 Lb. Boneless skinless sashiml-grade tune

1 Cup Sweet corn

3 Cups Baby spinach leaves

4 Plum tomatoes, chopped

2 Ripe avocados, cubed

Fresh cilantro for garnish, chopped

Combine the juices, garlic, jalapeno and salt in a blender and pulse until smooth. Cut the tuna into 1-inch cubes. Marinate the tuna with the mixture from your blender in the fridge for 1 hour. In a skillet melt the oil until hot. Flash fry the Tuna for 30 secs. and serve over the spinach.

SOUP

Soups are easy on digestion, which means the body can use more time healing itself instead of putting its effort into breaking down such a dense meal

CLASSIC GAZPACHO

Serves 4

6 Lrg. Plum tomatoes, quartered

½ Cucumber, peeled and chopped

½ Bell pepper, you color choice

2 Cloves garlic

2 Tbsp. Sea salt

1 Tsp. Cayenne pepper

2Tbs Goats cheese, optional

Place all ingredients in a food processor and blend until smooth. Garnish with some fresh basil and enjoy.

Rinse the noodles in warm water to bring them to room temperature. In a bowl toss all the ingredients together, garnish with fresh basil and goats cheese and serve.

WHITE BEAN SOUP

Serves 6

1-½ Cups Cannellini beans, soaked overnight

1 Bay leaf

5 Tbsp. Olive oil

1 Medium onion, chopped

1 Carrot, chopped

1 Celery stalk, chopped

3 Medium tomatoes, diced

2 Clove garlic, minced

1 Tsp. Fresh thyme, chopped

3 Cups Water, boiled

Sea salt and pepper to taste

Drain the beans and place in a large saucepan of water, bring to a boil and cook for 20 mines. Drain again and return the beans to the pan. Cover with cold water and add the bay leaf and cook for 1-2 hrs. Remove the bay leaf and puree ¾ of the beans in a food processor until you have a smooth paste. Heat the oil in a large frying pan; cook the onion until light golden brown. Add the carrot and celery and cook until softened. Stir in the tomatoes, garlic and thyme, and cook for a further 6-8 minutes. Next stir in the boiling water and add all the beans and stir until well combined. Simmer for 10-15 mins. Season with salt and pepper and serve.

TOMATO, LENTIL AND ONION SOUP

Serves 4-6

2 Tbsp. Olive oil

1 Lrg. Onion, chopped

2 Celery stalks, chopped

¾ Cup Split red lentils

2 Lrg. Tomatoes, roughly chopped

3-¾ Cups Low sodium veggie stock

2 Tsp. Dried Italian herbs

Sea salt and black pepper to taste

Fresh parsley, chopped

Heat oil in a large saucepan, add the celery and onion and cook until softened. Next add the lentils and cook the mixture for about 1 min. Then stir in the tomatoes, stock and herbs. Cover, bring to a boil and simmer for about 15-20 mins. When lentils are cooked let the soup cool down to room temperature, then puree in a food processor until smooth. Season with salt and pepper to taste, garnish it with the parsley and enjoy

PUMPKIN SOUP

Serves 4

1 Lb Pumpkin, diced into 1 inch cubes

4 Tbs coconut oil, melted

I Medium onion, chopped

3 Cups Low sodium veggie stock

2 Cups Rice milk

Pinch Nutmeg

Sea salt and black pepper to taste

Heat the cocnut oil in a pan, add the onion and cook until lightly golden. Stir in the pumpkin cubes and cook for approx 3-4 mins. Next add the stck and cook until pumpkin is soft, approx 15 mins, and remove from heat. Puree the mixture in a blender intil smooth, then return to pan. Gradually stir in the milk and add the nutmeg. When well combined, season to taste and enjoy.

VEGGIE POTATO SOUP

Serves 8

3 Tbsp. Coconut oil

1 Onion, sliced thinly

5 Potatoes, or sweet potatoes

4 Celery stalks

5 Small zucchinis, grated

2 Parsnips, grated

3 Garlic cloves, minced

6 Cups Low sodium chicken or veggie broth

1 ½ Tsp. Sea salt

Pinch of black pepper

1 Cup Fresh parsley, chopped

1 Cup Pinto beans

Heat coconut oil in a soup pot on a medium – high heat. Add onion, celery and garlic until golden brown. Then add all the other veggies and potatoes and stir well. Add broth, seasoning and beans, bring to a boil, and then simmer for 15 mins. Puree the soup in a food processor, garnish with fresh parsley and enjoy!!!

SWEET POTATO AND LEEK SOUP

Serves 8

3 Tbsp. Coconut oil or olive oil

2 Tbsp. Rice milk, or coconut milk

2 Onions, diced

4 Leeks, trimmed and diced

2 Parsnips, peeled and diced

2 Cups Cauliflower, diced

5 Small sweet potatoes, or regular, peeled and diced

2 Cloves garlic, minced

2 Tsp. Sea salt

8 Cups Low sodium chicken or veggie broth

Dash paprika

Dash Black pepper

In a soup pot heat the coconut oil or olive oil on a medium – high heat. Add onions, leeks, cauliflower, parsnips and garlic. Stir constantly until golden. Add the potatoes, seasonings and broth and bring to a boil. Reduce heat and simmer for 35-40 minutes, or until veggies are tender. Then puree in a food processor and enjoy.

Coconut milk makes it rich, thick and creamy. Whereas rice milk allows the sweet potato to take center stage with a subtle texture

CURRIED SWEET POTATO BISQUE

Serves 2

4 Lrg. Sweet potatoes, peeled and diced

4 Tbsp. Coconut oil, melted

5 Fresh basil leaves, chopped

6 Small garlic cloves

3 Tbsp. Curry powder

3 Tsp Sea salt

3 Tsp Dried dill

2 Handfuls spinach

1 ½ - 2 Cups boiling water, or coconut milk

Preheat oven to 400f. Toss together in a bowl, coconut oil, potatoes, basil, garlic cloves and curry powder. Then place the ingredients on a baking sheet and cook for 25 mins. or until tender. Let cool then toss in a bowl with sea salt, dill, and spinach. Place all ingredients in a blender with the water or coconut milk. Blend until smooth and enjoy. If the soup is to thick add more liquid.

BROCCOLI CREAM SOUP

Serves 4

1 ½ Lbs. Broccoli, chopped

2 Tbsp. Olive oil

2 Garlic cloves

2 Tbsp. Creamed coconut, a good brand is 'let's do organic'

Sea salt and black pepper to taste

In a pot of salted water, cook broccoli for 4 -6 mins. until soft, do not overcook. When cooked, drain and reserve 3 tbsp. of the water for later. In a large pot add olive oil and garlic; cook until garlic is lightly golden. In a blender puree the broccoli and the reserved water then transfer to the pot with the garlic and olive oil. Stir well and bring to a boil. Reduce the heat to a light simmer then add the cream. Add salt and pepper to taste, and then serve.

Creamed coconut is dehydrated meat of a coconut conveniently packed in a little rectangular box. I use it to add some serious flavor, creaminess and 'oh my goodness' to my recipes. I don't melt it when it's going into a soup or stew as it melts by itself in any hot liquid based recipe

1 POTATO, 2 TOMATO SOUP

Serves 4

2 Plum tomatoes

1 Onion chopped

1 Sweet potato, chopped

4 Garlic cloves, minced

¾ Cup Olive oil

4 Cup Low sodium chicken or Veggie broth

1 Tbsp. Basil

1 Tbsp. Dried oregano

1 Tsp. Sea salt

Pinch of black pepper

Preheat oven to 350f. Pour ¾ cup olive oil into a glass-baking dish. Place tomatoes, halved side down in the dish, place carrots, sweet potato, onion and garlic to the dish. Place a sheet of parchment paper on top of dish to cover veggies and roast for 45 mins. Remove from oven to cool. When cooled place ingredients to a soup pot, add the stock and bring to a boil reduce heat, stir and simmer for 10 – 15 mins. Puree in a food processer and season to taste.

ROASTED CAULIFLOWER AND GARLIC SOUP

2 Heads cauliflower, chopped

4 Tbsp. Olive oil

1 Garlic bulb

1 Sweet onion, chopped

2 Tbsp. Mirin (chinese rice wine)

2 Tsp. Sea salt

4 Cups Low sodium veggie stock

2 Tbsp. Fresh thyme

2 Tsp. Black pepper

Preheat the oven to 350f. In a baking dish place the cauliflower and drizzle with olive oil. Wrap the garlic bulb in foil after rubbing it with olive oil. Place both in the oven and roast for 1 hour. Remove form the oven and set aside. Once cooled separate the garlic bulb. In a large pot sauté the onion until translucent, next add the cauliflower, garlic, mirin, sea salt and stock. Bring to a boil and simmer for 5 mins. Remove from heat and puree until smooth. Return to the pan and heat through adding in the thyme, and whit pepper and simmer for a further 20 mins. Garnish with thyme leaves and serve.

CREAMY SPLIT PEA SOUP

Serves 6

1 Large onion, chopped

3 Stalks celery, chopped

1 Tbsp. Coconut oil

3 Tbsp., Mirin

3 Tbsp. Thyme

Sea salt to taste

White pepper to taste

3 Cups Split peas, rinsed

10 Cups Low sodium veggie stock

1 Lemon, zest and juice

Heat the coconut oil and sauté the onion and celery until translucent and golden brown. Next add the thyme, mirin and season to taste with salt and pepper. Add the peas and veggies, next incorporate the stock and bring to a boil. Reduce heat and simmer for 2 ½ hours. Remove from heat and mix in the lemon juice and garnish with the zest.

GINGER, SHIITAKE AND CABBAGE SOUP

Serves 6

12 Dried Shiitake mushrooms

8 Cups water

1 Tbsp. Fresh grated ginger

1 Large leek, chopped

1 Tbsp. coconut oil, melted

2 Cups Green cabbage, chopped

1 Carrot, grated

1 Cup Edamame beans

2 Tbsp. Tamari

1 Tsp. Plum vinegar

Boil the mushrooms until soft and retain the stock. When cooled, slice into thin strips. Set the mushrooms and stock aside. Sauté the ginger and leek until translucent. Next add the mushroom slices and sauté for a further 4-5 mins. Add the cabbage, carrots, beans, tamari and stock. Cover and simmer for 10 mins. Remove from heat, stir in the vinegar and enjoy.

SALMON AND CORN CHOWDER

1 Lb. Salmon fillets, or haddock cut into 1-inch cubes

2 Tbsp. coconut oil, non-melted

2 Tbsp. Olive oil

2 Shallots, minced

4 Cups Low sodium chicken stock

4 Red potatoes, unpeeled and cut into ½ inch cubes

2 Cups Sweet corn

1 Cup Creamed coconut

Sea salt to taste

Black pepper to taste

Fresh basil, chopped for garnish

In a frying pan, melt 1 Tbsp. coconut oil over a medium heat. Add the salmon and sauté until opaque on the outside, approx. 2-3 mines. In a large saucepan over a medium heat melt the remaining coconut oil and add the shallots. Sauté until translucent. Add the stock and bring to a boil. Reduce the heat add the potatoes and simmer for 15 mins. In a blender combine the ½ cup of sweet corn and the creamed coconut, puree until smooth. Add this mixture to the stock. Add the remaining creamed coconut and the remaining corn to the stock and simmer for a further 5 mins. Once simmered add the salmon and simmer for a further 2 mins. Season with salt and pepper and garnish with basil.

CORN CHOWDER

Serves 4

1 Tbsp. Coconut oil, melted

1 Onion, chopped

2 Stalks celery, chopped

2 Carrots, chopped

1 Medium potatoes, peeled and diced

¼ Cup Mirin*

½ Tsp. Sea salt

3 ½ Cups Corn, fresh or frozen

5 Cups Rice milk

Sea salt and pepper to taste

In a large pot over medium heat, melt the coconut oil and sauté the onions until soft. Add the celery, carrots, potatoes, mirin and sea salt. Sauté for 4-5 mins. Add corn and cover the ingredients in the pot with enough milk to cover. Reduce heat and simmer for 20 mins. Remove from heat and puree gently in a blender. Add water as needed to achieve desired consistency. Serve to taste with sea salt and pepper.

*Mirin is a Japanese rice wine

French Onion Soup

Serves 4 bowls

4 Onions, Chopped

2 - 32oz Vegetable broth (I use Pacific)

2 Tbsp. Coconut oil

6 drops Stevia

4 Kale Leaves, Diced

salt and pepper to taste

1 Tbsp. Coriander

1 tsp. dried Oregano

2 fresh Garlic cloves, minced

Preheat the oven to 400 degrees F.

Coat a Large glass baking dish with 1Tbsp coconut oil. Add in the onions and stir in the remaining 1 Tbsp. coconut oil, 2 Cups of the vegetable broth, stevia drops, garlic, and spices. Bake for approx. 20 minutes or until onions are tender.

Then transfer to a food processor. Pulse, until onions are in pieces (about half the size)

Topping options : half of an avocado, diced. Gluten free grain bread, cubed, goat cheese or vegan cheese (option is yours if you want to melt the cheese)

Serve and Enjoy!!

MOMS CLASSIC CHICKEN SOUP

Makes 1 large pot

1 (organic, free range) Whole Chicken, roasted and picked apart.

4 Carrots, sliced

3 Celery, sliced

1 Onion, diced

4 fresh garlic, minced

fresh parsley & thyme, chopped

2- 32oz organic Chicken broth

½ tsp. Garlic powder

½ tsp. Onion Powder

Black pepper to taste

2 Tbsp. Olive oil

Bake the chicken at 350 degrees for about 1hr and 10 minutes (or until fully cooked). Pick the chicken apart and transfer the pieces onto a dish.

(If you want to make homemade chicken broth, just fill a large pot with water, place in the chicken Carcass, 1 Tbsp. Balsamic vinegar (to release the minerals from the bones), same vegetables listed above (no need to dice anything tiny, you are going to get the flavor from everything than toss it out, reserving just the broth and adding in the same soup vegetables and reserved chicken pieces), 1 Tbsp. sea salt, fresh Parsley and Thyme. Bring to a boil than lower the heat. Simmer for 8-10 hrs. adding water continuously.

(Back to the actual recipe) In a large pot on medium flame, heat the olive oil. Sauté garlic and onions until lightly golden or until onions are translucent. Toss in carrots, celery, all remaining ingredients including the chicken broth and lastly the chicken pieces.

Bring to a boil then let simmer for 4-5 hrs. (I recommend serving it the next day, the flavors are aloud to increase by sitting together over night)

VEGETABLE DISHES

Do not underestimate vegetables. Usually a lot more often then not people look at vegetables and automatically label it bland and tasteless just because it's considered a powerful healthy food category. Anyone that comes into my house when I'm cooking veggies ask me what the occasion is and what I'm cooking because the aroma is sinful. That person leaves with chosen recipes that I present to you.

MOUTH WATERING ROASTED VEGETABLES

Serves 2-3

4 Carrots, chopped

2 Heads broccoli, chopped

2 Bell peppers

2 Lrg. Zucchini, chopped

¼ Cup Olive oil

1 Tsp. Garlic powder

1 Tsp. Onion powder

2 Tsp. Sea salt

1 Tsp. Black pepper

Preheat oven to 350f. Toss chopped vegetables and remaining ingredients in a bowl. Then transfer to a glass baking dish, 9x13, and bake for approx. 30 mins.

There is nothing like the scent and taste of roasted vegetables right out of the oven, they never reach the plate in my house as everyone picks at them on the baking dish

BAKED YAMS

Serves 2-3

2 Lbs. yams, chopped and peeled

2 Tbsp. Olive oil

2 Tsp. Sea salt

Preheat oven to 375f. Toss all the ingredients in a bowl, spread on a baking sheet and bake in the oven for 1 ½ hours, or until tender.

TUSCAN GRILLED ZUCCHINI AND TOMATOES

Serves 3-4

3-4 Kabob Skewers

2 Med zucchini, chopped

2 Med yellow squash, chopped

2 Tbsp. Olive oil

½ Tsp. Sea salt

½ Tsp. pepper

2 Tomatoes, quartered

6 Garlic cloves, 3 whole, 3 minced

In a bowl combine zucchini, squash, olive oil, salt and pepper, tomatoes and garlic. Place the whole garlic cloves, veggies and tomatoes on skewers, grill on a med-high heat until all sides are cooked till tender. When cooked remove from heat and prepare the Tuscan oil. When made, pour the Tuscan oil over the kabobs and serve.

-TUSCAN OIL:

3 Tbsp. Olive oil,

Juice and zest of a lemon

2 Tbsp. Fresh thyme, minced

2 Tbsp. Fresh parsley, minced

2Tsp Hot pepper flakes

1 Tbsp. Nutritional yeast

1 Tbsp. Mustard powder

1 Tbsp. Apple cider vinegar

BAKED SWEET POTATOES

Serves 2-3

2 Lbs. Sweet potatoes, chopped

2 Tbsp. Coconut oil, melted

1 Tbsp. Curry powder

1 Tsp. Turmeric

1 Tbsp. Oregano

1 Tbsp. Rosemary

1 Tsp. Sea salt

Preheat oven to 350f. Place sweet potatoes and coconut oil in a glass baking dish and mix together. Then add the spices and toss until even. Bake for 1 hr. 30 mins, or until tender.

ROASTED TOMATOES

Serves 2

6 Plum tomatoes, halved

¾ Cup Olive oil

Sea salt to taste

½ Cup Fresh basil leaves, chopped

Preheat oven to 350f. Line a baking dish with parchment paper; brush the tomato halves with the oil, sprinkle with seasoning and roast in the oven for 3 hrs. When roasted let cool and sprinkle with the basil. You can also blend in a food processor to make a super easy fresh tomato sauce, just sprinkle the fresh basil on after processing.

BEAUTY OF THE BEETS

Serves 2

5 Lrg. Beets, chopped 1-1/2 inches thick

2-3 Tbsp. Coconut oil

Sea salt to taste

Preheat oven to 350f. In a glass dish toss all the ingredients together and the place on a baking sheet. Bake for 45mins – 1hr, until tender and enjoy.

KOMBU NOODLE PASTA

Serves 2

12 Oz Kombu seaweed noodles

3 Plum tomatoes, finely chopped

1 Cup Fresh basil, chopped

1 Clove garlic, diced

1 Tbsp. Sea salt

Black pepper to taste

ROASTED RATATOULILLE

Serves 4

2 Small onions cut into ¼ inch thick half moons

2 Red bell peppers, peeled, cored and cut into ¼ inch strips

1 Medium eggplant cut crosswise into ½ inch slices

2 Medium zucchinis cut into ¼ inch rounds

15 Whole Garlic cloves

2 Cup spinach

½ Cup plus 2 Tbsp. olive oil

1Tsp Rosemary

Sea salt

4 Medium ripe tomatoes, peeled and chopped

¼ Cup Fresh basil

Preheat oven to 350f. In a pan stir fry the garlic, onion, and ¼ cup of olive oil until translucent. Add the remaining ingredients and cook until golden brown. Place the cooked vegetables in a baking dish along with the remaining olive oil and bake for 15 – 20 mins.

CABBAGE &CARROT STIR-FRY

Serves 6

1 ½ Tsp. Cumin powder

2 Tbsp. Olive oil

¾ Tsp. Ground coriander

½ Tsp. Black pepper

½ Jalapeno, finely chopped

6 Cups Thinly sliced green cabbage

2 Cups Grated carrots

2-½ Tsp. Sea salt

1 ½ Tsp. Agave

½ Cup Cilantro, chopped

3 Tbsp. fresh lime juice

Heat the oil in a wok and add the jalapenos, cook until softened. Then add the carrots and cabbage. Stir occasionally for approximately 3-4 mins. Stir in the cumin powder, salt and agave and cook for 30 secs. Remove from heat and add cilantro and lime juice. Serve at room temperature or cold.

This recipe is great to store in the fridge as leftovers. I usually have it for breakfast, lunch or dinner the next day over a large leafy green salad

LEMON GARLIC GREEN BEANS

3 Cups Green beans

3 Tbsp. olive oil

2 Tbsp. Lemon juice

5 Garlic cloves, minced

½ Onion

Heat pan on stove with olive oil, then add the onions and the garlic. Cook until golden. Add in remaining ingredients, sauté until tender. This acts as a great side dish with the herb crusted chicken recipe.

SAUTEED BUTTERNUT SQUASH

Serves 2-3

2 Tbsp. Olive oil

2 Tbsp. coconut oil, melted

3 Cups Butternut Squash, peeled and diced in ½ inch pieces

1 Tsp. Sea salt

1 Tsp. Black Pepper

¼ Cup Fresh flat leaf parsley, chopped

1/3 Cup Walnuts, chopped

1 ½ Tsp. Grated lemon zest

Heat the olive oil and coconut oil in a sauté pan. Add the squash, salt and pepper. Cook until squash is golden and tender, about 8-10 mins. Transfer squash to a serving bowl and toss in all the other ingredients, Serve immediately.

SPICY CITRUS ZUCCHINI NOODLES

3-4 Zucchini, spiralized into spaghetti

1 Grapefruit, juiced

3 Tbsp. Fresh lemon grass slices

1 Tbsp. Chili sauce

2 Tbsp. Sesame oil

1 Tbsp. Coconut sugar, sifted

1 Tbsp. Lemon juice

1 Tsp. dried ginger, or freshly grated

½ Cup Green onions, chopped

1 Tbsp. Brown rice vinegar

¼ Almond butter

Whisk together all the ingredients the zucchini's. When well combined, drizzle over the zucchini noodles. Great to serve with CFC Chicken recipe.

Make sure you make a note to yourself to purchase a spiralizer. It can be conveniently purchased online.

Let's just say you wont regret buying one when delicious flourless spaghetti is on your plate.

ROASTED RADISHES

Serves 4-6

3 Bunches Radishes, halved

1/8 Cup Olive oil

1/8 Cup Coconut oil, melted

¼ Tsp. Black pepper ¼ Tsp. Sea salt

Juice 1 Lemon

1 Tbsp. Fresh rosemary, chopped

Preheat oven to 475 f. Place radish halves in a bowl. Drizzle with oils, and coat evenly. Next add the remaining ingredients and combine well. Place the radish mixture evenly on a cookie sheet and bake in the oven for 15-20 mins. Season to taste.

TURNIP AND RUTABAGA FRIES

Serves 4

2 Rutabagas

2 Turnips

¼ Cup Olive oil

1 Tsp. Dried garlic

1 Tbsp. Dried rosemary

1 Tsp. Sea salt

Preheat oven to 450 f. cut the turnips and rutabagas into spears about ½ inch thick. Microwave for 8 mins. Transfer spears to a baking pan and sprinkle with garlic and salt. Bake for 15-18 mins, stirring 2 during cooking time so they don't burn.

VEGGIE KEBABS

Makes 4 kebabs

2 Bell peppers, sliced

12 Mushrooms

12 Grape tomatoes

3 Small Onions, quartered

1 Eggplant, cut into 1-inch cubes

MARINADE

1 Cup Olive oil

2 Tbsp. Coconut oil, melted

1 Cup Red bell pepper, chopped

Juice of 2 Limes

2 Tbsp. Grated ginger

2 Tsp Minced garlic

Sea salt to taste

1 Cup Fresh cilantro

Soak 4 wooden skewers in water for 30 mins. Thread the veggies on the skewers and arrange on a plate. Mix all the marinade ingredients, except the cilantro, in a blender until well combined. Next add the cilantro and pulse once or twice until incorporated. Marinade the kebabs for 2 hours. Grill on a medium heat until soft and lightly browned.

VEGGIE HASH

Serves4

1 Medium yellow onion

3 Garlic cloves, minced

3 Tbsp. Coconut oil, melted

2 Cups Sweet potato, grated

2 Cups Potatoes, grated

1 Cup Zucchini, grated

1 Cup Yellow summer squash, grated

¼ Cup Fresh parsley, chopped

Sea salt and black pepper to taste

Melt 1 tbsp. oil in a large skillet. Sauté the onion and garlic until caramelized. Add the sweet potato and white potatoes and sauté for a further 6 mins. Add the zucchini, squash and parsley and season to taste. Continue to sauté for a further 10 mins until veggies are cooked through. Turn broiler onto high, and place skillet under the heat until the hash has a crisp crust on the top. Remove from oven and flip the hash and return to the broiler until that side is crisp also. Serve and enjoy.

JERUSALEM ARTICHOKES WITH LEMON

Serves 4

8-10 Jerusalem artichokes

2 Tbsp. Coconut oil, melted

4 Garlic cloves, minced

2 Tbsp. Lemon juice

1 Tbsp. Fresh rosemary, finely chopped

Sea salt and black pepper to taste

Scrub the artichokes well, and slice widthwise. Melt the coconut oil in a large skillet and sauté the chokes for 2-3 mins. Add the Garlic and lemon juice and continue to sauté for a further 4-5 mins. Deglaze the pan with water. Next add the rosemary, salt and pepper and sauté until caramelized. Remove from heat and serve.

VEGGIE MEDLEY WITH CHILES

Serves 4

3 Medium sweet potatoes, peeled and chopped

1 Lb. Brussels sprouts, chopped

5 Parsnips, peeled and chopped

4 Shallots, quartered

8 Garlic cloves, peeled

4 Small hot chilies, halved

Coconut oil, melted

Corse sea salt

Preheat oven to 400f. Place all the veggies in a mixing bowl. Add the chilies to the bowl and drizzle with the coconut oil. Toss to combine, and spread the veggies onto a 9x13 glass casserole dish. Roast for 15 mins. and toss again. Roast for a further 15 mins. until veggies are soft. Season to taste and enjoy.

GREEN BEANS WITH GADO SAUCE

Serves 4

1 Lb. Green beans, topped and tailed and steamed

1 Tbsp. Coconut oil, melted

1 Sweet onion, sliced into rings

½ Sweet bell pepper, sliced thin

½ Cup Bean sprouts

3 Tbsp. Almonds, chopped

½ Cup Coconut milk

2 Tbsp. Nut butter

½ Lemon, juiced

2 Tsp. Coconut secret aminos or gluten free Tamari

2 Tsp. Ginger, minced

Pinch pepper flakes

To make the gado sauce mix the ginger and pepper flakes with the wet ingredients, except the coconut oil, thoroughly in a bowl and set aside. In a large wok sauté all the veggies, onion first, peppers second then the remaining veggies, until cooked. Add the beans sprout and nuts last. In a large bowl toss the cooked veggies with the prepared sauce and enjoy.

ASIAN VEGGIE NORI ROLLS

Serves 4

2 Sheets raw nori

4 Large collard green or romaine lettuce leaves

1-½ Cups Shredded carrots

1 ½ Cup Shredded daikon

1 Avocado, thinly sliced

8 Scallions, chopped

2 Cups Bean sprouts, chopped

¼ Cucumber, diced

1 Red bell pepper, chopped

Lay out the nori sheets on a clean dry surface. Arrange a collard green or lettuce leaf on top of each sheet. These leaves will prevent the nori sheet from becoming too moist from the veggies. Next layer your veggies, and then top with the daikon, avocado, scallions and sprouts in a line down the center. Wrap each sheet up like a burrito; moisten edges with a small amount of water and seal. Cut into two diagonally and enjoy.

ROASTED PARSLEY CARROTS

Serves 2-3

2 Cup Fresh carrots, chopped

1 Cup Fresh parsley, minced

5 Garlic cloves, minced

1 Tbsp. Coconut oil, melted

½ Tsp. Sea salt

¼ Cup Scallions, chopped

Preheat oven to 350 f. In a bowl toss carrots in oil and add the remaining ingredients. Place the mixture into a glass-baking dish for 15-20 mins. until tender

I serve these carrots with the Holy Mayan Roasted Chicken; it's to die for.

GARLIC MASHED POTATOES

4 Medium Sweet potatoes

1 Tbsp. Coconut oil

1 Tbsp. Fresh garlic, minced

1 ½ Cups Coconut milk

¾ Tsp. Sea salt

Black pepper

Preheat oven to 400 f. Bake the potatoes for 1 hour or until tender. Let them cool. Remove about half of the skin and mash the potatoes with the remaining skin. Melt the coconut oil in a large saucepan and over a medium heat sauté the garlic until golden brown. Add the potatoes and remaining ingredients to the pan and cook for 5-10 mins. stirring often.

SWEET POTATO SALAD

2 Lbs. Sweet potato, diced

6 Cups H2o

Sea salt

1 Cup Vegan gluten free mayo

4 Tbsp. Sweet pickle relish

2 Tsp. Onion, minced

2 Tsp. Yellow mustard

1 Tsp. Coconut vinegar

1 Tsp. Celery, minced

1 Tsp. Pimentos, diced

½ Tsp. Carrot, shredded

½ Tsp. Parsley, dried

¼ Tsp. Black pepper

Lightly peel the potatoes and cut into 1-inch cubes. Bring the water to a boil in a saucepan and cook the potato cubes until tender yet firm in the middle. In a medium bowl combine the remaining ingredients and whisk until smooth. Pour the drained potatoes in the bowl and combine with the dressing. Refrigerate for 4 hours.

ASPARAGUS WITH TOASTED PECANS AND MUSTARD

Serves 4

2 Lbs. Asparagus

¾ Cup Pecans

½ Cup Extra virgin olive oil

½ Cup Red wine vinegar

1 Tbsp. Whole Grain mustard

¼ Tsp. Sea salt

Fresh ground pepper

1 Tsp. Fresh Coriander, chopped

Preheat oven to 300F. In a small bowl whisk the vinaigrette ingredients together and set aside. Place pecans on a parchment lined cookie sheet and toast until lightly browned. Remove from oven to cool. To prepare the asparagus bend each stalk and snap off the tough end. Discard the ends and steam the asparagus until bright green. Remove from heat and place on a serving dish. Drizzle with the vinaigrette, top with the toasted pecans and enjoy.

ARTICHOKES, FENNEL AND OLIVES OVER ZUCCHINI NOODLES

Serves 4

3 Tbsp. Coconut oil, melted

1 Onion, diced

2 Garlic cloves, minced

1 Cup Canned artichoke hearts, quartered

½ Cup Kalamata olives, pitted

1 Fennel bulb, halved, cored and thinly sliced

1 Bunch arugula

1 Cup Freshly chopped tomatoes

½ Cup Fresh parsley, chopped

1 Tbsp. Lemon juice

Sea salt and black pepper to taste

Prepared zucchini noodles, in the veggie section of my book. Prepare the zucchini noodles as shown under the veggie section of my book. Meanwhile, in a large pot over medium heat, sauté the onions and garlic until soft. Add the artichokes, olives, fennel and arugula. Sauté until heated through and add the tomatoes and sauté for another 2 mins. Next add the parsley and lemon juice. Season to taste with salt and pepper, remove from heat and serve over the zucchini noodles.

GARLICKY ROASTED LEEKS AND VEGGIES

Serves 6

5 Tbsp. Coconut oil, melted

3 Leeks, chopped

2 Zucchinis

1 Cup Green beans, chopped

2 Carrots, diced

6 Garlic cloves, minced

1 Bell pepper, cut into strips

½ Cup Pearl onions

1 Tbsp. Fresh thyme, chopped

Sea salt and black pepper to taste

Preheat oven to 350 f. Prepare a lasagna dish with a light coat of oil. In a mixing bowl toss all the ingredients with the oil and place the mixture into the baking dish. Bake uncovered for 35 mins.

POTATOES ANNA

Serves 4

2 Sweet potatoes, thinly sliced

2 Medium Yukon gold potatoes

2 Tbsp. Coconut oil

2 Garlic cloves, minced

1 Tsp. Thyme

3 Fresh sprigs rosemary, chopped

1 Medium onion, chopped

Preheat oven to 425 f. Spray and ovenproof skillet with baking spray. In a bowl toss the sweet potatoes with half of the coconut oil, garlic and herbs. In another bowl toss the Yukon potatoes with the remaining oil, garlic and herbs. In the skillet layer the potato mixture evenly alternating between the sweet potatoes and the Yukon potatoes. Over a medium – high heat cook for 5 mins. Bake in the oven for 45, until tender. To serve flip the skillet upside down and cut into pie slices and enjoy.

ITALIAN PUMPKIN

1 Small cooking pumpkin

1 Tbsp. Coconut oil, melted.

1 Onion, chopped

2 Garlic cloves, minced

1 Tsp. Oregano

1 Tsp. Basil

Preheat oven to 350 f. Line a baking sheet with parchment paper. Wash the pumpkin and cut in halves. Scoop out the seeds and save to roast them later if desired. Place the pumpkin halves flesh side down on the baking sheet and prick the skin several times with a fork. Bake for 30 mins; remove from oven and let cool just enough so you can handle them. Peel off rind and cut into 1 ½ inch chunks. In a large frying pan over medium heat add the oil and onion, sauté until soft. Next add the garlic, cooked pumpkin and herbs. Season with sea salt and pepper and serve hot.

VEGETABLE COCONUT STEW

Serves 4

1Large Shallot, chopped

1 Cup Coconut, shredded

2 Garlic cloves, minced

1 Jalapeno, deseeded and cut in half

2 Tbsp. Coconut oil

1 Cucumber, diced

1 Head Caullflower, broken into florets

1 Carrot, sliced

2 Cups Green beans, halved

2 Tomatoes, diced

1 Tsp. Turmeric

½ Tsp. Cumin

1 ½ Cups Coconut milk

Sea salt to taste

½ Cup Creamed coconut

Combine the coconut flakes, shallot, garlic and jalapeno in a food processor and pulse until blended. In a deep saucepan warm the coconut oil and add the shallot mixture from the blender, sauté fro 5 mins. Next add the all the veggies and spices and sauté for a further 2 mins. Then add the coconut milk and creamed coconut. Bring to a rapid boil, cover and cook 8-10 mins.

GRILLED POTATO FRIES

Serves 4

2 Tsp. Sea salt

½ Tsp. Cumin

½ Tsp. Coriander

½ Tsp. Chili powder

½ Tsp. Paprika

½ Tsp. Allspice

½ Tsp. Thyme

½ Tsp. Black pepper

1 Lb. Sweet potatoes, cut length wise into wedges

3 ½ Tbsp. Olive oil

Preheat your grill to medium – high on one half; leave the other half of the grill at a low heat. Toss potatoes and olive oil in a bowl, coating evenly. Add the spices and combine well. Grill the potatoes on all side till golden brown. If you find potatoes burning move them to the low heat of the grill. When wedges are tender and crispy, remove and serve with the veggie patties.

GRAINS

Grains are powerful healing foods, when gluten free. Besides being delicious, grains offer some natural heaviness to ensure you stay on this lifestyle.

QUINOA AND SPINACH BOWL

Serves 1

1 ½ Cup Quinoa, cooked

¼ Onion, diced

¼ Red bell pepper, diced

2 Tbsp. Coconut oil, melted

1 Tbsp. Curry powder

½ Tbsp. Sea salt

2 Handfuls Spinach

2 – 3 Tbsp. House dressing

Add the coconut oil in a pan and heat. Sauté onion and pepper until golden and tender. Add the remaining ingredients, except the spinach and dressing, combine well. Serve on top of a bed spinach and drizzle with house dressing.

HOUSE DRESSING

¼ Cup Olive oil

2 Tbsp. Apple cider vinegar

1 Tbsp. Dried dill

1 Tbsp. Honey

1 Tbsp. Yellow mustard

Pinch Sea salt

Wisk all ingredients together in a bowl and drizzle over spinach and quinoa bowl.

MOLLY'S VEGGIE BURGERS

Serves 4

2 Tbsp. Coconut oil, melted

1 onion, diced

1 clove garlic, minced

3 green onions, diced

1/2 Tsp. cumin

3/4 Cup diced fresh mushrooms

15 Oz pinto beans

1 Tsp. Fresh parsley

Sea salt and black pepper to taste

2Tbs Olive oil

In a pan heat the olive oil and sauté the onions and garlic 3 to 5 minutes, until onions are lightly golden. Add the green onions, cumin and mushrooms and cook for further 5 minutes, until mushrooms are cooked. In a food processor pulse the beans until well mashed. Next add the mushrooms to the bean mixture and add parsley, salt and pepper. Stir until well combined. Shape the mixture into patties. Heat about two tablespoons of coconut oil and cook each side of the patty until golden brown, about 3 minutes on each side. Serve in lelluce wraps paired with my favorite grilled potato fries.

BAKED FENNEL WITH A CRUMB CRUST

Serves 4

3 Fennel bulbs, cut lengthways and quartered

2 Tbsp. Olive oil

1 Garlic clove, chopped

1 Cup Gluten free bread crumbs

2 Tbsp. Fresh Italian parsley, chopped

Sea salt and pepper to taste

Fennel sprigs for garnish

Preheat oven to 375f. Place the fennel in a baking dish and drizzle with olive oil. In a bowl mix together the garlic, breadcrumbs, parsley, and the remainder of the oil mix until well combined. Sprinkle the mixture evenly over the fennel and roast for 30 mins, until fennel is tender and the crumb topping is golden brown. Serve hot and garnish with fresh sprigs of fennel.

ZUCCHINI-TOMATO GRATIN

Serves 4

1 ½ Lb. Tomatoes, ¼ inch thick slices

2 Medium Zucchini, 1/8 inch slices

2 Tbsp. Olive oil

4 Garlic cloves, minced

2 Tbsp. Olives, chopped

¼ Cup Basil, chopped

3/4 Cup Vegan cheese or goat cheese, crumbled

Place tomatoes in a colander and sprinkle with salt, let drain for 45 mins. Spread the zucchini on a baking sheet and sprinkle with salt, and lest rest for 30 mins. Preheat oven to 375f. In a non-stick skillet heat 1 Tsp. oil and sauté the zucchini foe 3-4 mins. until golden brown. Layer half the zucchini in a casserole dish and top with half the tomatoes. Sprinkle half the garlic 1tbs olives and ¼ cup of cheese, then repeat. Season with salt and pepper. Drizzle olive oil over the top of the gratin. Cover with foil and bake for 10 mins. Then remove foil and bake for a further 20 mins. until cheese is melted and gratin is bubbling.

HEARTY LENTIL STEW

Serves 4

8 Lrg. Carrots, chopped

5 Celery stalks, chopped

1 Leek, chopped

1 Head broccoli, chopped

1 Zucchini, chopped

1 Cup Mushrooms, chopped

1-Cup Okra

½ Medium onion

6 Cups Low sodium veggie broth

Hot sauce to taste

½ Tsp. Curry powder

Sea salt and black pepper to taste

Place the veggies, okra and onions in a large pot with the stock. Bring to a boil, add the spices and simmer for 10-15 mins. until tender and season to taste. That's it. Serve with sprouted grain toast and organic butter drizzled with organic raw honey.

STUFFED MOCHI WITH BITTER BEANS

Serves 3-4

12 Fresh shiitake mushrooms, sliced thinly

1 Leek, sliced lengthwise

1 Tbsp. Coconut oil

1 Tbsp. Bragg's liquid aminos

1 Cup Grated carrots

1 Cup Grated daikon

1 Tbsp. Mirin

1 Large bunch Kale, chopped

1 Tbsp. Sesame seeds, toasted

12 Oz Garlic or onion mocha, cut into 12 squares

Preheat oven to 350f. In a large skillet heat the coconut oil sauté the leek until soft, add the mushrooms and sauté for 4-5 mins. Add the water and the liquid aminos 1 tbsp. at a time to deglaze the skillet. Continue to sauté the mushrooms until caramelized. Next add the carrots, daikon and mirin and cook until carrots are soft. Fold in the kale and cook until tender. Line a baking sheet with parchment paper and place the mochi squares on it. Bake until they puff. Remove from oven and carefully slice open each puff, stuff with the baked greens and enjoy.

RED PEPPER RISOTTO

Serves 6

3 Lrg. red bell peppers

2 Tbsp. Coconut oil, melted

3 Lrg. Garlic cloves, chopped

6 Tomatoes, chopped

2 Bay leaves

6 Cups Low sodium veggie stock

2-½ Cups Brown rice

6 Fresh Basil leaves, chopped

Sea salt and black pepper to taste

Broil the peppers until skins are blackened and blistered. Place them in a bowl and cover with damp paper towels and set aside for 10 mins. Next peel the skins off and slice thinly discarding the seeds and core. Heat the oil in a pan, add the garlic and tomatoes and cook over a gentle heat for 5 mins. Next stir in the pepper and bay leaves and cook for 15 mins, stirring occasionally. Meanwhile pour the stock in a large saucepan and heat until simmering. Add the rice to the pepper and tomato mixture, and then add 2-3 ladles off boiling stock and stir until all moisture is absorbed. Continue to add the stock gradually and stir. When the rice is tender season with salt and pepper to taste, garnish with the basil and enjoy.

RICE PILAF WITH NUTS

Serves 4

2 Tbsp. Avocado oil

1 Yellow onion, chopped

1 Large carrot, grated

2 Small zucchini, chopped

1 Garlic clove, minced

2 Tsp. Coriander

1 Cup Brown rice, cooked

2 Cups Low sodium veggie broth

¾ Cup Unsalted cashew nuts

Sea salt and black pepper to taste

In a large skillet heat the oil. Add the onion, carrot and zucchini and cook until translucent. Add the garlic and coriander and cook until fragrant. Add the rice and broth and bring to a boil. Simmer for 15 mins. Remove from heat and add the nuts and season to taste.

JEWELLED BROWN RICE

Serves 4

4 Tbsp. Coconut oil, melted

1 Cup Red onion, chopped

½ Cup Sweet bell pepper, chopped

¼ Cup Carrot, chopped

½ Cup Parsnip, peeled and chopped

½ Cup Celery, chopped

½ Cup Butternut squash, chopped

½ Cup Zucchini, chopped

½ Cup Mushrooms, chopped

½ Cup Leeks, chopped

½ Cup Low sodium chicken stock

2 Tsp. Tamari

Sea salt and black pepper to taste

6 Cups Brown rice, cooked

1 Cup Fresh herbs, parsley, cilantro, basil and oregano

In a large skillet heat the oil and sauté all the veggies until soft. In a hot wok add the veggies, rice stock and tamari and heat through for 10 mins. Add the chopped herb mixture and serve.

DIRTY RICE

Serves 4

2 Tbsp. Coconut oil

2 Large onions, chopped

2 Garlic cloves, minced

2 Tbsp. Cajun spice

1 Cup Brown rice, cooked

2 Cups Low sodium veggie stock

½ Cup mushrooms, chopped

Preheat oven to 350f. In a skillet sauté the onions and garlic and cook until soft. Next add the spices and cook until fragrant. Add the rice and cook for 5 mins. then add the stock. Transfer the entire mixture into a casserole dish and bake for 15 mins.

POMEGRANATE AND SAFFRON PILAF

Serves 4

20 Threads of saffron

¼ Cup Dried currants

2 Tbsp. Coconut butter, melted

1 Cup Brown rice, cooked

2 Cups Low sodium veggie stock

½ Cup Orange juice (fresh if possible, or 100% organic O.J)

¼ Cup Silvered almonds, toasted

¼ Cup Pomegranate seeds

1 Tsp. Cinnamon

Preheat oven to 350f. Prepare a medium sized casserole dish and place the coconut butter in the dish. Add the rice, water, stock and orange juice. Add the saffron, currants and sugar and mix well. Bake in the oven until all the moisture is absorbed, approx. 30 mins. Remove from oven and add the almonds, pomegranate seeds and cinnamon and serve.

ORZO SUMMER SALAD

Serves 6

6 Cups Water

2 Cups Orzo, cooked

2 Tbsp. Coconut oil, melted

1 Tsp. Sea salt

1 Tsp. Black pepper

1 Medium onion, chopped

¼ Cup Low sodium veggie stock

2 Cups Roasted plum tomatoes, chopped

1 Garlic clove, minced

½ Cup Fresh basil leaves

Toss the orzo in a bowl with the oil, salt and pepper. Sauté the onions, when translucent add the tomatoes and the garlic. Next add the stock and water and simmer for 5 mins. Add the orzo to the skillet and toss well, heat through. Add the basil and serve.

QUINOA WITH ALMONDS AND CURRANTS

Serves 4

1 ½ Cups Quinoa

2 ¼ Cups H20

¼ Cup Currants

Pinch Sea salt

1 Tbsp. Coconut oil, melted

1 Red onion, diced

¼ Tsp. cinnamon

¼ Tsp. Ginger

¼ Tsp. Coriander

¼ Tsp. Turmeric

¾ Tsp. Cumin

3 Tbsp. Toasted sliced almonds

¼ Cup Fresh parsley, chopped

Sea salt and fresh ground pepper to taste

Rinse quinoa and place large pot with water, currants and sea salt. Bring to a boil, then reduce heat and simmer 15 minutes or until all water is absorbed. Let cool and fluff with fork. In a skillet over medium heat, sauté onion and spices until soft. Fold into cooked quinoa with the almonds and parsley. Season to taste with salt and pepper.

ZESTY BASMATI RICE WITH CINNAMON AND CUMIN

Serves 6

1 ½ Cups Brown basmati rice

3 Cups Veggie stock, low sodium

1 Cinnamon stick

½ Tsp. Ground cumin

¼ Tsp. Sea salt

Zest of 1 orange

1 Tbsp. Toasted Sesame oil

½ Cup Toasted Cashew pieces

¼ Cup Fresh cilantro, chopped

Soak Rice for 1 Hour in a bowl with water. Drain and place in a large pot with the stock, cinnamon stick, cumin, salt and orange zest. Bring to a boil, cover, reduce heat and simmer until all water is absorbed. Remove from heat and discard cinnamon stick. Fluff with a fork, toss with sesame oil, cashews and cilantro. Let cool slightly and serve.

JASMINE RICE WITH SWEET PEAS

Serves 6

2 Cups Brown jasmine rice

4 Cups Low sodium veggie stock

Pinch Sea salt

1 ½ Cups Fresh or frozen peas

2 Tbsp. Lemon juice

1 Tbsp. Lemon peel, grated

1 Tbsp. Fresh parsley, chopped

Rinse and drain rice 3-4 times until water runs clear. Place in rice cooker with 2 cups of water and salt and cook until liquid is absorbed. Place peas in a strainer, bring 2 cups of water to a boil and pour over peas to blanch or thaw. Fold in peas, lemon juice and lemon peel into cooked rice. Top with chopped parsley and serve.

WILD RICE AND SUNFLOWER SEED PILAF

Serves 4

2 Tbsp. Coconut oil, melted

1 Cup Raw sunflower seeds

½ Tsp. Dried sage

1 Tsp. Dried thyme

1 Tsp. Sea salt

3 Tbsp. Olive oil

1 Leek, chopped

1 Sweet bell pepper, chopped

¼ Cup Dried Cranberries

2 Zucchinis, chopped

2 ½ Cups wild rice, cooked

5 Cups Low sodium chicken or veggie stock

Freshly ground black pepper

Preheat oven to 350 f. Spray a casserole dish with non-stick spray. In a large skillet heat the olive oil and sauté the leek, pepper, zucchini's and cranberries until sift. Add the rice, salt and stock and bring to a boil. Reduce the heat and simmer for 40 mins. Put the rice mixture into a casserole dish and bake in the oven for 30 mins. until all the liquid is absorbed. Season to taste.

APPLE STUFFING

Serves 2

4 Slices of gluten free bread

1 Apple, diced

1 Celery Stalk, diced

1 Tbsp. Coconut oil

½ Cup String beans chopped

1 Tsp. Poultry seasoning

1 Tsp. Sea salt

½ Tsp. Celery salt

1 Tsp. Mustard powder

2 Tbsp. Sliced almonds

1 Tbsp. Pistachios, chopped

½ Tsp. Thyme

½ Tsp. Dill

½ Tsp. Garlic powder

½ Tsp. Onion powder

In a blender make the breadcrumbs from the gluten free bread. Sauté the apple and all the veggies in a pan with coconut oil. Cook until tender. When cooked, mix all the ingredients together in a well-oiled 9x9 glass-baking dish. Bake for approx. 25-30 mins. or until golden and crunchy in a 350f oven.

Wholly stuffing! How did I.....? Ssshhh, no questions, just let the recipe do the talking.

POLENTA AU GRATIN

Serves 6

1 Lb. Prepared polenta

1 Tbsp. Coconut oil, melted

2 Cups of prepared Pasta sauce

½ Cups H20

FILLING

1 Tbsp. Extra virgin olive oil

1 Garlic cloves, minced

1 Large onion, thinly oil

1 Sprig rosemary leaves, minced

1 Cup Mushrooms, thinly sliced

1 Bunch Swiss chard, chopped

¼ Cup Rice Parmesan, grated

Sea salt and pepper to taste

Cut polenta into small pieces and heat 1 tbsp. of coconut oil in a large pot, over medium heat. Sauté for 1 min. Add 3 Tbsp. of pasta sauce and water and heat for 5 mins, until polenta starts to fall apart. Cream the polenta with a fork. Remove from heat, cover and set aside. Heat 1 Tbsp. Coconut oil in a large skillet over medium heat; add garlic, onion and rosemary, sauté until soft. Next add the mushrooms and chard. Cover and cook for 3-4 mins. Season with salt and pepper. Next lightly oil an 8x8 inch casserole dish and spread half the polenta over the bottom. Cover with half the remaining pasta sauce, chard and then polenta. Layer with the remaining polenta, pasta sauce and cheese. Cover with foil and bake for 15 mins. Uncover then bake for another 10 mins. Uncover and let cool and serve.

FURTHER READING

Here are my favorite books that I highly recommend to the ambitious person who wants to increase there knowledge on health.

-Eating for Beauty- David Wolfe

-Sun food Diet Success System- David Wolfe

-The Beauty Detox Solution- Kimberly Snyder, C.N

-Colon Health Key to Vibrant Life- Dr. Norman W. Walker

-Diet & Salad- Dr. Norman W. Walker

-Fresh Vegetable and Fruit Juices: What's missing in your body? - Dr. Norman W. Walker

-The Natural way to Vibrant Health- Dr. Norman W. Walker

-Food Combining & Digestion- Steve Meyerowitz

-Mucusless Diet Healing system- Arnold Ehret

-The Grape Cure- Johanna Brandt

-All of Natalia Rose's Books

Made in the USA
Middletown, DE
29 January 2018